THE CHRISTOLOGY OF
MARK'S GOSPEL

THE CHRISTOLOGY OF MARK'S GOSPEL

Jack Dean Kingsbury

FORTRESS PRESS   PHILADELPHIA

Library of Congress Cataloging in Publication Data

Kingsbury, Jack Dean.
    The Christology of Mark's Gospel.

    Includes bibliographical references and indexes.
    1. Jesus Christ—History of doctrines—Early church,
ca. 30–600.   2. Bible. N.T. Mark—Criticism, interpretation, etc.   I. Title.
BT198.K535   1983   232   83–5576
ISBN 0–8006–0706–6

120B83   Printed in the United States of America   1–706

To
Amelia Kingsbury McMullen
Anna Kuster Kingsbury
Samuel Boyd Kingsbury

CONTENTS

PREFACE

The aim of this book is to explore the christology of Mark. In the present climate of Marcan studies, however, this is perhaps an "untimely" venture. For one thing, the topic that has garnered more scholarly attention than any other in the recent past is that of discipleship. For another thing, one senses that, because of a preoccupation with christology on the part of scholars in past decades, a pall of ennui has settled over the subject. This is all the more the case when it comes to an examination of titles of majesty. The mood in some quarters appears to be that if one investigates christology, one should do so apart from any concentration on titles. But this position, too, is reductionistic. In the case of Mark, titles of majesty occur at strategic points throughout the story. Hence, if scholars are to find a solution to the seemingly intractable problem of Marcan christology, they will have to arrive at some agreement as to what these titles connote and what purpose they serve within Mark's story. Still, the position is doubtlessly well-taken that, if one is to probe the Marcan titles of majesty, one does well not to do so in the abstract but in consideration of the plot of Mark's story. In recognition of this, I have undertaken a balancing act in Chapter 3: while keeping the reader in touch with the plot of Mark by tracing the development of the motif of the secret of Jesus' identity, I have also attended to what I perceive to be the more stubborn problem of ascertaining the meaning and function of major titles of majesty.

Determinative of the plan of the book are two factors: the history of Marcan research in this century and the analysis of the story of Mark. Chapter 1 is a discussion of the motif of the secret of Jesus' identity. What necessitated such a chapter is the fact that while almost all Marcan scholars assert that there is an aura of secrecy surrounding the identity of Jesus in Mark's story, the disagreement over the nature or extent of this secrecy is enormous. At a minimum, scholars acknowledge that the motif of the secret of Jesus' identity encompasses some five passages (1:24–25, 34; 3:11–12; 8:29–30; 9:9). Extend the motif beyond this grouping, however, and the question immediately arises as to whether this or that passage "breaks" the secret. For example, does Bartimaeus's appeal to Jesus as the Son of David "break" the secret? Does the narrative comment that the Jewish leaders perceived that Jesus had told the parable of the wicked husbandmen against them "break" the secret? Does the high priest's question of whether Jesus is the Messiah, the Son of the Blessed, "break" the secret? What of Jesus' public references to himself as "the Son of Man" (2:10, 28; 8:38); do they "break" the secret? The reason these questions cannot be dismissed but must be answered is that they place in doubt the viability of the motif of the secret of Jesus' identity. To the extent that there may be "breaks" in the secret, to that extent the secret is undermined as a motif and emptied of its significance as a factor that gives shape to Mark's story. In the final analysis, it is only by probing the text of the Gospel itself for literary clues as to how Mark would have the reader construe the motif of the secret of Jesus' identity that one can assess the nature, scope, and importance of this motif for coming to grips with the christology of Mark. My firm conviction is that this motif is vital to the understanding of Mark's christology and that Mark invites the reader to regard it as remaining in force from baptism to crucifixion (and resurrection).

Chapter 2 focuses on the "corrective approach," which is the dominant method by which scholars, certainly in North America, have interpreted the christology of Mark in the last quarter century. In the form it generally takes, the guiding notion is that the titles "Son of God" or "Messiah" or both are defective, the first because it is burdened with a theology of glory which has no truck with suffering, and the second because it connotes, in Peter's confession, for example, a king of national political stripe. To combat the false views "Son of God" and "Messiah" connote, Mark brings to bear upon his story his own theology of the cross and, say some, also employs "the Son of Man" to "correct," "reinterpret," or "give right content to" these titles. After sketching the history of the corrective approach, I monitor the problematic associated with it. In this connection, one point that begs to be stressed is that the contention that the title "Son of God" is to be thought of as being defective until it has been reinterpreted cannot, on literary-critical grounds, be sustained; for if one postulates this, then one is forced to take the untenable position that God's baptismal affirmation that Jesus is his Son is of the nature of an "unreliable comment."

Chapters 3 and 4 are the heart of the book. In Chapter 3, I investigate the christology of Mark in keeping with the motif of the secret of Jesus' identity. The sustained probe of Mark's story accounts for the great length of this chapter. Important conclusions I reach are the following: In fullest measure, Mark identifies Jesus as being the Davidic Messiah-King, the Son of God. Although the titles that stand behind this designation partly overlap in meaning, each has its distinctive coloration. Thus, Jesus is the "Anointed One" ("Messiah," "Christ"), and what Mark understands by this in any given instance he indicates by means of the context, wider or immediate. Jesus is also the Son of David, for he stands in the line of David and fulfills (e.g., in healing Bartimaeus) the eschatological expectations associated with David. Again, Jesus is the "King of the Jews (Israel)," for he is God's anointed ruler of Israel who wields his authority, ironically, by submitting to the mockery of Gentile and Jew and embracing death. Still, Mark takes pains to bind the secret of Jesus' identity more narrowly to his divine sonship, which underscores the critical factor of the unique filial relationship Jesus has to God. This secret, that Jesus is the royal Son of God, remains in force from baptism to crucifixion (and resurrection). Ask Mark, therefore, who the Jesus is whom God empowers with his Spirit, calls Son, and chooses for messianic ministry (1:1–13), who authoritatively preaches, calls disciples, teaches, heals, and exorcizes demons (1:14—8:26), and who journeys to Jerusalem and suffers, dies, atones for sins, and is raised by God (8:27—16:8), and Mark's answer is that he is the royal Son of God. (Then, too, because Jesus, raised by God, remains the royal Son of God in the time between the resurrection and the Parousia, it is also as such that he fulfills the role at the Parousia of the Son of Man of OT prophecy.) And what purpose does the motif of the secret of Jesus' identity serve? Its purpose is to show, through the medium of the story Mark tells, under what circumstances it comes about that a human character at the end of the story, namely, the centurion, "thinks" about Jesus in the same way as God affirms, at the beginning of his story, that he "thinks" about Jesus, namely, as his royal Son.

Chapter 4 corroborates the results of Chapter 3 by detailing the use Mark makes of "the Son of Man." In my judgment, there is overwhelming indication that "the Son of Man" is without content as far as the topic of the identity of Jesus is concerned: Mark does not utilize "the Son of Man" to inform the reader of "who Jesus is." As a result, Jesus' public references to himself as "the Son of Man" do not "break" the secret of his identity. But despite the fact that Mark does not utilize "the Son of Man" to explain "who Jesus is," he does make of it a technical term, or title, for he applies it exclusively to Jesus and in conformity with the unique contours of his life and ministry: earthly activity; suffering, death, and rising; and return for judgment and vindication. The distinctiveness of this title lies in the way in which it functions within Mark's story. It is of the nature of a "public title" in the sense that it is the title by means of which Jesus refers to himself "in public" or in view of the "public," or "world" (Jews and Gentiles, but especially his opponents). The purpose for which Jesus employs it is to point to himself as "the man," or "the human being" (earthly, suffering, vindicated), and to assert his divine authority in the face of opposition. In translating this title, one can perhaps capture its force in Mark's story by rendering it as "this man," or "this human being." Overall, the impact this title has upon Mark's story is that it emphasizes the twin elements of conflict with the "public," or "world," and of vindication, at the Parousia, in the sight of the "world."

It now gives me great pleasure to express my gratitude to those who have contributed, directly or indirectly, to the successful completion of this project: to President T. Hartley Hall, IV, of Union Theological Seminary in Virginia and Dean Patrick Miller, Jr., for supporting my request to the Board of Trustees for a year's sabbatical during which I finished the manuscript; to the Board of Directors of the American Council of Learned Societies, for voting me a fellowship for the academic year 1981–82; to Frederick Danker, for his ready willingness to explore ideas on important aspects of this book; to John Trotti, the Librarian, Martha Aycock, Reference Librarian, and Cecelia Clark, Assistant Reference Librarian, for an immense amount of assistance in securing books and articles; to Norman Hjelm, Director of Fortress Press, and John Hollar, Academic Editor, for commissioning this project; to David Bauer, my graduate assistant, for pre-

paring the indexes; and, above all, to my wife Barbara, for her un-
flagging support during the long period of research and writing.

J.D.K.

Union Theological Seminary in Virginia
Pentecost, 1982

ABBREVIATIONS

AB   Anchor Bible
ATANT   Abhandlungen zur Theologie des Alten und Neuen Testaments
BAG   W. Bauer, W. F. Arndt, F. W. Gingrich, and F. W. Danker,
            Greek-English Lexicon of the NT
BETL   Bibliotheca ephemeridum theologicarum lovaniensium
Bib   *Biblica*
Bib Leb   *Bibel und Leben*
BJRL   *Bulletin of the John Rylands Library*
BKAT   Biblischer Kommentar: Altes Testament
BZ   *Biblische Zeitschrift*
BZNW   Beihefte zur *ZNW*
CBQ   *Catholic Biblical Quarterly*
CBQMS   Catholic Biblical Quarterly—Monograph Series
CGTC   The Cambridge Greek Testament Commentary
CRB   Cahiers de la Revue Biblique
EKKNT   Evangelisch-katholischer Kommentar zum Neuen Testament
ET   English translation
EvQ   *Evangelical Quarterly*
EvT   *Evangelische Theologie*
Exp Tim   *Expository Times*
FB   Forschung zur Bibel
FRLANT   Forschungen zur Religion und Literatur des Alten und Neuen
            Testaments
GNT   Grundrisse zum Neuen Testament
HibJ   *Hibbert Journal*
HTKNT   Herders theologischer Kommentar zum Neuen Testament
HTR   *Harvard Theological Review*
Int.   *Interpretation*
JAAR   *Journal of the American Academy of Religion*
JBL   *Journal of Biblical Literature*
JR   *Journal of Religion*
JSNT   *Journal for the Study of the New Testament*

JSNTSup	Journal for the Study of the New Testament—Supplement Series
JTS	*Journal of Theological Studies*
LD	Lectio divina
LUĂ	Lunds universitets årsskrift
LXX	Septuagint
MeyerK	H. A. W. Meyer, Kritisch-exegetischer Kommentar über das Neue Testament
MTS	Marburger Theologische Studien
NICNT	New International Commentary on the New Testament
NovT	*Novum Testamentum*
NovTSup	Novum Testamentum, Supplements
NT	New Testament
NTAbh	Neutestamentliche Abhandlungen
NTD	Das Neue Testament Deutsch
NTS	*New Testament Studies*
OT	Old Testament
RAC	*Reallexikon für Antike und Christentum*
RelSRev	*Religious Studies Review*
SANT	Studien zum Alten und Neuen Testament
SBB	Stuttgarter biblische Beiträge
SBLDS	SBL Dissertation Series
SBLMS	SBL Monograph Series
SBM	Stuttgarter biblische Monographien
SBS	Stuttgarter Bibelstudien
SBT	Studies in Biblical Theology
SBTheol	*Studia Biblica et Theologica*
SCHNT	Studia ad corpus hellenisticum novi testamenti
SNT	Studien zum Neuen Testament
SNTSMS	Society for New Testament Studies Monograph Series
ST	*Studia theologica*
Str-B	[H. Strack and] P. Billerbeck, *Kommentar zum Neuen Testament*
SUNT	Studien zur Umwelt des Neuen Testaments
TBü	Theologische Bücherei
TDNT	G. Kittel and G. Friedrich (eds.), *Theological Dictionary of the New Testament*
THKNT	Theologischer Handkommentar zum Neuen Testament
TLZ	*Theologische Literaturzeitung*
TTZ	*Trierer theologische Zeitschrift*

TynBul	*Tyndale Bulletin*
UNT	Untersuchungen zum Neuen Testament
WMANT	Wissenschaftliche Monographien zum Alten und Neuen Testament
ZNW	*Zeitschrift für die neutestamentliche Wissenschaft*
ZTK	*Zeitschrift für Theologie und Kirche*

1   THE SHAPE OF THE PROBLEM

The Secret of Jesus' Identity in Mark

Each field of study has its giants. In this century, the giant of Marcan studies is William Wrede. Whether strongly supported or vigorously opposed, Wrede has had more influence on the way in which the Gospel according to Mark[1] has been interpreted than perhaps any other scholar.

Wrede is famous, of course, for his theory of the messianic secret. The purpose of this chapter is to explore this theory. What, briefly stated, is it? What modifications has it undergone at the hands of other

---

1. The Gospel according to Mark is a story, and literary theorists distinguish in analyzing a story between the "real author," the "implied author," and the "narrator" (cf., e.g., Booth, *Rhetoric of Fiction,* pp. 70–76; Chatman, *Story and Discourse,* pp. 147–51; Rhoads, "Narrative Criticism," pp. 9–11). The "real author" is the historical person who actually creates, or has created, any given story. In the act of creating a story, however, the real author also creates a "literary version" of himself, a "second self," which the reader comes to know through the medium of the story. This second self is the "implied author." The "narrator," in turn, is the "voice" the reader hears as he peruses the story, the one who "tells" the reader the story. One of the principal reasons literary theorists distinguish between the "implied author" who stands behind the whole of a story and the "narrator" who tells the story is that a narrator can prove himself to be "unreliable." The "unreliable narrator" is the narrator who is found to be at odds with the implied author. This occurs, for example, when the narrator does not espouse the same system of knowledge, values, beliefs, or norms which undergirds and informs the story. In the case of the Gospels, however, the reader encounters only "reliable narrators," i.e., narrators who are in accord with the implied authors. For this reason, the need to distinguish between narrator and implied author in Gospel studies appears to be less pressing. In this study, at any rate, I shall designate both narrator and implied author as "Mark," "Matthew," or "Luke." By so doing, I can retain a familiar nomenclature. When referring to those historical personages who were the real authors of the Gospels, I shall employ the term "(first or second or third) evangelist." Because earlier generations of scholars made no distinction, say, between the "historical Mark" and "Mark as the implied author or narrator," it is not always possible in discussing their work (cf. Chaps. 1 and 2) to achieve terminological precision in this regard.

scholars? Is it still viable in some form today as a vehicle for understanding Mark's portrait of Jesus?

THE MESSIANIC SECRET:
FROM WREDE TO THE PRESENT

Wrede's theory of the messianic secret has been rehearsed so often since he first proposed it in 1901[2] that one needs only to recall the essentials. Basically, Wrede's theory is an aggregate of three interrelated contentions.

Wrede's Theory of the Messianic Secret

Wrede's first contention has to do with the matter of "context": the Gospel of Mark, and therefore the messianic secret, can properly be discussed only against the broad background of the development of early Christian thought.[3] Within the NT, the place of Mark is between two poles. The one pole comprises such passages as Acts 2:36; Romans 1:4; and Philippians 2:6–11. These passages give expression to the Christian belief that it was at his resurrection that Jesus first became the Messiah.[4] Because this view of Jesus' messiahship is the earliest one known, it necessarily presupposes that Jesus did not, during his earthly ministry, present himself publicly as the Messiah.[5] In other words, the character of Jesus' life on earth was in fact non-messianic.[6]

The second of the two poles is the Gospel according to John. Here Jesus, in stark contrast to the first view, is unabashedly portrayed as being the Messiah already in the course of his historical existence.[7]

Situated as it is between these two poles, Mark incorporates within it the tension between them.[8] Like the Fourth Gospel, Mark too portrays Jesus as the Messiah.[9] But under the influence of the earliest

---

2. Wrede, *Messiasgeheimnis*, passim (ET, *Messianic Secret*, passim).
3. Ibid., pp. 5–6, 207–51 (ET, pp. 7–8, 209–52).
4. Ibid., pp. 214–15 (ET, pp. 216–17).
5. Ibid., pp. 216, 229 (ET, pp. 218, 230).
6. Ibid.; pp. 214, 216–17 (ET, pp. 216, 218).
7. Ibid., p. 216 (ET, p. 217).
8. Ibid., pp. 222, 227–28 (ET, pp. 223, 228–29).
9. Ibid., p. 125 (ET, p. 126).

Christian view, Mark also describes Jesus as keeping his messiahship secret. Mark's "messianic secret," therefore, is in essence the product of the wedding of these two perspectives. In the form the evangelist has given it, it is the notion that Jesus, although he is the Messiah, nonetheless does not divulge his identity.[10]

The second of Wrede's three main contentions concerns the "scope" of the messianic secret: so comprehensive is it that it pervades the whole of Mark.[11] Thus, the messianic secret extends not only to the identity of Jesus but also to his activity of teaching and miracle-working and to his suffering, death, and resurrection.[12] By the same token, there are certain features of Mark which point directly to the messianic secret, such as the following: (a) Jesus issues "commands to silence" to demons (1:25, 34; 3:12), to persons whom he heals,[13] and to the disciples (8:30; 9:9) to the effect that they should not reveal his messianic dignity or otherwise tell of him; (b) Jesus delivers his teaching to the crowds in parables, that is, in speech they cannot comprehend (4:10–13); and (c) as a corollary to the preceding, the disciples, although they are the recipients of divine revelation and of private instruction from Jesus, are nevertheless said not to understand the things that they see and hear.[14]

The last of Wrede's three main contentions pertains to the phenomenon of "contradictions": throughout Mark's narrative, there are those places where the messianic secret is manifestly broken.[15] Examples of such contradictions can be found, for instance, in the miracle-stories. Cases in point are those passages where the evangelist juxtaposes a command of Jesus to silence with the notation that this command is promptly ignored and public proclamation is made of his mighty act (1:44–45; 7:36; cf. 7:24). In the evangelist's overall scheme, however, "contradictions" are not idle mistakes but perform

---

10. Ibid., pp. 79–81, 114, 125–26 (ET, pp. 80–81, 113–14, 126).

11. Ibid., p. 114 (ET, pp. 113–14).

12. Ibid., pp. 80, 114 (ET, pp. 80, 113–14).

13. Cf. Mark 1:43–45; 5:43; 7:36; 8:26.

14. Cf. Mark 4:13, 40–41; 6:50–52; 7:18; 8:16–21; 9:5–6, 19; 10:24; 14:37–41. Wrede, *Messiasgeheimnis*, pp. 33–65, 93–114 (ET, *Messianic Secret*, pp. 34–66, 92–114).

15. Wrede, *Messiasgeheimnis*, pp. 124–29 (ET, *Messianic Secret*, pp. 124–29).

a necessary function. They are the "fissures" in the all-pervasive messianic secret through which he permits the revelation of Jesus' messiahship to shine forth. Indeed, it is exactly these fissures that anticipate the goal towards which the evangelist aims the whole of his story, namely, the full disclosure of the messianic secret at the resurrection (9:9).

In summary of Wrede's theory, Mark is perceived to be a document of the latter part of the first century (A.D. 60–70) which was written for the purpose of describing the earthly Jesus as the Messiah.[16] At the time it arose, the non-messianic nature of the life and ministry of Jesus had not yet been forgotten but was rapidly fading from sight. Increasingly, the notion was asserting itself that if the risen Jesus is the Messiah "now," then he has always been the Messiah, also during his life on earth. As spokesman for this view, the second evangelist wrote of the life of Jesus in such fashion that he gave a messianic cast to the non-messianic traditions of the sayings and deeds of Jesus by presenting the earthly Jesus as the Messiah who was intent on keeping his messiahship a secret.

The Attack upon Wrede's Theory

Wrede's theory sparked a vigorous debate. Until as recently as the 1960s, in fact, scholars reacted to it in the main by aligning themselves with one of two schools of thought.[17] What distinguished the two schools is their conception of the Gospel of Mark. The one school, for example, was convinced that Mark is to be construed as a reliable historical account, though not necessarily a biography, of the life of Jesus of Nazareth; the interest here was to enlist Mark in the life-of-Jesus research. With few exceptions, it was British scholars who adopted this position. And because in Wrede's theory Mark functions as a primary witness to the theology of the evangelist but only as a fragmentary witness to the historical life of Jesus, the scholars of this school took a rigorous stand against it.

16. Ibid., pp. 6–7, 125–26, 227–29 (ET, pp. 8–9, 126, 228–30).

17. For a concise but excellent survey of these two schools of thought, the one British and the other Continental, cf. Powley, "Messianic Secret," pp. 309–10. For more detailed overviews of scholarly reaction to Wrede's theory of the messianic secret, cf. Ebeling, *Messiasgeheimnis*, pp. 1–113; Percy, *Botschaft Jesu*, pp. 271–99; Minette de Tillesse, *Le secret messianique*, pp. 9–34; and Räisänen, *Messiasgeheimnis*, pp. 27–48.

The leader of the attack upon Wrede's theory was Albert Schweitzer. In his celebrated book *Von Reimarus zu Wrede* (1906),[18] Schweitzer emphatically dismissed Wrede's theory on the grounds that Mark admits to being read as genuine history and that the notion that Jesus is the Messiah originated, not with the resurrection appearances, but in Jesus' own self-consciousness.[19]

Especially in Great Britain, Schweitzer's negative assessment of Wrede's theory found a ready reception. Indeed, for three generations it effectively forestalled any truly positive appraisal of Wrede's work by British scholarship.[20] Thus, quick to pick up on Schweitzer's critique of Wrede, William Sanday roundly declared in 1907 that Wrede's entire construction, because it traces belief in Jesus' messiahship to the resurrection but not to his earthly ministry, is "not only very wrong but also distinctly wrong-headed."[21] In echo of Sanday's position almost fifty years later, T. W. Manson bluntly stated in 1956 that, owing to the thoroughgoing skepticism one finds in Wrede's theory about the possibility of ever recovering from Mark a historically reliable picture of the ministry of Jesus, the "farther we travel along the Wredestrasse [Wrede-street], the clearer it becomes that it is the road to nowhere."[22] And in a remark that brought the

---

18. Schweitzer's book was translated into English in 1910 under the title *The Quest of the Historical Jesus*.

19. Schweitzer, *Von Reimarus zu Wrede*, pp. 334, 337–47, 367–95 (ET, *Quest of the Historical Jesus*, pp. 335, 338–48, 368–95).

20. It should be observed, however, that if British scholarship tended to be uncompromising in its rejection of Wrede's theory, there were those scholars, most notably A. E. J. Rawlinson (*St Mark*, pp. 260–62) and V. Taylor ("The Messianic Secret in Mark," pp. 147–50; "W. Wrede's The Messianic Secret in the Gospels," pp. 248–50; and "The Messianic Secret in Mark: A Rejoinder," pp. 245–48), who did find a "residuum of truth" in it. As Taylor ("The Messianic Secret in Mark," pp. 149–50) defined it, this residuum of truth is the insight that the secret that Jesus is the Messiah is integral to the whole of Mark's portrait of Jesus because it was integral to the person and ministry of the earthly Jesus himself. In other respects, two British scholars of reputation who endorsed Wrede's theory were R. H. Lightfoot (*History and Interpretation,* pp. 16–22) and T. A. Burkill (cf. *Mysterious Revelation*).

21. Sanday, *Life of Christ*, pp. 69–76. Following in the footsteps of Schweitzer and Sanday, A. S. Peake, speaking for his generation, flatly asserted in an article in 1924 ("Messiah," p. 57) that Wrede's theory of the messianic secret is "untenable."

22. T. W. Manson, "Life of Jesus," pp. 216, 220–21. As irony would have

consistent repudiation of Wrede's theory by British scholarship full circle, Stephen Neill opined in 1964 that Sanday had, at the outset, "said all that really needs to be said about Wrede."[23]

However it may be judged, the British critique of Wrede's theory was not without result. Its insistence, for example, that the ultimate source of the notion that Jesus is the Messiah is not simply the resurrection but the historical Jesus himself gradually won the assent of NT scholars almost everywhere. Significant in this respect was the rise of the New Quest of the historical Jesus. In a seminal article published in 1954, Ernst Käsemann contended that, whether the earthly Jesus applied the category of Messiah to himself or not, it is nonetheless the only category that does justice to the unparalleled claim to authority that resides in his words.[24] And in 1956, Günther Bornkamm, whose *Jesus von Nazareth*[25] has been more widely read perhaps than any other book produced by the New Quest, asserted that although he cannot see that the historical Jesus laid claim to any messianic title for himself, he surely did awaken in his followers the belief that he was the Messiah they had been hoping for.[26] Taken together, these statements by Käsemann and Bornkamm strike at the heart of that aspect of Wrede's theory which the British critique, too, had challenged. If Jesus' claim to authority was messianic in nature if not in name, it follows that the notion that Jesus is the Messiah ultimately derives from Jesus himself and that it is mistaken to think that there ever existed a "non-messianic" tradition of the sayings and deeds of Jesus.[27]

But even on the dubious matter of treating Mark as "genuine his-

---

it, it was Norman Perrin, who had studied under Manson, who turned Manson's harsh judgment against him by writing in a review article in 1966 ("Wredestrasse becomes the Hauptstrasse," pp. 297–98) that, on the contrary, the "Wredestrasse has become the Hauptstrasse [main street], and it is leading us to new and exciting country."

23. Neill, *Interpretation of NT*, p. 248 n. 1.

24. Käsemann, "Problem des historischen Jesus," p. 206 (ET, "Problem of the Historical Jesus," pp. 37–38).

25. ET, *Jesus of Nazareth*.

26. Bornkamm, *Jesus*, p. 158 (ET, *Jesus*, p. 172).

27. Cf. ibid., pp. 157–58 (ET, p. 172). If in the view of Käsemann and Bornkamm the historical Jesus was "implicitly" the Messiah in that he spoke and acted with (divine) authority, in the view of such scholars as the following the historical Jesus was "explicitly" the Messiah because he possessed a "messianic consciousness": O. Betz, "Frage nach dem messianischen Bewusstsein Jesu," pp. 34–48;

tory," the British critique cannot be said to have been without effect. True, in faulting Wrede because he argued that Mark is theological in nature and not fundamentally historical, it clearly was in the wrong. Still, it is apparent that at least a variation of the historical approach to Mark enjoys currency in some quarters today. Thus, there are those who hold that the second evangelist was a "conservative redactor"[28] who, in working with primitive traditions, did relatively little to change them. But if this was in fact the case, should it not be possible to employ the Second Gospel as a tradition-critical vehicle for working one's way back, in most instances, even to the historical Jesus? Rudolf Pesch has posed this question, and answered it in the affirmative with his massive commentary on Mark.[29] Ironically, therefore, the approach to Mark which Wrede wrote his book some eighty years ago to combat continues to exert a strong appeal.

The Adoption of Wrede's Theory

As was stated above, two major schools of thought sprang up in reaction to Wrede's theory. If the one school, under the tutelage of Schweitzer, discounted Wrede's theory, the other one was positively disposed towards it. Scholars who may be said to represent this school of thought are Martin Dibelius, Rudolf Bultmann, Hans Jürgen Ebeling, and Georg Strecker.[30] Their writings on the messianic secret spanned the time from the rise of NT form criticism following World War I to the mid '60s.

What is characteristic of these four scholars is that, in contradis-

---

Aune, "Messianic Secret," pp. 20–31; Longenecker, "Messianic Secret," pp. 210–15; and Dunn, "Messianic Secret," pp. 110–17.

28. Cf., e.g., Simonsen, "Problematik," pp. 6, 11, 13, 16, 22–23; Best, "Preservation of the Tradition," pp. 33–34; Theissen, *Wundergeschichten*, pp. 189–96, 198–201, 211–21; Pesch, *Markusevangelium*, I, 15–32; Räisänen, *Messiasgeheimnis*, pp. 14–16, 167–68. On a different note, J. Meagher ("Principle of Clumsiness," p. 471) has described the second evangelist as a "clumsy, if talented and creative, storyteller." For an assessment of the evangelist's use of tradition which contrasts sharply with that of the scholars just cited, cf. Kelber, "Oral Tradition," pp. 7–55.

29. Pesch, *Markusevangelium*, I–II.

30. Dibelius, *Formgeschichte*, pp. 225–32 (ET, *Tradition to Gospel*, pp. 223–30); Bultmann, *Geschichte der synoptischen Tradition*, pp. 370–76 (ET, *History of the Synoptic Tradition*, pp. 345–50); Ebeling, *Messiasgeheimnis*, pp. 95–115, 144–46, 178–79, 192–93, 219–24; Strecker, "Messiasgeheimnistheorie," pp. 190–210. Cf. also Burkill, *Mysterious Revelation*, passim.

tinction to Schweitzer and the British scholars mentioned above, they did not look upon Mark principally as a quarry from which to mine facts concerning the historical Jesus. Instead, they regarded it as a literary work in its own right, although all except Strecker stressed that it is the unsophisticated product of a "compiler" and not the creation of an "author."[31] As to its nature and purpose, Mark is kerygmatic and was written to proclaim the gospel for the age in which the evangelist himself lived. As Wrede correctly saw, the interpretive key to this gospel is the "messianic secret," the idea that although Jesus, who is the Messiah, desires to keep his divine glory hidden, it nevertheless bursts forth in secret epiphanies. Moreover, as Wrede also correctly saw, the messianic secret is comprehensive in scope. It encompasses all the major motifs of Mark's narrative, to wit: (a) the commands to silence that Jesus issues to demons, healed persons, and the disciples; (b) the custom of Jesus of speaking in parables, that is, in speech that "those outside" are unable to grasp; and (c) the persistent inability on the part of the disciples to understand the very words and deeds of Jesus to which they bear witness.

Owing to the prestige of especially Bultmann and Dibelius, Wrede's theory of the messianic secret enjoyed its years of greatest influence in the decades following 1920. Whatever the diversity of opinion among Marcan scholars on the Continent, the majority was convinced that the messianic secret is in fact the theme around which the second evangelist organized his Gospel. Not only that, but in time some scholars began to view the messianic secret in still more exalted terms. In a much-quoted article published in 1957, for example, Hans Conzelmann apparently spoke for many when he declared that the theory of the messianic secret, as conceived by the second evangelist, is the factor that gave rise to the Gospel genre itself.[32]

Redefining the Scope of the Messianic Secret

In the 1960s, however, a new trend of events began to take shape in Marcan studies. Up to this time, scholars who had been disposed

---

31. Dibelius, *Formgeschichte*, pp. 231–34 (ET, *Tradition to Gospel*, pp. 229–32); Bultmann, *Geschichte der synoptischen Tradition*, p. 375 (ET, *History of the Synoptic Tradition*, p. 350); Ebeling, *Messiasgeheimnis*, p. 115. By contrast, cf. Strecker, "Messiasgeheimnistheorie," pp. 200–207.

32. Conzelmann, "Gegenwart und Zukunft," pp. 293–95.

to find in Wrede's theory an avenue of approach to Mark had also been disposed to accept his judgment that the messianic secret is an inclusive concept that gives unity to the whole of Mark's narrative. But this judgment of Wrede now became the object of scrutiny, and what resulted was the dismemberment of his inclusive concept. On Wrede's view, such basic features of Mark's story as Jesus' commands to silence, his speaking in parables, and the ignorance of the disciples are all of a piece with one another. On the opposing view, these features are to be seen instead as separable motifs. Significantly, Albert Schweitzer, in his critique of Wrede at the turn of the century, had argued the selfsame point.[33]

Ulrich Luz, in dependence on H. J. Ebeling, is one of those who initiated this new trend in Marcan studies.[34] Focusing on Jesus' commands to silence, Luz distinguished between the ones Jesus directs to demons and his disciples (1:34; 3:11–12; 8:30; 9:9) and the ones he directs to persons he has healed (1:44–45; 7:35–37). The former commands, because they have to do with Jesus' identity as the Messiah, properly constitute the motif of the "messianic secret." By the same token, the latter commands belong to a different motif. The striking thing about them is that they are not kept but broken (1:45; 7:36–37). This, however, is indicative of the purpose they serve: such breaking of Jesus' commands is meant by Mark to attest to the fact that so overwhelming is the divine power which inheres in Jesus' miracles that people who have experienced or witnessed them cannot but proclaim him throughout the land. Not the hiddenness of Jesus, therefore, but the public proclamation of him is the point of this motif.[35] Indeed, the passage 7:24, though not found in a miracle-story, gives trenchant expression to this motif.

---

33. Schweitzer, *Von Reimarus zu Wrede*, pp. 343–47 (ET, *Quest of the Historical Jesus*, pp. 344–48).

34. Luz, "Geheimnismotiv," pp. 9–30. Cf. also Trocmé, *Mark*, p. 124 n. 1. For an incisive analysis of some of the problems associated with Wrede's thesis that the messianic secret is an inclusive concept in Mark, cf. W. C. Robinson, "Secret Messiah," pp. 10–30.

35. Unlike the passages 1:44–45 and 7:35–37, Jesus issues a command to silence following a miracle in 5:43 (cf. also 8:26) which is not disobeyed. Räisänen (*Messiasgeheimnis*, pp. 82–89) reasons that because the commands of 5:43 and 8:26 remain intact, they must be seen as serving a different purpose in Mark from the commands given in 1:44 and 7:36, namely, they are intended to dampen rumors about Jesus as a miracle-worker. If this is correct, then it would appear that commands to silence following miracle-stories serve contrasting purposes in Mark:

If Luz demonstrated that the commands to silence which Jesus gives to healed persons belong to a motif that is distinct from that of the messianic secret, Theodore Weeden and others argued that the persistent inability of the disciples to understand comprises yet another distinguishable motif in Mark's story.[36] Interestingly, Wrede himself had tacitly acknowledged this, but placed this theme in the service of the messianic secret anyway.[37] By contrast, Weeden took the opposite tack and insisted that the disciples' lack of comprehension, and consequently not the messianic secret, is the dominant motif of Mark's narrative.[38] Mark is polemical in nature, and by attending to the motif of the disciples' ignorance one can discern its message. Although Weeden's thesis that Mark portrays Jesus as repudiating the disciples has not gone uncontested,[39] his contention that the disciples' failure to comprehend Jesus is a motif in its own right is generally acknowledged by scholars today.

The third main element in Wrede's broad concept of the messianic secret has to do with Jesus' speaking in parables. In his attack upon Wrede's theory, Albert Schweitzer had already described the inclusion of this element in the messianic secret as "one of the weakest points of the entire construction."[40] As Schweitzer put it, the parabolic speech of Jesus in Mark concerns "the secret of the Kingdom of God" (4:11). However integrally Jesus himself may be related to the Kingdom, there is no justification for restricting the secret of the Kingdom to the secret of Jesus' messiahship. Wrede notwithstanding, the two are not coterminous. Now, decades later, Marcan scholars were again urging, in echo of Schweitzer, that Jesus' speaking in parables and the secret of his identity be treated as two motifs.[41]

---

the motif of "publicity" on the one hand and of "secrecy" on the other. On the various functions of commands to silence in ancient miracle-stories, cf. Theissen, *Wundergeschichten*, pp. 143–54.

36. Cf. Tyson, "Blindness of the Disciples," pp. 261–62; Trocmé, *Mark*, pp. 107–37 (esp. p. 124 n. 1); and Weeden, "Heresy," p. 145.

37. Wrede, *Messiasgeheimnis*, pp. 114, 208–9, 235 (ET, *Messianic Secret*, pp. 113–14, 210, 236).

38. Weeden, "Heresy," pp. 145–58.

39. Cf., e.g., Best, "Role of the Disciples," pp. 377–401; Tannehill, "Disciples in Mark," pp. 396–405; Petersen, "End," pp. 151–66.

40. Schweitzer, *Von Reimarus zu Wrede*, p. 345 (ET, *Quest of the Historical Jesus*, p. 346).

41. Cf. Aune, "Messianic Secret," p. 25; Dunn, "Messianic Secret," p. 95;

Accordingly, by the mid '70s the "messianic secret" no longer existed as the pretentious construct Wrede had made of it. As Wrede saw it, there presents itself in the Gospel of Mark only one overarching motif—the idea that Jesus, although he is the Messiah, nevertheless keeps his messiahship a secret—and every facet of the Gospel stands in the service of this one motif. But so formulated, Wrede's thesis had proved itself to be overdrawn. Instead of being the sole motif of the Gospel, the messianic secret is in reality one motif among others. At its core, it consists of the several commands to silence which Jesus directs to demons (1:34; 3:11–12; cf. 1:24–25) and to the disciples (8:29–30; 9:9) to the effect that they should not divulge his identity. What is noteworthy about these commands is that they are kept and not broken. Of course, although it may be admitted that the messianic secret is only one motif among others, this does not mean that it will not develop in concert with other motifs. Indeed, the interpreter can expect that other motifs will, at points, reinforce it or even extend it. The ignorance of the disciples and Jesus' speaking in parables may be motifs that can be distinguished from the messianic secret, but it is obvious that they can also enhance and further it.

Questioning the Viability of the Messianic Secret

Though it was seen to be only one motif among others, scholars nonetheless continued to be of the opinion that the messianic secret played a vital role in Mark's story. But in a lengthy monograph published in 1976, Heikki Räisänen charged that to take this position is to misread the data. He maintained that, on the contrary, the messianic secret is a motif of little consequence in Mark.[42]

To understand Räisänen's thinking, it is helpful to return briefly to Wrede's theory. Wrede incorporated into his theory a key provision concerning "contradictions."[43] His contention was that the element of contradiction is integral to the second evangelist's gospel-story. It is so because the evangelist intended to hold in tension two themes that are, to say the least, paradoxical: (a) that Jesus is the Messiah;

Brown, "Secret of the Kingdom," pp. 60–74; Räisänen, *Messiasgeheimnis*, p. 53.

42. Cf. Räisänen, *Messiasgeheimnis*, pp. 143–68.

43. Wrede, *Messiasgeheimnis*, pp. 69, 124–29 (ET, *Messianic Secret*, pp. 70, 124–29).

and (b) that he keeps his messiahship a secret. To do justice to both themes, the evangelist had no choice but to portray Jesus as the secret Messiah who nevertheless intermittently reveals his messiahship.

Now Räisänen does not contest the view that the "true messianic secret," that is, that handful of passages in which Jesus forbids demons or the disciples to make his messiahship or divine sonship known (1:24–25, 34; 3:11–12; 8:29–30; 9:9), is in fact one of the motifs which characterizes Mark's story.[44] What he contests is the notion that he believes sits all too easily with Wrede and other scholars as well, namely, that the second evangelist fashioned a story that does indeed successfully hold in tension both the messianic secret and its contradictions.[45] Literarily, the problem is that the evangelist, by intermittently permitting the secret of Jesus' messianic identity to be divulged to outsiders and even to the Jewish leaders, compromised the integrity of the motif of the messianic secret.[46]

As early as 2:10 and 2:28 the Marcan Jesus, asserts Räisänen, openly refers to himself as "the Son of Man," and at 2:19–20 as the "bridegroom." At 10:46–52 and 11:1–10, Jesus stands forth in public as the "Son of David," and at 12:35–37 he speaks of himself indirectly as the "Lord" who is greater than David. In 12:1–12, Jesus narrates a parable his opponents seem to understand (cf. 12:12), making obvious allusion to himself as God's "Son," and at 14:61–62 he plainly acknowledges before the Jewish Sanhedrin that he is the "Messiah, the Son of the Blessed." Finally, at 9:9 Jesus appears to designate the resurrection as the point after which the secret of his divine sonship will be lifted, but this idea is blatantly contradicted by the centurion's confession at 15:39 that he is the "Son of God."

Räisänen's analysis leads him to conclude that the evangelist thus put together a story in which he worked at cross purposes with himself. On the one hand, he did in fact imbue his story with the messianic secret according to which Jesus periodically commands demons and his disciples to silence as regards his identity. On the other hand, the evangelist likewise included episodes that indicate that Jesus' messianic dignity is no secret whatever to outsiders and even to his oppo-

---

44. Cf. Räisänen, *Messiasgeheimnis*, p. 159.
45. Cf. ibid., p. 144.
46. Cf. ibid., pp. 143–58.

nents. But if the evangelist did proceed in this manner, what does this say of him as a writer? It suggests, Räisänen maintains, that he was not the original thinker that most scholars make him out to be.[47] On the contrary, he was much more a "transmitter" of traditions, as the early form critics recognized.[48] And as far as the secret of Jesus' messianic identity is concerned, this plainly was not so important a motif to the evangelist that he was prepared to free it of the tensions, inconsistencies, and contradictions that deprive it of its literary and theological effectiveness.[49]

THE MESSIANIC SECRET:
A REAPPRAISAL

Along with Wrede's own book, Räisänen's monograph rates as one of the five or six most comprehensive treatments of the topic of the messianic secret in Mark.[50] While his point of departure is an observation that is not new (the motif of the messianic secret seems to be burdened in Mark with the element of contradiction), the conclusion he arrives at is radical (the second evangelist undermined one of his own motifs). Be that as it may, the case Räisänen makes against the messianic secret as being a viable motif is so immediately relevant to any probe of the christology of Mark that it cannot simply be dismissed. In what follows, therefore, I shall take up Räisänen's arguments, but do so with a view towards gaining further insight into both the nature of the messianic secret and the way in which Mark develops this motif.

Initial Considerations

The first thing to note is that Räisänen consistently designates the secret of Jesus' identity as the "messianic secret." He does this because this is the term Wrede made current.[51] But this bow to conven-

---

47. Cf. ibid., pp. 14–16.
48. Cf. ibid., pp. 167–68.
49. Cf. ibid., pp. 14–15, 158, 160, 167–68.
50. In addition to the volumes by Wrede and Räisänen, cf. Ebeling, *Messias-geheimnis* (1939); Sjöberg, *Menschensohn* (1955); Burkill, *Mysterious Revelation* (1963); and Minette de Tillesse, *Le secret messianique* (1968).
51. Räisänen, *Messiasgeheimnis*, p. 27.

tion notwithstanding, the secret of Jesus' identity in Mark has to do more specifically with his divine sonship. To make this observation is, of course, not new,[52] but this fact neither diminishes the importance of the observation nor makes it any less imperative that one state on what basis it is being made.

As I see it, the reason the secret of Jesus' identity is to be understood as a secret about his divine sonship is that Mark more typically associates the twin features of "identity" and "secrecy" with "Son of God" throughout his story than with any other title. In his narrative comment of 1:1, Mark exclusively informs the reader that Jesus Christ is the Son of God.[53] In the baptismal scene, God affirms to Jesus alone that he is his beloved Son (1:11). In the course of Jesus' ministry in Galilee, the demons cry out that Jesus is the Son of God, but their shouts are systematically suppressed (1:24–25, 34; 3:11–12) or uttered in private confrontation (5:7). Atop the high mountain, God causes Jesus to be transfigured before Peter, James, and John and declares to them that Jesus is his beloved Son, but the three disciples are unable to grasp this revelation and, after it has occurred, Jesus enjoins the disciples to speak to no one about it (9:2–9). In hostile encounter with the Jewish leaders, Jesus designates himself as the "beloved son," but he does so in parabolic speech (12:1, 6). At his trial before the Sanhedrin, Jesus replies "I am!" to the question of whether he is the Messiah, the Son of the Blessed (God), but his reply is labeled as blasphemy so that, ironically, because of the willful ignorance of the Sanhedrin, his divine sonship remains unperceived (14:61–64). Finally, however, the centurion, seeing Jesus expire on the cross, bursts through the element of "secrecy" surrounding Jesus' "identity" as the "Son of God" by exclaiming openly, "Truly this man was the Son of God!" (15:39).

My contention is not that the title "Messiah" never exhibits these twin features of "identity" and "secrecy." On the contrary, at

---

52. Cf. Vielhauer, "Christologie des Markusevangeliums," pp. 201, 203; also Haenchen, *Weg Jesu*, p. 133; Kertelge, *Wunder Jesu*, p. 192; Gnilka, *Jesus Christus*, p. 145; Moule, "Messianic Secret," pp. 242–43; Luz, "Geheimnismotiv," p. 23.

53. According to the 26th edition of Nestle-Aland, *Novum Testamentum Graece*, the best manuscript evidence supports the inclusion of "Son of God" in Mark 1:1 as constituting the correct reading.

8:29–30 Peter confesses Jesus to be the Messiah and Jesus responds by issuing a command to silence. Still, this does not alter the fact that this combination of features does not constitute the hallmark of "Messiah." "Messiah" is the most general of Mark's christological categories, and what characterizes it are diversity of use and need for definition. To illustrate its diversity of use, "Messiah" can serve as a name (9:41), or as a name that is also a title (1:1), or as a title (8:29; 12:35; 13:21; 14:61; 15:32). And as for its need for definition, of the seven times Mark ascribes "Messiah" to Jesus, five times he explains how it is to be understood. Four times Mark defines "Messiah" in terms of either "Son of David" (12:35), or "King of Israel" (15:32), or "Son of God (the Blessed)" (1:1; 14:61), and one time he defines it, as we shall see in Chapter 3, by means of the context with which he associates it (8:29). Only twice, in fact, does "Messiah" appear as an "adequate" title for Jesus: once when it functions as a name ("because you are Christ's"; 9:41);[54] and once when it connotes "the Jesus of Mark's story" whose Parousia is awaited (13:21). Accordingly, in view of the way in which Mark deals with the title of "Messiah" as opposed to the title of "Son of God," it is a misnomer that obscures the true focus of the motif of the secret of Jesus' identity to term it a "messianic secret."

Recognition of the fact that the secret of Jesus' identity in Mark is not, finally, a "messianic secret" but the secret that he is the Son of God will, of course, affect the way in which one judges the cogency of the arguments Räisänen lodges against the literary and theological viability of this motif. Nonetheless, it is important to observe that, quite apart from this matter of terminology, not all of Räisänen's arguments are of equal weight. Räisänen contends, for instance, that Jesus' use of the term "bridegroom" in 2:19–20 constitutes a public disclosure of the mystery of his person.[55]

But "bridegroom" in 2:19–20 is a metaphor,[56] and as such it must

---

54. Cf. Hahn, *Hoheitstitel*, p. 224 n. 1.

55. Räisänen, *Messiasgeheimnis*, pp. 147–48.

56. Cf. Dewey, *Public Debate*, p. 118. In their exposition of Mark 2:19–20, recent commentators have been greatly influenced by the arguments of Jeremias (cf. *Gleichnisse*, p. 49 ns. 2–3 [ET, *Parables*, p. 52 ns. 13–14]) and Gnilka (cf. "Bräutigam," pp. 298–301; *Markus*, I, 114), who claim that in Mark 2:19a the term "bridegroom" is to be understood in its literal sense but that in 2:(19b)–20 it can be seen to have become a metaphor either for "Jesus" or for Jesus as the

first be deciphered for its meaning to be known. Does it refer to Jesus as the "Messiah," as it does in the Gospel of John (3:28–29)?[57] In the parable of the ten virgins in Matthew, it refers to Jesus as the coming "Son of Man" (25:1–13). Does it, then, refer here in Mark to Jesus as the earthly Son of Man (cf. 2:19 to 2:10; 2:28) and the suffering Son of Man (2:20)? Or are there yet other options to be considered? The point is, within the world of his story Mark leaves the meaning of "bridegroom" open. Except for the fact that one can surmise that it alludes to Jesus, it remains an undefined metaphor. But if "bridegroom" is an undefined metaphor, one cannot legitimately claim that Mark presents Jesus, in using this term, as making public the secret of his identity.

Three of Räisänen's other criticisms are likewise tenuous. He maintains, for instance, that the passage 9:9 is contradicted by 15:39.[58] At 9:9, Mark has Jesus stipulate that the resurrection will be the event after which the secret of his identity will no longer be in force. At 15:39, on the other hand, the centurion blatantly violates this stipulation by declaring at the foot of the cross that Jesus is the Son of God.

This criticism represents a misreading of 9:9. A look at this passage reveals that it portrays Jesus as enjoining Peter, James, and John (9:2) not to tell anyone of the things they have just witnessed atop the mountain of the transfiguration until he shall have risen from the dead. The passage 9:9, then, concerns an injunction Jesus gives to disciples. Moreover, if one traces the development of Mark's story, one discovers that this injunction is in fact kept. Not until the disciples shall have seen the crucified but risen Jesus at their projected meeting in Galilee (14:27–28; 16:6–7) can the reader assume that they attain to a proper understanding of what it is that they have experienced at the transfiguration (cf. 9:5–6, 9–10). But again, all of this concerns disciples of Jesus. The words of 9:9 are in no wise tantamount to the dictum that no character whatsoever in Mark's story will be permitted to comprehend that Jesus is the Son of God prior to the resurrection.

"Messiah." A major problem in interpreting Mark 2:19–20 is the simple fact that "bridegroom" seems not to have been used in OT and inter-testamental literature as a metaphor for the "Messiah" (cf. Jeremias, "Nymphē," pp. 1101–2).

57. Cf., e.g., Taylor, St. Mark, pp. 210–11.

58. Räisänen, Messiasgeheimnis, p. 154.

As these words read, they do not at all envisage the centurion. Hence, it cannot be said that his "confession" of Jesus at 15:39 amounts to a contradiction of them.

Again, Räisänen also contends that the secret of Jesus' identity becomes public knowledge through his narration of the parable of the wicked husbandmen (12:1–12).[59] This is evident, Räisänen says, because Mark lets it be known after Jesus has finished the parable that the Jewish leaders, to whom he has delivered it (11:27), "recognized that he had spoken the parable with reference to them."[60]

Here, too, Räisänen claims too much. In 12:1, Mark says of Jesus that "he began to speak to them [the Jewish leaders] in parables." Earlier in his story, Mark has had Jesus explain that his speaking in parables, that is, his parabolic speech, is mysterious speech (4:11–12).[61] It is so because such speech must not only be grasped by the mind but also appropriated by the heart.[62] When this happens, true understanding takes place, as in the case of "insiders"; when it does not, such speech condemns rather than illuminates, as in the case of "outsiders" (3:23; 4:2, 10–12).[63]

In the parable of the wicked husbandmen, Mark calls attention to both dimensions of parabolic speech. On the one hand, he does indeed state that the leaders of the Jews recognize that Jesus has told the parable with reference to them (12:12). In so doing, he informs the reader that the Jewish leaders have grasped only too well that Jesus has identified them with the rebellious and murderous tenants and himself with the beloved son (12:1–9). On the other hand, Mark likewise reports that the response of the Jewish leaders to Jesus' parable is that they want to seize him and only hold back for fear of the crowd (12:12). With this comment, Mark informs the reader that the Jewish leaders have rejected the truth-claim that Jesus' parable makes upon them. Their understanding of the parable is thus "obdurate understanding":[64] having heard the truth, they cannot receive the truth

---

59. Ibid., pp. 145–46.

60. This translation of Mark 12:12c is that of BAG, p. 710.

61. On the parable as mysterious speech in Mark, cf. Boucher, *Mysterious Parable*, pp. 24–25, 44, 83–84.

62. Cf. ibid., pp. 83–84.

63. Cf. Carlston, *Parables*, p. 179.

64. Cf. Pesch, *Markusevangelium*, II, 223, Cf. also the remarks of Boucher

and so repudiate it and are in turn condemned by it (cf. 4:12). In Mark's scheme of things, therefore, the parable of the wicked husbandmen does not become a vehicle for publicly unveiling the secret of Jesus' identity.

In the trial of Jesus before the Jewish Sanhedrin (14:55–65), Räisänen finds yet another instance in Mark where the secret of Jesus' identity comes to light. This occurs as Jesus responds with the words, "I am!" to the question of the high priest, "Are you the Messiah, the Son of the Blessed?" (14:61–62).[65] What Räisänen has overlooked, however, is the role that irony plays in Mark's depiction of Jesus' trial.[66] The secret of Jesus' identity is in fact embedded in the words of the high priest's question. But as Mark shows, the high priest poses his question in the conviction that it can only be answered rightly if it is answered in the negative (14:63–64). Hence, it is in the ignorance that attends repudiation that he utters the truth about Jesus' identity, which explains why, when Jesus answers him in the affirmative, he charges him with blasphemy (14:64). The trial of Jesus before the Sanhedrin does not result in the lifting of the secret of his divine sonship.

At this juncture, there are two further passages in Mark I should touch on even though Räisänen does not adjudge them to be contradictions to the secret of Jesus' identity. They are 5:7 and 13:32. The alleged problem with 5:7, which is located in the pericope on the Gerasene demoniac (5:1–20), is that it seems to be anomalous to the pattern Mark establishes in 1:24–25; 1:34; and 3:11–12. That is to say, although the man possessed of demons addresses Jesus as "Son of the Most High God," Jesus does not command him to silence.[67]

But the problem is more apparent than real. In the section 5:2–13, Mark depicts Jesus as being alone with the demoniac;[68] he commands the unclean spirit to leave the man (5:8), and the unclean spirits (now said to be legion) are destroyed as the pigs they enter rush into the sea and drown (5:13). Not until 5:14–20 do the herdsmen become

---

(*Mysterious Parable*, p. 60) on the topic of "hardness of heart" relative to parabolic speech.

65. Räisänen, *Messiasgeheimnis*, pp. 146–47.

66. On Mark's use of the literary device of irony in the passion narrative, cf. Juel, *Messiah and Temple*, pp. 47–48.

67. Cf., e.g., Boobyer, "Secrecy Motif," p. 229.

68. Cf. Lohmeyer, *Markus*, p. 98.

involved in the action, and from then on the narrative focuses on the impact the healing of the demoniac has both on the people of the region and on the life of the man himself. It may be that one will want to fault the evangelist for not having told this miracle-story more skillfully,[69] but the clear intention of the text to present Jesus and the demoniac in private encounter in 5:2–13 makes the need for a command to silence superfluous.[70]

To turn to 13:32, the context and the subject matter of the passage prevent the reader from sensing in the reference to "the Son" a break in the secret of Jesus' identity.[71] Whereas the secret holds until the crucifixion (15:39), Mark has Jesus speak to the four disciples in chapter 13 about matters of the future which lie well beyond the cross and resurrection: the destruction of the temple and the course of events that will issue in the coming at the end of time of Jesus in his role as the Son of Man. Literarily, by associating this reference to "the Son" with this "distant setting," Mark effectively removes it from the flow of his story that moves between baptism and crucifixion—resurrection.

Further Considerations

Thus far I have denied that the several examples of contradictions to the secret of Jesus' identity which Räisänen has cited are valid. But there is yet another group of examples he cites, and here the situation changes to a degree.

Räisänen insists, for instance, that the secret of Jesus' identity surfaces in all three of the pericopes that point to him as the Son of David (10:46–52; 11:1–11; 12:35–37).[72] In two of these pericopes, those on Jesus' entrance into Jerusalem (11:1–11) and on the question about David's son (12:35–37), such disclosure of the secret is indirect. But in the pericope on the healing of blind Bartimaeus (10:46–52), it is strikingly apparent. Because in this group of pericopes it is the one on Bartimaeus that is critical to Räisänen's argument, we can restrict our discussion to it.

As Mark describes it, Bartimaeus, a blind beggar, twice appeals for

---

69. Cf. Meagher, *Clumsy Construction*, pp. 67–74.

70. Cf. further Burkill, *Mysterious Revelation*, p. 89; Koch, *Wundererzählungen*, pp. 63–64; Moule, "Messianic Secret," p. 243.

71. In Chapter 3, I discuss why I believe that "the Son" in Mark 13:32 refers to Jesus as the Son of God.

72. Räisänen, *Messiasgeheimnis*, pp. 148–54.

mercy to Jesus as the Son of David in the presence of both the disciples and a large crowd, and Jesus responds to his appeal by granting him his sight (10:46–52). Consequently, one is surely correct in maintaining that Jesus is portrayed in this scene as being revealed in public to be the Son of David.[73]

But Räisänen to the contrary, the public revelation of Jesus as the Son of David does not put an end to the secret of Jesus' identity. The reason for this is that this secret focuses, as I have observed, not on Jesus' Davidic, but on his divine, sonship. Indeed, in Chapter 3 I shall note that in the third main part of his story (8:27—16:8), Mark guides the reader through a progressive unveiling of Jesus' identity: the reader witnesses, respectively, Peter confess Jesus to be the Messiah, Bartimaeus appeal to him as the Son of David, and, finally, the centurion penetrate what for Mark is the essential secret of Jesus' person, his divine sonship.

If Räisänen contends that the secret of Jesus' identity comes to light in the Son-of-David pericopes, he advances the same argument relative to the occurrence of "the Son of Man" in 2:10 and 2:28. As far as Räisänen is concerned, the appearance of "the Son of Man" in these passages undermines from the outset of Mark's story any notion of secrecy concerning Jesus' identity.[74]

Again, in one respect Räisänen is absolutely right in the observation he makes regarding 2:10 and 2:28: there is no hint of secrecy in Jesus' use of "the Son of Man" in these passages. In fact, the passage 8:38 might also be cited as a third example of this same kind. Thus, it is in the presence of the "crowd" and "some of the scribes" in the first instance (2:2, 4, 6, 12), in the presence of "the Pharisees" in the second instance (2:24), and in the presence of the "crowd with the disciples" in the third instance (8:34) that Jesus publicly refers to himself as the Son of Man.

But from this correct observation Räisänen draws a false conclusion. It does not follow that because Jesus publicly refers to himself in 2:10; 2:28; and 8:38 as the Son of Man, Mark has "sabotaged" (from the beginning of his story) the motif of the secret of Jesus' identity. An inference that better commends itself is simply that the title of "the

---

73. Cf. also the discussion of Mark 10:46–52 in Chapter 3.
74. Räisänen, *Messiasgeheimnis,* pp. 144–47.

Son of Man" does not function in Mark in the same way as does the title of the "Son of God." If this is in reality the case, then Mark's use of "the Son of Man" need not be such as to conflict with the motif of the secret of Jesus' identity.

Concluding Remarks

When Wrede first proposed his thesis concerning what he designated as the "messianic secret" at the turn of the century, he used it as an inclusive concept that allegedly governs every facet of Mark. Since then, Wrede's inclusive concept of the messianic secret has been pruned considerably. In the 1960s, scholars cautiously began to regard it as one motif among others, but by the '70s there were those who held that it encompasses no more than those few passages in which Jesus directs "commands to silence" to demons (1:24–25, 34; 3:11–12) and to his disciples (8:29–30; 9:9) to the effect that they should not reveal his identity. In what is to date the last major treatment of this topic, Räisänen acknowledged that these latter passages do indeed comprise what he calls the "true messianic secret" *(das eigentliche Messiasgeheimnis),* but he also reached the more significant conclusion that, literarily and theologically, the second evangelist so compromised the integrity of the messianic secret through contradiction and inconsistency that it plays only an inconsequential role in his gospel-story. In other words, according to Räisänen the vaunted "messianic secret" promulgated by Wrede had, after seventy-five years, proved to be a motif of next to no significance at all for understanding even the Marcan presentation of Jesus, let alone the entire Gospel of Mark.

I have discussed Räisänen's criticisms for two reasons: to show that these criticisms are not as compelling as they may appear; and, much more importantly, to use this discussion as a springboard for defining afresh, on literary-critical grounds, the nature and scope of the motif of the secret of Jesus' identity in Mark.

The secret of Jesus' identity in Mark is not, characteristically, a "messianic" secret but the secret that Jesus is the Son of God. This secret remains in force from the time Jesus first appears at his baptism to the time of his crucifixion (15:39) and resurrection (16:6–7). To preserve this secret intact, the most prominent device the evangelist employed is in fact the "commands to silence" which Jesus gives to the demons (1:24–25, 34; 3:11–12) and to his disciples (8:29–30; 9:7, 9) to the end that they should not make him known.

But the evangelist also employed a variety of other devices to safeguard the integrity of the secret. Thus, in the first verse of his Gospel he makes use of the "editorial comment" ("The beginning of the gospel of Jesus Messiah, the Son of God"), to which the characters in his story are of course not privy. At two places, he draws on the narrative feature of "privacy": in the baptismal scene, it is solely to Jesus that the heavenly voice affirms that he is "my [God's] Son" (1:10–11, RSV); and in the pericope on the Gerasene demoniac, the demoniac is alone with Jesus when he addresses him as "Son of the Most High God" (5:7; cf. 5:2–13, RSV). Again, to extend the motif of the secret of Jesus' identity, the evangelist furthermore avails himself both in a general way and at specific places of other motifs, such as those of Jesus' speaking in parables and of the ignorance of the disciples, without at the same time compromising the distinctiveness of these motifs. Examples of the pointed use of these other motifs are the notation in the parable chapter that "those outside" are blind and bereft of spiritual insight (4:10–12), the attribution of "obdurate understanding" to the Jewish leaders in Jesus' telling of the parable of the wicked husbandmen (11:27; 12:1–12), and the "narrative comment" concerning the fear and incomprehension that befall the three disciples as they bear witness to the transfiguration of Jesus (9:6). In other respects, the evangelist likewise brings into play the literary device of irony to sustain the secret of Jesus' identity: at Jesus' trial before the Sanhedrin, the high priest, asking Jesus who he is, utters the mystery of his person (14:61); still, the high priest does not penetrate this mystery, for he remains ignorant of the truth he has spoken (14:63–64). Incidentally, the same element of irony colors the narrative of Jesus before Pilate and on the cross, for neither Pilate nor the Jewish leaders nor the Jewish people believe that Jesus is in fact "the Messiah, the King of the Jews (Israel)" (cf. 15:2, 9, 12, 18, 26, 32). And last, the evangelist in one instance safeguards the secret of Jesus' identity through his use of the prophetic mode of speech: when Jesus refers to himself as "the Son" in his eschatological discourse (13:32), the predictive nature of his speech situates this reference in a context that lies beyond the crucifixion and resurrection and envisages the time before the Parousia.

Thus far little has been said about "the Son of Man." In any attempt to come to grips with the christology of Mark, one of the central problems one faces is how to relate the title of "the Son of Man" to the title of the "Son of God." Since the time of Wrede, Marcan scholarship has had much to say about this problem. Indeed, in the last years one solution has become dominant. A discussion of this solution is therefore mandatory.

2   THE SHAPE OF THE PROBLEM

Corrective Christology
in Mark

In the course of the last years, the so-called "corrective" approach to the christology of Mark has become dominant in scholarly circles, especially in North America. According to this approach the second evangelist, for one or more adduced reasons, regarded the title "Son of God" (with which "Messiah," too, is aligned) as defective for conveying the true meaning of the person of Jesus. As a result, a major part of the program the evangelist set for himself in writing his Gospel[1] was to "correct" the title Son of God. This he did, through his espousal of a theology of the cross and the use he made of the title "the Son of Man." In the Gospel of Mark, therefore, the interpreter encounters what may be termed a "corrective christology." In this chapter, I aim to survey the history of this approach to Mark's christology. This will shed light on the problematic associated with it and pave the way for the alternative approach to be pursued in Chapter 3.

CORRECTIVE CHRISTOLOGY:
FROM WREDE TO THE PRESENT

The notion that "Son of God" in Mark is defective for explaining who Jesus is until it has been corrected by "the cross" and "the Son of Man" is bound up with the further notion that "Son of God" is to be interpreted in terms of the Hellenistic concept of "divine man" *(theios anēr)*. But this view, in turn, presupposes a prior view, namely, that the second evangelist found the concept of "divine man," for reasons we shall soon explore, to be flawed as a vehicle for describing Jesus. The latter view, however, has become current in Marcan studies

---

1. For a brief overview of the "accomplishment" of Mark, cf. Kingsbury, *Jesus Christ*, pp. 28–60.

only relatively recently. Before it asserted itself, in fact, Marcan studies went through a period during which "Son of God" was correlated
with "divine man" in a highly positive fashion. It is with this period,
therefore, that our survey begins.

The First Phase

The work of William Wrede is once again a convenient place to
begin since his book on the messianic secret is, as I noted in the last
chapter, a watershed in Marcan studies. Wrede properly recognized
that the baptismal scene is, as he put it, "extraordinarily important"
to Mark's presentation of Jesus.[2] In this scene, Jesus sees the Spirit
descend upon him and hears the voice from heaven announce to him
that he is God's beloved Son (1:9–11). To discern the significance of
this event, it is idle, Wrede believed, to turn to the theocratic categories
of Jewish messianism, for Jesus ceases at the baptism to be a mere
human being and becomes instead a supernatural being. Through the
reception of the Spirit he, the Messiah, becomes endowed with a
supernatural nature by virtue of which he will perform miracles and
impart through his teaching heavenly wisdom and knowledge.

Wrede does not attach the label of "divine man" to this characterization of Jesus. On the contrary, he even questions in passing whether
Mark's Jesus can be equated with a "son of the gods" or a "hero"
of the ancient world.[3] Yet, his understanding of the Marcan Jesus is
such that Rudolf Bultmann, in his *Theologie des Neuen Testaments*[4]
(the first installment of which appeared in 1948), appropriated it and
designated it as divine-man christology of the first type.[5] For its part,
Bultmann's use of the term "divine man" presupposed, as his citation
of the scholarly literature shows,[6] the two-volume study published by
Ludwig Bieler in 1935–36 and entitled *Theios Anēr*.[7]

By his own account, Bieler was the first to delineate the ancient

---

2. Wrede, *Messiasgeheimnis*, pp. 71–79 (ET, *Messianic Secret*, pp. 72–79).

3. Ibid., p. 76 (ET, p. 76).

4. ET, *Theology of the New Testament*.

5. Bultmann, *Theologie*, pp. 132–33 (ET, *Theology*, I, 130–31).

6. Cf. ibid., p. 123 (the references to scholarly literature cited in the German
edition have been omitted from the English edition).

7. For bibliographical details, cf. the Selected Bibliography.

Greco-Roman concept of the "divine man" *(theios anēr)*.[8] According to Bieler this concept, long in developing, first became fixed in the age of Hellenism, when it became commonplace in religious and philosophical thought.[9] As presented by the sources, the "divine man" is a person of genius, or "superman" *(Uebermensch)*, who, though human, is indwelt by the divine.[10] By nature, therefore, the divine man is one who possesses extraordinary gifts and abilities. Among other things, he distinguishes himself both by his divine wisdom and by his divine power to perform miracles.[11]

This thumbnail sketch of the divine man, abstracted from Bieler's discussion,[12] tallies well with Wrede's description of the baptized Jesus. This no doubt explains in large part why Bultmann could so easily adopt Wrede's understanding of the Marcan Jesus and designate it as "divine-man christology." In Bultmann's eyes, the Gospel of Mark was at home in the Hellenistic churches of Pauline persuasion.[13] The. accomplishment of the second evangelist is that he united the "Hellenistic kerygma about Christ, whose essential content consists of the Christ-myth [cf. Phil. 2:6–11] . . . , with the tradition of the story of Jesus."[14] Christologically, therefore, the "Son of God" of the Gospel of Mark is the same figure as the "Son of God" of Pauline theology. The one difference between them is that the second evangelist neglected to incorporate into his christological portrayal of the Son of God the notion of preexistence.[15] In recognition of this omission, it is thus

---

8. Cf. Bieler, *Theios Anēr*, I, 4–5. By the same token, Bieler (ibid., I, 5 n. 10) does not neglect to acknowledge the contributions made to the study of his subject matter by such scholars as G. P. Wetter (cf. *Sohn Gottes*) and H. Windisch (cf. *Paulus und Christus*). For an instructive survey of the pertinent literature dealing with "divine man" and related topics, cf. Smith, "Prolegomena," pp. 174–99.

9. Bieler, *Theios Anēr*, I, 2–3.

10. Ibid., I, 129, 141; II, 113.

11. Ibid., I, 73–97.

12. For other definitions of "divine man," cf. H. D. Betz, "Divine Man," p. 116; and Achtemeier, "Divine Man," p. 187.

13. Bultmann, *Geschichte der synoptischen Tradition*, p. 372 (ET, *History of the Synoptic Tradition*, p. 347).

14. Ibid.

15. Ibid., p. 374 (ET, p. 348).

preferable to designate his conception of Jesus as "divine-man christology of the 'first type.' " Nevertheless, the fact remains: through
his reception of the Spirit at the baptism, the Marcan Jesus becomes
Son of God, that is, divine man.[16]

In 1956, Willi Marxsen inaugurated the era of redaction criticism
in Marcan studies with the publication of his well-known monograph,
Der Evangelist Markus.[17] Unlike Bultmann, Marxsen does not conceive of Mark as having been read in the Hellenistic churches of Paul
but as having served the needs of a Christian community in Galilee
awaiting the imminent Parousia of the resurrected Jesus.[18] But on the
matter of christology, Marxsen adheres faithfully to the views of Bultmann. For him, too, the line that runs between Paul and Mark is
straight, and one indication of this is the message Mark proclaims in
the passion narrative: "the Risen Lord—the Son of God—goes to the
Cross."[19] As one could expect, therefore, Marxsen nowhere hints that
he demurs at Bultmann's correlation of Son of God in Mark with the
idea of divine man.

The Second Phase

Accordingly, what is noteworthy about the first period of the divine-
man approach to Mark's christology is that the concept of divine man
was clearly being used in a positive sense in order to claim that, except
for the idea of preexistence, Mark's understanding of Jesus as the
Messiah (Christ), the Son of God, is fundamentally the same as that
of Paul. The second period of this approach began in the late 1950s
and runs to the present. This period, however, has been marked by
a striking change: theologically, the Hellenistic concept of divine man,
as it finds expression in the Gospel of Mark, has no longer been
adjudged to be a positive factor but a negative one. What this means
concretely is that scholars have taken one of two positions on the way
in which the second evangelist developed his christology: some have
maintained that he himself became a spokesman for the Hellenistic,
divine-man christology he received from the tradition, the upshot being

---

16. Bultmann, *Theologie*, p. 133 (ET, *Theology*, I, 131).

17. ET, *Mark the Evangelist*.

18. Marxsen, *Markus*, pp. 59–61 (ET, *Mark*, pp. 92–94).

19. Marxsen, *Einleitung*, p. 123 (ET, *Introduction*, p. 137). Cf. also Marxsen,
Markus, pp. 98–100, 145–47 (ET, *Mark*, pp. 146–49, 213–16).

that the christology of his Gospel is "inferior" to that of either Paul or John; or, conversely, others have maintained that the evangelist took over this Hellenistic, divine-man christology only in order to combat and to correct it.

Dieter Georgi and Siegfried Schulz appear to advocate the first of these two positions. In his influential study on the opponents of Paul in 2 Corinthians, Georgi argues that the tradition the evangelist inherited, as seen in some of his miracle-stories and in the story of the transfiguration, presents Jesus uneschatologically as a supernatural being and superior miracle-worker, that is, as a divine man of Jewish-Hellenistic stripe, and that christologically the evangelist continued in this tradition.[20] For his part, Schulz avers that the evangelist's debt to the divine-man concept of Jewish-Hellenistic Christianity was such that, although he pictures the Son of God who performs miracles as also going the way of the cross, he nevertheless converted the "theology of the cross" into a "theology of glory."[21]

A greater number of scholars, however, have taken the second position and insisted that the evangelist combated and reinterpreted the Hellenistic, divine-man christology of his tradition by subordinating it to his understanding of Jesus as one who must suffer and die on the cross. In which part of the tradition is the divine-man christology that the evangelist allegedly combated to be found? Scholars have pointed above all to the miracle-stories.

For example, Johannes Schreiber asserts in a probe of Mark's christology that the evangelist "reshaped" the divine-man christology he encountered in such traditional stories as the exorcisms, miracles, and debates of Jesus by depicting the cross, and not these other events, as the place where the Son of God decisively defeats the forces of Satan.[22] Ulrich Luz, in turn, claims in his investigation of the messianic secret that the strategy of the second evangelist was not to eliminate the divine-man christology of the miracle-stories but to utilize these stories to extol the glory of a Jesus whose true majesty lies in going the way of the cross.[23] Again, Leander Keck states in his study of

---

20. Georgi, *Gegner des Paulus*, pp. 210, 213–16.

21. Schulz, *Stunde der Botschaft*, pp. 54–59, 64–79, esp. 77.

22. Schreiber, "Christologie," p. 158.

23. Luz, "Geheimnismotiv," pp. 28–30.

Mark 3:7–12 that the evangelist can be seen to have appropriated a traditional cycle of miracle-stories, which were imbued with a Hellenistic, divine-man christology focusing on the manifestation of the divine power of the Son of God, and to have "restricted" the significance of these stories by interpreting the life of Jesus as a whole in the light of the cross.[24] On a slightly different note, Hans Dieter Betz contends in his study of Jesus as divine man that, although the evangelist persisted in adhering to the divine-man christology of his sources, he employed such elements as the theory of the messianic secret, the account of the passion of Jesus, and a stress on eschatology in order to "reinterpret critically" this divine-man christology on the basis of the kerygma of the cross and resurrection of Jesus.[25] In a similar vein as Keck, Paul Achtemeier argues in his analysis of the pre-Marcan tradition that the evangelist drew on two cycles of miracle-stories, which originally formed part of a liturgy celebrating "an epiphanic Eucharist" based on bread broken with the divine-man Jesus, and that he sought to "overcome" this view of Jesus and of the Eucharist by inserting these cycles into a different framework, namely, one that calls attention to the importance of Jesus' death.[26] And last, Ludger Schenke maintains in his study of the miracle-stories in Mark that the theological accomplishment of the second evangelist is that he penned a "history of Jesus" whereby he pictures the true epiphany of the Son of God as taking place, not in the divinely wrought, glorious miracles he performs, but in his death in hiddenness and humility on the cross.[27]

One can observe from the latter survey that, in the 1960s and '70s, the notion obtained in some quarters that the second evangelist stood at considerable theological distance from a part of his tradition, especially some or all of the miracle-stories, and that this reflects itself

---

24. Keck, "Mark's Christology," pp. 349–51, 354, 357–58.

25. H. D. Betz, "Divine Man," pp. 121–25. Cf. also idem, "Gottmensch II," pp. 300–302. I should gratefully like to acknowledge the receipt from Hans Dieter Betz of an offprint of this latter article which, unfortunately, reached me after the manuscript for this book had been completed. As far as Mark is concerned, Betz's position in this article is the same as that expressed in his earlier piece on "Jesus as Divine Man," cited above in this footnote.

26. Achtemeier, "Origin and Function of the Pre-Marcan Miracle Catenae," pp. 198, 220–21.

27. Schenke, Wundererzählungen, pp. 393–95.

in the circumstance that he counteracted the divine-man christology this tradition proclaimed. Seizing on this notion of "christological tension" between the evangelist and his tradition, Theodore Weeden has attempted to parlay it into a comprehensive thesis that will explain the whole of the evangelist's theological program. Depending heavily on Georgi's sketch of the opponents of Paul in 2 Corinthians, Weeden suggests that the evangelist wrote his Gospel in order to combat "false prophets" and "false Christs" who had invaded his community. These individuals, announcing Christ to be a great *theios anēr* and claiming that he was present in them and spoke through them, insisted that authentic Christian existence finds meaning and fulfillment not in suffering servanthood, but in the pneumatic glory of divine-man existence.[28] The evangelist met this heresy, Weeden claims, by depicting Jesus, who functions in effect as the evangelist's spokesman and espouses the theology of the cross, as discrediting the disciples, who become in effect surrogates for the evangelist's opponents and advocates of their theology of glory.[29]

Of the Marcan scholars in North America, Norman Perrin has perhaps been more influential in recent years than anyone else. With Weeden's work serving as a "catalytic agent" for his own,[30] Perrin, too, took the position that the evangelist was in christological tension with his tradition and that he resolved this by "correcting" the tradition's false picture of Jesus as divine man. How did he do this? The clue to answering this lies, in Perrin's eyes, in determining precisely how the evangelist relates the title "the Son of Man" in his Gospel to the title "Son of God." Specifically, the evangelist employs the title the Son of Man to "interpret and to give a correct content to the belief in Jesus as Son of God" by playing down the divine-man connotations of the latter title and emphasizing the necessity of suffering.[31]

With Perrin, other scholars have also taken up the view that, of the christological titles that occur in the Gospel of Mark, "the Son of Man" is the only one the second evangelist found adequate to meet

---

28. Weeden, "Heresy," pp. 153–55.
29. Ibid., pp. 150, 155–58.
30. Perrin, "Christology of Mark," p. 110 n. 16.
31. Ibid., pp. 92–93, 112–13.

his purposes. To return to Weeden, he flatly declares in his book of 1971 that the "Son-of-man title is the only christological title in Mark that is not censored or cloaked in secrecy."[32] For his part, John Donahue affirms in his analysis of the trial narrative that "the Son of Man" is the title par excellence in Mark because, unlike the titles "Christ," "Son of God," "Son of David," and "Lord," it is "never associated with false or inaccurate meanings."[33] Similarly, Paul Achtemeier writes in his study of Mark that the one christological title that the evangelist found to be neither "ambiguous" ("Christ," "Son of God") nor "inadequate" ("Son of David," "prophet") but suitable to express the meaning of Jesus of Nazareth is that of "the Son of Man."[34] In a different vein, Norman Petersen states in his book on literary criticism that the Marcan narrator invites the reader to regard Jesus' own "divine" understanding of himself as being the Son of Man as the opposite of the erroneous "human" notion of the disciples that he is the king.[35] And to round things out with an opinion that is the obverse of those just cited, Werner Kelber opts in his investigation of the Kingdom of God in Mark for a form of corrective christology that finds no fault with "Son of God" but associates "the Son of Man," understood apocalyptically, as expressive of a false christology that was being touted by Jerusalem-oriented Jewish Christians with whom the second evangelist was in conflict.[36]

To recapitulate, from Wrede to the present there has been a prominent trend among Marcan scholars to identify the attitude the second evangelist took towards the Hellenistic concept of divine man as the interpretive key for unlocking his christology. The historical survey of the work of these scholars divides itself into two phases. In the first phase, the term "divine man" was used positively to argue the thesis that the second evangelist intended nothing else than to proclaim the

---

32. Weeden, *Mark*, p. 65 n. 20; cf. p. 67.

33. Donahue, *Christ*, pp. 182, 184; cf. also pp. 89–90, 95, 178–80. It should be noted, however, that Donahue's doctoral dissertation is not his latest word on the christology of Mark. In a more recent essay ("Royal Christology," pp. 72–78), he argues that Mark's christology is to be interpreted in the light of Jewish royal messianism and he illustrates how he believes Davidic motifs and expectations have been applied in Mark to Jesus.

34. Achtemeier, *Mark*, pp. 41–47.

35. Petersen, *Literary Criticism for New Testament Critics*, pp. 62–64, 67–68.

36. Kelber, *Kingdom in Mark*, pp. 22, 64–65, 80, 135–37.

same kerygma as Paul. But in the second phase, the term "divine man" has been seen as a concept in need of correction. Thus, where it is held that the second evangelist followed the lead of his tradition and simply appropriated the Jewish-Hellenistic, divine-man (Son-of-God) christology that had come down to him, there the evangelist himself has become the target of criticism owing to his alleged advocacy of a theology of glory. By contrast, where it is held that the second evangelist adopted a critical stance over against the Jewish-Hellenistic, divine-man (Son-of-God) christology of his tradition or of persons in his community or of both, there the evangelist has been seen as having combated and corrected this christology through his advocacy of a theology of the cross and his use of the title the Son of Man.

CORRECTIVE CHRISTOLOGY:
A REAPPRAISAL

Over the years, the view that the attitude the second evangelist took towards the Hellenistic concept of "divine man" is pivotal to a proper grasp of his christology has not, of course, gone uncontested.[37] Indeed, in the last decade the scholarly criticism of this view has been steadily mounting. In this section, I aim both to review this criticism and to raise additional questions. Four problem areas will receive attention: matters related to the term *theios anēr* ("divine man") itself; the scholarly probe of the pre-Marcan tradition; the inclination to find the interpretive key to Marcan christology outside the Second Gospel; and the viability of the contention that the second evangelist employed one christological title, namely, that of the Son of Man, to "correct" another, namely, that of Son of God.

The Debate over the Term "Divine Man"

The reason the term *theios anēr* has itself become the object of debate is that those who have used it to characterize the christology of Mark or of the pre-Marcan tradition have tended to work with it as though it were a fixed concept with precise meaning. We recall that

---

37. For the criticism of an earlier generation, cf. Manson, *Jesus the Messiah*, pp. 43–46; and Bieneck, *Sohn Gottes*, pp. 70–74.

the divine man of Hellenism is said to be an extraordinary personage,
or "superman," who is indwelt by the divine and consequently possesses both supernatural wisdom and the supernatural power to perform miracles.[38] Recent investigations, however, have challenged the
notion that the term *theios anēr* ever achieved the status of a fixed
concept in the ancient world. In his survey of the pertinent Greek
literature, for example, the philologist Wülfing von Martitz points out
that "divine man" is a comparatively rare term in ancient Greek
literature, that it is not associated in any firm way with those extraordinary personages to whom some form of divinity is ascribed, and
that it is also not clear from the texts that such "divine persons" were
usually held to be "sons of gods."[39] The overall conclusion von
Martitz reaches is that *theios anēr*, in the pre-Christian era at any rate,
never was a "technical term" or "fixed expression."[40] But if this is
in fact the case, it also follows that neither could "son of god" have
been a title by which the "divine man" was known.[41]

Other scholars have taken the same stand as von Martitz.[42] Moreover, his conclusions appear to have been corroborated by the studies
of David Tiede and Carl Holladay. Tiede, for instance, shows how
precarious it is to suppose that *theios anēr* was a fixed concept in
Hellenism by demonstrating that, until the second century A.D. at the
least, one can distinguish in ancient Greek thought, including Hellenistic Judaism, not one type but "two (discrete) types" of heroes said
to be divine: whereas the one type is said to be divine by reason of
his great wisdom and moral virtue, the other type is said to be divine
by reason of his great power to perform miracles.[43] Implicitly, there-

---

38. Cf. above, notes 10, 11, and 12, p. 27.

39. Von Martitz, *"Hyios,"* pp. 338–40.

40. Ibid., p. 339.

41. Cf. Hengel, *Sohn Gottes,* p. 50 (ET, *Son of God,* p. 31).

42. Cf., e.g., Lentzen-Deis, *Taufe Jesu,* pp. 273, 276; O. Betz, "Divine
Man," pp. 229–40; Schweizer, "Markus-Forschung in USA," pp. 535–37; Kee,
"Aretalogy," pp. 402–22; Roloff, "Kuhn: Aeltere Sammlungen," p. 519; Berger,
"Messianität Jesu," pp. 6–7; Theissen, *Wundergeschichten,* pp. 262–73, 277–82;
Hengel, *Sohn Gottes,* pp. 50–53 (ET, *Son of God,* pp. 31–32); Egger, *Frohbot-
schaft,* pp. 138–41; Pesch, *Markusevangelium,* I, 277–81; Danker, *Benefactor,*
p. 492.

43. Tiede, *Charismatic Figure,* pp. 4–13, 98–99, 289, 291.

fore, Tiede's study calls into question the notion that Mark's portrait of Jesus as the Son of God has its source in ancient Greek traditions concerning divine heroes because, in bridging these discrete traditions Tiede has described, Mark's portrait can be seen not to conform to them.

Still, Tiede does not deal with the expression *theios anēr* per se. Holladay, however, does deal with it, concentrating his attention on its use in Jewish-Hellenistic literature (Philo, Josephus, and Artapanus). His reason for investigating this literature is that some scholars have rather easily assumed, especially in the aftermath of Georgi's imposing study concerning the opponents of Paul in 2 Corinthians, that the Hellenistic concept of divine man entered early Christian theology under the influence of Hellenistic Judaism. Do the results of Holladay's investigation support the thesis that behind the title "Son of God" in the Gospel of Mark there stands a concept of "divine man" as mediated by Hellenistic Judaism? The answer is negative. For one thing, *theios anēr* in Hellenistic Judaism was, again, no fixed concept but a fluid expression, as can be seen from the fact that it could vary dramatically in meaning and signify a "divine man," an "inspired man," a "man related to God," or an "extraordinary man."[44] For another thing, miracle-working in Mark's Gospel is integral to what it means for Jesus to be "Son of God," and yet, surprisingly, it does not appear that in Hellenistic Judaism such miracle-working was even essential to the notion of a hero's being a divine man.[45]

The debate over the term *theios anēr* has not run its course. But at the present time, it does seem to have had one noticeable effect on Marcan studies: scholars have become more cautious than once was the case about assuming that *theios anēr* was, at the time the second evangelist wrote, a fixed concept with a prescribed meaning and so well known that the Marcan title of Son of God can readily be correlated with it. Indeed, in the recent past one of the questions urgently raised in Marcan studies has been: Against what background is the

---

44. Holladay, *Theios Anēr*, p. 237.
45. Ibid., pp. 236–39, 241.

title Son of God to be interpreted? In response to this question, several scholars have been looking to traditions that run through Judaism back to such OT passages as 2 Samuel 7 and Psalm 2.[46] Yet, one of the burdens of this approach has consistently been that scholars have been unable to document the use of "son of God" in pre-Christian Judaism as a title for the Messiah. As late as 1969, for instance, W. G. Kümmel still held fast to an argument he had advanced in 1950, namely, that "son of God" cannot be construed as a name for the Messiah at the time of Jesus because there is "not a single, sure piece of evidence" *(nicht einen einzigen, sicheren Beleg)* in pre-Christian Judaism to show that "son of God" was a messianic title.[47]

Since then, however, the ongoing analysis of texts from Qumran has shed new light on this question, although the scholarly measurement of the amount of light differs. Thus, C. F. D. Moule states, in an appeal to three of these texts, that "it is certainly demonstrable that to be God's son was . . . recognized as one of the Messiah's characteristics."[48] Matthew Black, in turn, is bolder than Moule, declaring that 4Q Flor. has made "fully certain" the messianic use of the whole christological concept of the Son in pre-Christian Judaism.[49] Joseph Fitzmyer, on the other hand, is more guarded in his claims, for he believes that no direct connection has yet been established in pre-Christian Judaism between "son of God" and Jewish messianology.[50] At the same time, what Fitzmyer does assert in a discussion of a find at Qumran is that "son of God" can be seen to be both "titular" and "royal" (applied to a son of an enthroned king who is possibly a Davidic heir) and that, if this title is not directly connected to messianic expectations, it is even less connected "with a *theios anēr* of a miracle-working setting."[51] On balance, although the latter statement by Fitz-

---

46. Cf., e.g., Schweizer, *"Hyios,"* pp. 367–68, 378–79; O. Betz, "Divine Man," pp. 234–40; Donahue, "Royal Christology," pp. 71–78; Kee, *Jesus in History,* pp. 150–52; Juel, *Messiah and Temple,* pp. 77–116; Steichele, *Sohn Gottes,* passim; Matera, *Kingship of Jesus,* passim.

47. Cf. Kümmel, "Gleichnis von den bösen Weingärtnern," p. 215; *Theologie,* p. 68 (ET, *Theology,* p. 76).

48. Moule, *Christology,* p. 28.

49. Black, "Christological Use of the OT," pp. 2–4.

50. Fitzmyer, *Wandering Aramean,* pp. 105–6.

51. Ibid., pp. 106–7.

myer does not envisage Marcan studies, it would appear to capture rather well the current trend of things: to the same extent that the Hellenistic expression *theios anēr* seems to have become less plausible as the key for understanding the title Son of God in the Gospel of Mark, the OT background of the title and the traditions that flow from it seem to be growing in significance.

The Probe of the Pre-Marcan Tradition

The second problem-area associated with the view that the door to a proper understanding of Mark's christology is the Hellenistic concept of divine man has to do with the pre-Marcan tradition. We have seen that there are those scholars who contend that the second evangelist assumed a negative stance towards part of his tradition because it was imbued with a divine-man christology. To prove the truth of this contention, one must be able to delineate the contours of this tradition and to describe the situation-in-life in which it arose. But on both counts, the results achieved have proved to be unsatisfactory or tenuous or conflicting.

As far as delineating the tradition with which the evangelist was at odds is concerned, some scholars have contented themselves with merely making vague references, for example, to the miracles of Jesus[52] or to his miracles and debates[53] or even to the entire first half of Mark's Gospel.[54] By contrast, other scholars, such as Leander Keck,[55] Paul Achtemeier,[56] and Heinz-Wolfgang Kuhn,[57] have in fact made notable attempts to isolate one or more cycles of miracle-stories in Mark and to show how they believe the evangelist overcame the divine-man christology inherent in them. But aside from the fact that their findings do not dovetail as neatly as one would want,[58]

---

52. Cf., e.g., Bultmann, *Geschichte der synoptischen Tradition*, p. 256 (ET, *History of the Synoptic Tradition*, pp. 240–41); Schulz, *Stunde der Botschaft*, pp. 64–79.

53. Cf., e.g., Schreiber, "Christologie," p. 158.

54. Cf., e.g., Weeden, "Heresy," p. 148.

55. "Mark's Christology," pp. 341–58.

56. "Origin and Function of the Pre-Marcan Miracle Catenae," pp. 198–221.

57. *Aeltere Sammlungen*, pp. 191–213.

58. Cf. with one another, e.g., the results achieved by Keck ("Mark's Christology," p. 349), Achtemeier ("Isolation of Pre-Markan Miracle Catenae," p.

Kuhn[59] admits to some ambivalence as to how certain he is that the cycle of pre-Marcan miracle-stories he has uncovered ever existed in that form, and Dietrich-Alex Koch[60] and Ludger Schenke,[61] who have also made detailed studies of the miracle-stories in Mark, either flatly deny that the evangelist took from the tradition any blocks of miracle-stories or else insist that he only drew upon a loose grouping of oral units that had not as yet been made to serve any single "intention." These widely differing results evoke a practical question: To what degree can one permit the hypothesis—that it was a fundamental goal of the second evangelist to correct a heretical, divine-man christology that was embedded in a significant portion of the miracle-tradition he appropriated—to govern one's understanding of his "christological program" when this heretical tradition is as elusive and difficult to pin down as these studies apparently indicate?

As for the situation-in-life in which the divine-man tradition of Mark presumably emerged, the inclination has been simply to co-opt Georgi's description of the divine-man heresy Paul faced in the A.D. 50s at Corinth and to postulate the same heresy as having afflicted the community out of which the Second Gospel eventually arose around A.D. 70.[62] Justification for making this postulate is the hypothesis that itinerant Christian missionaries of Jewish-Hellenistic stripe spread the heresy of Corinth from place to place throughout the Roman Empire. But Ludger Schenke, who otherwise also draws on Georgi's work, objects to this facile ascription of the Corinthian heresy to the Marcan community. It rests on an assumption he finds highly improbable, namely, that the opponents of Paul at Corinth can be made representative of the whole of the Jewish-Hellenistic Christian missionary movement, and this over a longer period of time.[63] Whatever one may think of Schenke's demurral, it does underline how conjectural any

---

291), and Kuhn (*Aeltere Sammlungen*, p. 203). Cf. further Fowler's critique of efforts to isolate pre-Marcan cycles of miracle-stories (*Loaves and Fishes*, chap. 1).

59. *Aeltere Sammlungen*, pp. 203, 209, 214.

60. *Wundererzählungen*, p. 39.

61. *Wundererzählungen*, pp. 384–86.

62. The work of Kuhn (*Aeltere Sammlungen*, pp. 211–13) and of Weeden ("Heresy," pp. 150, 153–54; *Mark*, p. 60) reflects this view particularly well.

63. Schenke, *Wundererzählungen*, pp. 386–87.

attempt to reconstruct the situation-in-life in which the pre-Marcan tradition developed necessarily must be.

But now a word of clarification is in order. There is no intention in the preceding discussion to claim that the gospel miracle-stories were immune in the course of their transmission from the influences of the Greco-Roman world. On the contrary, it is common knowledge that the miracle-stories attributed to Jesus exhibit structural and stylistic features that parallel those found in the miracle-stories attributed to such figures as Apollonius of Tyana,[64] the itinerant Neo-Pythagorean philosopher, or to Hanina ben Dosa, a Jewish rabbi.[65] No, the issue is rather this: Do the very shape and style of these miracle-stories (cf., e.g., Mark 4:35—6:52) make them the bearers of a non-eschatological theology of glory and divine-man christology that a theologian of the cross, such as the second evangelist, *would have to see himself as "correcting" if he took them up into his Gospel?* Apparently, there are any number of scholars who have entertained this question and answered it in the affirmative. But in so doing, they have opted for an approach to the christology of Mark that is difficult to sustain.

To begin with, this approach is of course tradition-critical in nature. That is to say, it is from the miracle-tradition lying behind the Gospel of Mark that one comes to the Gospel. What makes this approach objectionable, however, is the fact that the interpreter who chooses it knows, virtually in advance of his having read the Gospel of Mark in terms of itself (= literary criticism), what the christological program of the second evangelist will be, namely, that of "correcting" the heretical christology of his miracle-tradition. Moreover, because "Son of God" is the title that is reputedly to be associated with this miracle-tradition, the interpreter likewise knows (again, virtually in advance of his having read the Gospel) that the second evangelist will also be concerned to "correct" this title. To speak methodologically, the problem with the approach to the christology of Mark we are discussing is that the tradition-critical method dictates how the literary-critical method is to be applied.

Without doubt, it is some form of the tradition-critical method, coupled with some view of the political, social, and religious history of the NT era, that has determined how the Gospel of Mark has been

---

64. Cf., e.g., Petzke, *Apollonius von Tyana,* passim.
65. Cf., e.g., Vermes, *Jesus the Jew,* pp. 72–78.

interpreted in this century.[66] Literary criticism, by whatever name and however naively or sophisticatedly it has been practiced, has been handmaiden to tradition criticism. But suppose one undertakes to read the Gospel of Mark on its own terms apart from the obvious dictates of tradition criticism. One could well arrive at different conclusions regarding the significance (or insignificance) in Mark of a "corrective christology" and the status and function of the title "Son of God." Ideally and in the long run, of course, the results of the application of both the literary-critical and the tradition-critical methods can be expected to confirm and reinforce one another. But if at the present the results of the application of the two methods conflict, it may turn out that it is our tradition-critical perceptions that are in need of revision.

The Key to Mark's Christology as Lying outside the Second Gospel

The third problem-area to be considered in connection with the view that the Hellenistic concept of divine man plays a critical role in the correct understanding of Mark's christology is not unrelated to what we have just said. Specifically, it concerns the fact that, on this view, it is the concept of divine man, and not the text of Mark itself, which provides the interpretive key to Mark's presentation of Jesus.

To illustrate this, it is instructive to observe how scholars who hold to the Hellenistic concept of divine man treat the story of the baptism of Jesus (1:9–11). This story is at the heart of the prologue of the Gospel of Mark and depicts Jesus as seeing the Spirit descend upon him from heaven, after which he is declared by a heavenly voice, in quotation of Psalm 2:7 and Isaiah 42:1, to be God's Son. As these scholars interpret this story, the decisive point of reference for them is not, say, these OT passages and related traditions. Instead, it is the Hellenistic concept of divine man. As they see it, the baptism is the place where the man Jesus is filled with the "supernatural substance" of the Spirit which, in turn, transforms him into the Son of God, that is, into a "supernatural being," or Hellenistic divine man.[67] To be

---

66. For a survey of biblical studies in the last century that underscores this point, cf. Petersen, "Literary Criticism," pp. 25–50.

67. Cf., e.g., Wrede, *Messiasgeheimnis*, pp. 73–75 (ET, *Messianic Secret*, pp. 73–75); Bultmann, *Theologie*, pp. 131–33 (ET, *Theology*, I, 128–31); Schulz, *Stunde der Botschaft*, p. 55.

sure, these scholars will differ over the attitude they believe the second evangelist himself assumed towards this "divine-man Jesus" of the baptism. Those who think that he simply adopted the christology of his tradition will see him as affirming this portrayal of Jesus as divine man.[68] Those who think that he radically modified or repudiated the divine-man christology of his tradition will see him as reinterpreting this baptismal portrait in the course of his Gospel by depicting Jesus as one who must suffer and die. Yet either way, the fact remains that it is the Hellenistic concept of divine man which serves as the point of departure for determining how the evangelist formulated his christology. In principle, however, any thesis that dictates that the interpretive key to Mark's christology is to be found outside the Second Gospel may be said to be suspect from the outset. In effect, what we have before us is a "clash" between a tradition-critical approach to Mark and a literary-critical approach.

"Son of Man" as Correcting "Son of God"

The fourth problem-area relative to the view that Mark's christology is oriented, positively or negatively, towards the Hellenistic concept of divine man pertains to the notion that the second evangelist employed one title, namely, "the Son of Man," in order to "correct" another title, namely, "Son of God."

Norman Perrin is perhaps the most eloquent spokesman for this position.[69] Acknowledging his debt to Weeden and Keck,[70] Perrin maintains that, as the title Son of God came to the second evangelist in the tradition, it was inadequate to express his own christology. This was due, among other things, to its divine-man associations. Hence, taking up this title, the evangelist utilized it "to establish rapport with his readers" but then "corrected" it as he moved through his gospel-story by drawing on the title the Son of Man to picture Jesus as a figure of authority who must nevertheless suffer and die but who will also rise and come again at the end of time.

Two particulars of this thesis call for comment. The one has to do with the idea that the second evangelist employed the title Son of God in the first part of his Gospel "to establish rapport with his readers"

---

68. Cf., e.g., Schulz, *Stunde der Botschaft*, pp. 54–59, 73–74.
69. Cf., e.g., Perrin, "Christology of Mark," pp. 108–21.
70. Cf. ibid., pp. 110 n. 16, 113 n. 20.

only to "correct" it in the second half of his Gospel. If this idea is right, it means that the evangelist, in telling the story of the baptism of Jesus (1:9–11), did not hesitate to cast Jesus in a "faulty" light. Literarily, however, the story of the baptism is the crown of the Marcan prologue (1:1–13). Here the reader of the Second Gospel listens in as God himself affirms the identity of Jesus (1:11), and this affirmation is in no wise characterized as being, in literary-critical terms, "unreliable" in nature. Accordingly, to attribute a negative purpose to the story of the baptism and therefore to the prologue of Mark's Gospel flies in the face of literary-critical method. It becomes comprehensible only when one recognizes that the interpreter has not derived this idea from the Gospel of Mark but has brought it to the Gospel from elsewhere.

Second, if the cardinal purpose of the evangelist's christological scheme was to use "the Son of Man" to correct "Son of God," one would think that the evangelist would have given explicit indication of this in the Gospel itself. That he did not do so suggests that "correcting" the one title with the other is not what he was about. Moreover, this conclusion becomes all the more compelling when one observes that the evangelist did, in fact, correct in explicit fashion an estimate of Jesus which he believed to be defective or "faulty." In the gospel-story, King Herod holds Jesus to be (the prophet) John the Baptizer raised from the dead, and the Jewish public is divided in its mind over whether Jesus is John or Elijah or another of the prophets of old; in sharp contrast to these views, Jesus is declared by Peter to be "the Messiah" (cf. 6:14–16 and 8:27–28 with 8:29). Given this example, one can only conclude that the evangelist's silence concerning any intention to correct the title Son of God with the title the Son of Man weighs against the thesis that he did so.

Concluding Remarks

From the time of Wrede to the present, scholars have interpreted Mark along tradition-critical lines. That is to say, they have first reconstructed the development of early Christianity within its first-century environment and then have assigned Mark its place within this development and have read it in this light. Such attempts to reconstruct the course of early Christianity in the world in which it arose are of course necessary. The art of approaching a document with such a tradition-critical scheme, however, consists in not permitting the scheme to predetermine the message of the document. In the case of Mark, this art has not always been practiced well.

One tradition-critical way of approaching the christology of Mark, which can be traced to Bultmann and, in rudimentary form, to Wrede, is in terms of the Hellenistic concept of "divine man." According to this concept, the divine man is a person of genius, or "superman," who, although human, is indwelt by the divine and hence distinguishes himself both by his supernatural wisdom and by his supernatural power to perform miracles. Bultmann applied this concept of divine man to the Marcan Jesus in a benign fashion to advance the thesis that, although the second evangelist made no mention of preexistence, the Son of God in Mark is to all intents and purposes the same figure as the Son of God in Paul.

In the 1960s, however, a notable change took place. Unlike Bultmann, a number of Marcan scholars now construed the divine man in singularly negative terms. They saw him as a non-eschatological figure symbolizing a theology, not of the cross, but of glory. Because most of these scholars regarded the second evangelist as a theologian of the cross whose situation was characterized by the fact that he had to contend with a view that made of Jesus a divine man, they understood his task to be that of correcting a heretical christology. To accomplish this task, the evangelist gave pride of place to his theology of the cross and employed the title "the Son of Man" for the purpose of giving a proper interpretation to the title "Son of God," the Marcan correlate of divine man.

This approach to the christology of Mark has, in some variation, been the dominant one in recent years. Yet in the minds of an increasing number of scholars, it has become vulnerable. Thus, there are those who dispute the contention that "divine man" *(theios anēr)* was either a fixed term or in popular religious use in the Hellenistic world of the first century A.D. Although the debate over this issue among the historians of religion continues, one thing seems clear: it is not possible at the present time, as once was the case, simply to assume that the concept of divine man is the proper avenue of approach to Mark's christology; indeed, it appears that the shoe has even been placed on the other foot: the scholar who would interpret Mark's christology in terms of the concept of divine man now bears the burden of proving that it is legitimate to do so.

Any uncertainty about the hermeneutical viability of the concept of divine man for understanding Mark's christology, however, threatens the downfall of the entire divine-man approach to Mark. Without the cornerstone of "divine man," for example, the title "Son of God" can no longer be made the simple correlate of "divine man." Neither can one argue that, because "Son of God" is to be identified with "divine man," "Son of God" is therefore defective or inadequate for expressing a "right" christology in Mark but must first be corrected by "the Son of Man." Again, the notion that the second evangelist formulated his christology either in line with, or in opposition to, the divine-man christology of his tradition or of opponents in his community also becomes subject to question. And in this connection, the subsidiary notion that the evangelist stood at odds with his miracle-tradition and that he had to overcome the theology of glory inherent in it likewise begs for reassessment.

Still, even if one were to suppose that "divine man" was to prove to be as firm a fixture of first-century Hellenistic religion as those who advocate it claim, there is to my mind yet another trenchant reason for questioning the soundness of the divine-man approach to Mark's christology. As an approach that has been shaped by tradition-critical and history-of-religion considerations, it dictates how Mark is to be read irrespective of literary-critical considerations that appear to controvert it. For one thing, the second evangelist in no wise intimates that the purpose of the baptismal scene in the prologue of his Gospel is to cast Jesus in a "faulty" or "ambiguous" light, yet this is the manner in which the baptism is made to function in the most prominent version of the divine-man, or corrective, approach to Mark's christology. For another thing, the evangelist also does not indicate in any pointed fashion that the reader is to construe the title the Son of Man as correcting the title Son of God, yet in some divine-man approaches the two are made to relate to each other in this way almost as if it were literarily and theologically self-evident instead of unusual in the extreme. In the third place, the evangelist has made no use in his Gospel of the term "divine man" *(theios anēr)*, yet it is said that this term is the key to a proper understanding of his portrait of Jesus. And last, the evangelist nowhere reveals in any explicit terms that he stood opposed to the christology of his tradition, yet such alleged opposition is made the basis for determining an important part of his "christological program," namely, overcoming this false christology.

Against the backdrop of this critique, I shall now turn to the Gospel of Mark itself and broach the question of Mark's christology. The task is not to read the Gospel in the light of a reconstruction of pre-Marcan traditions or of the alleged heresy of the Marcan church, but to follow the contours of Mark's story. My principal (though not exclusive) method, then, is that of literary criticism, and by this I mean no more than that I shall endeavor to read Mark by looking to the story it tells for the primary clues of meaning.

3 THE CHRISTOLOGY OF MARK

The Davidic Messiah-King, The Son of God

PRELIMINARY CONSIDERATIONS

In this chapter I aim to explore the christology of Mark, but to do so in keeping with the way in which Mark develops the motif of the secret of Jesus' identity. Before I turn directly to Mark's story, however, several preliminary matters call for comment. These concern, respectively, the concept of "evaluative point of view," the structure of the Second Gospel, "Jesus" as protagonist, and items of a procedural nature.

Point of View

In his article on "point of view" in the Second Gospel, Norman Petersen observes that Mark so narrates his story as to create a "world of values" as well as of events.[1] Specifically, Mark imbues his story with an "ideological (evaluative) point of view" (i.e., a particular way of construing reality; a system of attitudes, beliefs, values, and norms),[2] which the reader, in order to involve himself in Mark's story, contracts to adopt. By the same token, Mark is also at pains to identify his own evaluative point of view with that of the protagonist of his story, namely, Jesus.[3] Hence, as Mark depicts it there is only one correct way in which to view things: the way of Jesus, which is also Mark's own way.[4]

This description of "evaluative point of view" in Mark is, as far as it goes, sound. The problem, however, is that it basically leaves

---

1. Petersen, "Point of View," pp. 107–8.

2. Cf. Uspensky, *Poetics of Composition*, pp. 8–16; Booth, *Rhetoric of Fiction*, pp. 73–74; Chatman, *Story and Discourse*, pp. 151–58.

3. Petersen, "Point of View," pp. 107–8.

4. Concerning the notion that Gospel texts admit to only two ideological points of view, the "true" and the "untrue," cf. Lotman, "Point of View," pp. 341–43.

out of account the factor that is most crucial. It is not solely with the evaluative point of view of Jesus that Mark identifies his own evaluative point of view. He goes further and makes certain that both his evaluative point of view and that of Jesus are in accord with the evaluative point of view of God.

This raises the question of how Mark goes about bringing God's evaluative point of view to bear upon his story. One thing Mark does not do: he does not deal with God in the same manner in which he deals with the other characters of his story. With respect to the latter, Mark assumes the posture of the "omniscient narrator."[5] As an invisible observer, he is present in each scene of his story, and the characters, including Jesus, have no thoughts, feelings, or motives to which he is not privy. With respect to God, however, Mark does not permit the reader to imagine that he has "unmediated access" either to heaven—God's abode (11:25)—or to his "mind." There are no scenes in Mark's story whose settings are in heaven, and there are no freely fashioned suppositions about what God thinks, feels, or wills.

Instead, Mark's procedure for incorporating God's evaluative point of view into his story is a dual one. Primarily, Mark colors his story with references and quotations from the OT. In so doing, however, he shows that he is concerned, not just that God's evaluative point of view should be represented in his story, but that it should be afforded normative status. This is evident from several factors. For one thing, because the story Mark has to tell is about "(John and) Jesus," Mark reveals through his quotation of the prophetic word in 1:2–3 ("Behold, I [God] send my messenger [John] before you [Jesus] . . .") that God's evaluative point of view is normative for the entire story he relates. For another thing, Mark twice has God enter the world of his story as "actor" in order to address other characters directly, and both times God speaks in words drawn from the OT. In the one instance, it is Jesus whom God addresses, and he solemnly affirms his station and mission (1:11). In the other instance, it is the three disciples atop the mountain of the transfiguration, and he enjoins them to give heed to his beloved Son (9:7). The significance of these two scenes is twofold: they attest, again, to the normative status that Mark accords God's evaluative point of view in his story; and they portray God as

5. Cf. Petersen, "Point of View," pp. 105–18.

making of Jesus the supreme exponent of his evaluative point of view. This latter circumstance, in turn, likewise squares with yet another observation, namely, that Mark works with OT references in such a manner that all but a small number of them occur in the mouth of Jesus.[6] In any event, it is plain to see that Mark makes use of the OT, not simply to air God's evaluative point of view, but to establish it as normative.

Secondarily, Mark also incorporates God's evaluative point of view into his story while at the same time highlighting its central importance by depicting Jesus, in sayings which do not stem from the OT, as aligning his evaluative point of view with that of God. To illustrate this, consider the following "non-OT" sayings of Jesus. In conversation with the rich man who addresses him as "Good Teacher" in the one instance and with James and John in the other instance, Jesus openly affirms for himself a position that makes him subordinate to God ("Why do you call me good? No one is good but God alone" [10:18]; "but to sit at my right or at my left is not mine to grant, but it is for those for whom it has been prepared [by God]" [10:40]; cf. 13:32). In prayer to God in Gethsemane, Jesus closes by submitting his own evaluative point of view to that of God ("Abba, Father, all things are possible to you; remove this cup from me; yet not what I will, but what you will"; 14:36; cf. 8:31). In rebuking Peter for repudiating the notion that he must suffer, Jesus stresses that as far as the disciples, too, are concerned, it is God's evaluative point of view that sets the standard ("you are not thinking the things of God but of men"; 8:33d). And in debate with the leaders of the Jews, Jesus similarly asserts, albeit in sharply negative terms, that for them as well, the norm is God's evaluative point of view ("You have a fine way of rejecting the commandment of God, in order to keep your tradition"; 7:9).

Consequently, on the subject of "evaluative (ideological) point of view" in Mark's Gospel, the thing to note is not only that Mark aligns his evaluative point of view as narrator with that of Jesus but, beyond this, that Mark furthermore aligns both his own evaluative point of view and that of Jesus with the evaluative point of view of God. It is,

---

6. OT references in Mark which do not occur in the mouth of Jesus are such as the following: 1:2–3, 11; 9:7; 11:9–10 (cf. also 12:32–33; 15:26, 36).

in Mark's eyes, God's conception of reality, his system of values, that is normative in the gospel-story.

The circumstance that Mark establishes God's evaluative point of view as normative for his gospel-story has far-reaching consequences for any probe of Mark's christology. In principle, it means that the conception of Jesus which is normative in Mark's story is God's conception. Accordingly, the central question facing the interpreter is not, strictly speaking, how Mark, as narrator, conceives of Jesus or even what Jesus' conception of himself is, but, again, what God's conception of Jesus is. But if this is the central question, then the task of the interpreter, too, becomes clear. For one thing, the interpreter must obviously ascertain what God's conception of Jesus in Mark's story is. For another thing, he must also ascertain what the other conceptions of Jesus are which arise within this story, including those that Mark attributes to Jesus and to himself as narrator, so that he can compare them all to the conception God has of Jesus. And third, the interpreter must likewise define, to the extent he can, the literary and theological objectives Mark pursues by the fact that he chooses to make God's conception of Jesus normative for his story.

Structure

Scholars have not as yet achieved a consensus of opinion on the structure of Mark's Gospel.[7] Still, Mark himself has laced his narrative with summary-passages that point to a division of at least three main parts. The first main part (1:1–13 [15])[8] comprises frame material,[9] narrowly conceived (1:1, 2–3), and the beginning of the narrative proper, in which the reader is told of the ministry of John and is introduced to Jesus. The second main part (1:14—8:26) treats Jesus'

---

7. Two recent studies devoted to the problem of the structure of Mark, which also contain references to the pertinent literature, are those of Petersen ("Composition of Mark 4:1—8:26," pp. 185–217) and of Robbins ("Summons and Outline in Mark," pp. 97–114).

8. Mark 1:14–15 are transitional verses that go with both what precedes and what follows. In this study, I shall construe them with what follows (= 1:14—8:26). For a review of the arguments for and against associating vv. 14–15 with 1:1–13, cf. Keck ("Introduction to Mark's Gospel," pp. 352–70), who is an advocate of the larger section, and Steichele (*Sohn Gottes,* p. 41 n. 4), who speaks against it.

9. On the function of the "frame" of a literary work, cf. Uspensky, *Poetics of Composition,* pp. 137–40, 146–51.

ministry of preaching, calling disciples, teaching, healing, and exorcizing demons in and around Galilee.[10] And the third main part
(8:27—16:8) treats Jesus' journey to Jerusalem and his suffering,
death, and resurrection.[11] For my purposes, it will suffice to work
within the confines of these three main parts.

Protagonist

The personal name of the protagonist of Mark's story is "Jesus"
(Iēsous).[12] Mark not only introduces Jesus to the reader by this name
(1:1) but also, as narrator, regularly uses it himself. Indeed, there are
only three instances in which Mark permits characters in his story to
address Jesus as such. Twice it is demoniacs, who utter his name in
order to show that they know who he is so they can gain power over
him (1:24; 5:7),[13] but once it is blind Bartimaeus, who shouts aloud
Jesus' name in order to obtain healing (10:47). The most typical way
in which Mark identifies Jesus is by means of the expression "Jesus
the Nazarene."[14] What this expression conveys is that the man Jesus
comes from the city of Nazareth of Galilee.[15] In fact, even the speech
of Jesus betrays him as being "Galilean."[16] In Nazareth, the townspeople know him to be a "carpenter" by trade (6:3) and are well
acquainted with his family: his mother is "Mary"; his brothers are
"James," "Joses," "Judas," and "Simon"; and he has "sisters"
(6:3). Since leaving Nazareth and embarking on his public ministry
(1:9), Jesus has taken up residence, if anywhere, in "Capernaum"
(2:1; 9:33). Principally, however, he is an itinerant preacher
(1:38–39), teacher (10:1), and healer and exorcist;[17] he attracts the
crowd and wanders about the synagogues, villages, and regions of
Galilee,[18] traveling across the sea and back,[19] and occasionally seeking

---

10. Cf. Mark 1:14–15, 16–20, 21–22, 32–34, 38–39; 2:13, 14; 3:7–12, 13–19;
6:6b, 34, 53–56.
11. Cf. Mark 8:31; 9:31; 10:32–34; also 11:18; 12:1–12; chaps. 14—16.
12. The name "Jesus" occurs some eighty-one times in Mark's Gospel.
13. Cf. Theissen, *Wundergeschichten*, pp. 94–98.
14. Cf. Mark 1:24; 10:47; 14:67; 16:6; also 1:9.
15. Cf. Mark 1:9; 14:70 to 14:67.
16. Cf. Mark 14:67 to 14:70.
17. Cf. Mark 1:32–34; 3:10–11; 6:55–56.
18. Cf. Mark 1:33, 38–39, 45; 2:13; 3:7–8; 4:1; 5:21; 6:6b, 33, 56; cf. 8:27.
19. Cf. Mark 4:35; 5:1, 21; 6:45; 8:13.

out deserted places[20] or the isolation of the mountain.[21] Alienated from his natural family (3:21), Jesus has created a new family that consists of those whom he has called to follow him.[22] Alienated from the Jewish leadership, he can be found to redefine custom, tradition, or even law,[23] to recline at table with tax collectors and sinners (2:15–17), and to have dealings with Gentiles[24] or outcasts.[25] A "charismatic" figure,[26] Jesus perceives the thoughts and feelings of others,[27] and his words or deeds command assent[28] or, more often, "amaze,"[29] "frighten,"[30] "confound,"[31] or "offend."[32] Then, too, unlike the Matthean Jesus in large part, the Marcan Jesus is also a man of emotion, exhibiting compassion,[33] anger (3:5), wonder (6:6), pneumatic frenzy (8:12), indignation (10:14), love (10:21), and anxiety, distress, a sense of abandonment, and trust in God in the face of death (14:33–34; 15:34). Still, of all the traits that Mark ascribes to Jesus, the one he is concerned to mention first, when Jesus steps onto the stage of his story (1:9), and also last, when the angel speaks of Jesus to the women (16:6), is, again, that he is the man who comes from Nazareth (of Galilee).

Procedure

As I stated previously, my goal in this chapter is to explore the christology of Mark with an eye to the motif of the secret of Jesus' identity. To pursue this goal one must attend to the meaning and function of the titles Jesus bears which one encounters in moving

---

20. Cf. Mark 1:35, 45; 6:31–32.
21. Cf. Mark 3:13; 6:46; 9:2.
22. Cf. Mark 3:31–35; 10:28–30.
23. Cf. Mark 2:18; 2:23—3:6; chap. 7; 10:1–9.
24. Cf. Mark 3:8; 5:1–20; 7:25–30, 31–37; 8:1–9.
25. Cf. Mark 1:40–45; also 5:25–34.
26. Cf. Mark 1:21–22, 27; 11:21–27.
27. Cf. Mark 2:5, 8; 8:17; also 5:34; 10:52.
28. Cf. Mark 1:17–18, 20; 2:14; 12:28, 31.
29. Cf. Mark 1:22, 27; 2:12; 5:20, 42; 6:2, 52; 7:37; 9:15; 10:24, 26; 11:18.
30. Cf. Mark 4:41; 5:15, 33; [9:6]; 9:32; 10:32; 11:18.
31. Cf. Mark 4:13; 6:52; 7:18; 8:17, 21.
32. Cf. Mark 6:3; 14:27.
33. Cf. Mark 1:41; 6:34; 8:2.

through Mark's story. Yet, to attend to these titles is not to suggest that the examination of titles per se exhausts the investigation of Mark's christology.[34] What it does suggest, however, is that the examination of these titles remains an indispensable part of such an investigation. Unless scholars can reach some measure of agreement on the vexing issue of how Mark employs titles, no solution to the persistent problem of his christology is possible. Then, too, if the principal version of the "corrective approach" to the christology of Mark dictates that one title, namely, "the Son of Man," is to be seen as radically reinterpreting another title, namely, "Son of God" or "Messiah" (or both), then it is imperative in probing Mark's understanding of Jesus to ascertain the role that the titles of Jesus do in fact play in his Gospel.

The assigned task obliges one to concentrate, not on every designation for Jesus, but on the so-called major titles. Thus, scattered throughout Mark's story are several designations that either play only a minor christological role or are without titular significance. Cases in point are such terms as "bridegroom," "shepherd," "coming one," "prophet," "teacher-rabbi," and "Lord" (or "lord").

"Bridegroom," for example, is an uncommon metaphor about which one can say little more than that it stands for Jesus (2:19–20).[35] "Shepherd," because of its rich associations with both God and David in the OT, has the potential for being a major christological title,[36] but Mark employs it only twice, both times in quotation of the OT:

---

34. It is particularly literary critics who rightly warn against an approach to the christology of a Gospel which simply identifies the christological task with the study of the titles of Jesus. Cf., e.g., the comments Rhoads makes on this point ("Narrative Criticism," p. 7). For his part, Tannehill ("Narrative Christology," pp. 57–95) attempts to get at the christology of Mark by "learn[ing] who Jesus is through what he says and does in the context of the actions of others" (ibid., p. 58). The other side of the coin, however, is that the study of the titles of Jesus will always remain fundamental to the study of the christology of a Gospel, for two obvious reasons: (a) these titles play a vital role in the gospel-narratives themselves; and (b) these titles have a history, and thus serve to situate an evangelist's presentation of Jesus within a much broader religious context than merely that of his own document. One literary critic, who advocates a modified version of "corrective christology," who is sensitive to the importance of titles in Mark's story is Norman Petersen (cf., e.g., *Literary Criticism for New Testament Critics*, pp. 60–68).

35. Cf. our discussion of this term in Chapter 1.

36. Cf. Jeremias, *"Poimēn,"* pp. 487–93.

once to describe Israel as having no leader (6:34); and once to characterize Jesus as the one about to be put to death (14:27). The "coming
one," used once, appears to possess no christological significance of
itself but only as it alludes to Jesus as the bearer of "the coming
Kingdom of our father David" (11:9–10). "Prophet," applied once
by Jesus to himself in a proverb (6:4), appears to be devoid of titular
connotations. To be sure, Jesus often prophesies, but this does not in
itself make of "prophet" a christological title. Indeed, the notion that
Jesus is a "prophet" will, as we shall see, prove itself to be an
erroneous view some segments of the Jewish public hold (6:15; 8:28).
"Teacher," or "rabbi," is also non-titular and serves as a term of
human respect.[37] In Mark's scheme, the Jesus who "teaches" and is
called "teacher" is the royal Son of God (cf. 1:22 to 1:1, 11;
11:27–33). And finally, "Lord" or "lord" *(kyrios),* when it refers to
Jesus and not to God, tends to function in one of two ways: (a) it
becomes a surrogate for another title, or for "Jesus," or simply means
"sir" or "owner," as in 1:3 ("Lord" = "Jesus Messiah, Son of
God" [1:1]), 7:28 ("lord" or "Lord" = "sir" or "Jesus"), 11:3
("Lord" or "lord" = "Jesus as Son of David" or "owner," "master"), 12:36 ("Lord" = "Messiah"), and 13:35 ("lord of the house"
= Jesus in his role as "the Son of Man"); or (b) it ascribes to Jesus
divine authority, as in 2:28 (". . . the Son of Man is lord even of
the sabbath"). As far as the meaning of *kyrios* in 12:37 is concerned,
I shall discuss it in treating the pericope on the question about David's
son (12:35–37).

---

37. Mark makes frequent use of this term. Some fourteen times disciples (4:38;
9:38; 10:35; 13:1; 9:5; 11:21), strangers (5:35; 9:17; 10:17, 20, 51), and opponents
(12:14, 19; 14:45; cf. 12:32) call Jesus "teacher" or "rabbi." Once Jesus himself
tells two of his disciples to refer to him, in dealing with the man at whose house
they are to make preparations for eating the passover, as "the teacher" (14:14).
"Teaching" is the principal activity in which Jesus engages during his public
ministry, the thing he "was accustomed" to do (10:1). Only once, in fact, is it
said of the disciples that they "teach" (6:30). And what Jesus teaches is "new"
(1:27), for he speaks with divine "authority" (1:22, 27) and is the direct mouthpiece of God in these last times in a way that places him above even Moses
(10:2–9). Still, none of these observations alters the circumstance that "teacher"
in Mark functions as no more than a term of human respect. What distinguishes
Jesus as "teacher" is the divine authority with which he speaks (1:22, 27). Such
divine authority is his, however, because God has empowered him with the Spirit
(1:10). But the one whom God empowers with his Spirit he also affirms to be his
Son (1:11). The one who authoritatively "teaches" and is called "teacher" in
Mark's Gospel, therefore, is Jesus, the royal Son of God (1:1, 11; 9:7; 11:27–33).

The major christological titles Mark applies to Jesus in his story are "Messiah," or "Christ" ("Anointed One"; *christos*),[38] "King of the Jews (Israel)" *(basileus tōn Ioudaiōn [Israēl]),*[39] "Son of David" *(hyios tou Dayid),*[40] "Son of God" *(hyios tou theou),*[41] and "the Son of Man" *(ho hyios tou anthrōpou).*[42] If one looks at the way in which Mark works with these titles, one can discern a clear division among them. Next chapter we shall return to this point. Suffice it to say that the division is between "the Son of Man" on the one hand and "Messiah," "King of the Jews (Israel)," "Son of David," and "Son of God" on the other. The latter four titles comprise a group, related to one another by being directly related to "Messiah." To illustrate this, consider how Mark employs the titles "King of the Jews (Israel)," "Son of David," and "Son of God" in order to interpret the title "Messiah": (a) "the Messiah, the King of Israel" (15:32); (b) ". . . the Messiah is the Son of David" (12:35); and (c) "Jesus Messiah, the Son of God" (1:1);[43] and "the Messiah, the Son of the Blessed" (14:61). In sharp contrast to this procedure, Mark never places "the Son of Man" in apposition to "Messiah," and never does he write that "the Messiah is the Son of Man." Plainly, the title "the Son of Man" stands apart from these other "messianic" titles. Consequently, as I investigate the titles of Jesus, I shall take account of this division among them by first attending to Mark's portrait of Jesus as the Davidic Messiah-King, the Son of God, and by then turning next chapter to the sayings in which Jesus refers to himself as the Son of Man.

THE MINISTRY OF JOHN AND THE PRESENTATION OF JESUS (1:1–13)

The Caption-Summary

Whether Mark's opening verse is the "title" of his Gospel[44] or

---

38. Cf. Mark 1:1; 8:29; 12:35; 13:21; 14:61; 15:32; also 9:41.

39. Cf. Mark 15:2, 9, 12, 18, 26, 32.

40. Cf. Mark 10:47, 48; 12:35, 37.

41. Cf. Mark 1:1, 11; 3:11; 5:7; 9:7; 12:6; 13:32; 14:61; 15:39.

42. Cf. Mark 2:10, 28; 8:31, 38; 9:9, 12, 31; 10:33, 45; 13:26; 14:21, 41, 62.

43. According to the 26th edition of Nestle-Aland, the best manuscript evidence clearly favors the inclusion of "Son of God" in Mark 1:1. In this study, then, I shall follow Aland's example and read 1:1 as containing this title.

44. So Pesch, *Markusevangelium*, I, 74–75.

not,[45] it does alert the reader to the content of his story.[46] His entire narrative, Mark states, will treat the "beginning of the gospel."[47] And the focus of this narrative will be on "Jesus Christ (Messiah), Son of God."[48]

Rhetorically, this verse is critical already in informing the reader of Mark's own conception of Jesus (i.e., his own "evaluative point of view" concerning Jesus' identity). Addressing the reader both directly and programmatically, Mark tells him that he holds Jesus to be the "Messiah, the Son of God." Unless Mark should prove himself to be an "unreliable narrator,"[49] the reader has no grounds for assuming, or even suspecting, that these titles for Jesus are "false" or "defective." While Mark can be expected to elaborate them in the course of his story, they are nonetheless "correct."

The Prophetic Word of God

Following his caption-summary (1:1), Mark cites a massive, composite quotation from the OT (1:2–3; cf. Mal. 3:1; Exod. 23:20; Isa. 40:3). This quotation stands forth as the prophetic word attaining to its eschatological fulfillment (1:2a). Both formally and materially, it merits careful scrutiny.

Formally, v. 2 differs noticeably from v. 3. Whereas v. 3 intones the prophecy of Isaiah, v. 2 assumes the form of a direct address by God ("*I* send") to Jesus ("before *you*"). The emphasis, therefore, is on v. 2. Nonetheless, the entire passage functions as an epigraph and is of the nature of frame material.[50] Instead of contributing to the development of the story Mark narrates, it stands apart from it and provides the reader with information so that he can enter into the story's world and involve himself in it.

As an epigraph, the quotation 1:2–3 captures to a remarkable degree

---

45. So Gnilka, *Markus,* I, 42.

46. Cf. Haenchen, *Weg Jesu,* pp. 38–39; Gnilka, *Markus,* I, 42–43.

47. For a discussion of this expression, cf. Keck, "Introduction to Mark's Gospel," pp. 359, 366–68.

48. Cf. above, n. 43.

49. Mark is, of course, a "reliable narrator"; for a helpful statement on what it means to attribute "reliability" to Mark, cf. Fowler, *Loaves and Fishes,* p. 229 n. 23.

50. Concerning the "frame" of a story, cf. Uspensky, *Poetics of Composition,* pp. 137–38, 146–51.

the essence of Mark's story. Its focus is on three of Mark's main characters: God, John the Baptizer, and Jesus.

Through the medium of OT scripture, Mark depicts God ("Behold, I send") as presenting himself as the sole initiator and guide of the action that will take place in the ministries of John and of Jesus (1:2). Because these ministries, especially that of Jesus, comprise the stuff of Mark's story, Mark points to God, that is, his "will" or "evaluative point of view," as being determinative of the norms governing his story. But if Mark, who is a "reliable narrator," points to God as the one who determines the norms of his story, he indicates thereby that his own "evaluative point of view" will be in alignment with that of God. And since Mark has told the reader in 1:1 that Jesus is the Messiah, the Son of God, the reader can rest assured that this understanding of Jesus will have the sanction of God in Mark's story and hence be the "normative" understanding.

God designates John as "my messenger" (1:2) and Jesus as "Lord" (= Messiah, Son of God; cf. 1:3 to 1:1). As "God's messenger," John will be the forerunner of Jesus, and as "Lord," Jesus will be the one for whom John prepares the way (1:2–3). As "God's messenger" and as "Lord," both John and Jesus will undertake their ministries as the agents of God, speaking and acting on his divine authority. They will be the ones upon whom God confers his "badge of reliability."[51]

Interestingly, no reference is made in this quotation constructed from the OT to the other main characters in Mark's story: the "Jewish leaders," the "crowd," and the "disciples." Is there a hint in such omission that God will not confer on them his "badge of reliability"? As the rest of Mark's story reveals, this is exactly the case, for these characters will all prove themselves, though with vastly different outcome, to be "blind" and "without understanding" (4:11–12; 8:17–18).

We mentioned that this OT quotation characterizes the prophetic word as attaining to its eschatological fulfillment (1:2).[52] This theme of eschatological fulfillment touches on the matter of the temporal context in which Mark situates his story, his scheme of the history of salvation. According to Mark, from beginning to end the history of

---

51. Cf. Booth, *Rhetoric of Fiction*, pp. 16–20.
52. Cf. also J. M. Robinson, *History in Mark*, pp. 24–26.

salvation stands under the aegis of God (1:2b, 15a; 13:32). Nevertheless, Mark distinguishes in it between the time of the OT, which is
the "time of prophecy" (1:2a), and the "time of fulfillment" (1:2b–3;
cf. 1:15: "the time is fulfilled"). The time of fulfillment, however,
is better termed the "time of the gospel."[53] It encompasses the ministry to Israel of John (1:4–8) and of Jesus and the pre-Easter disciples,[54] and the ministry to all the nations of the post-Easter disciples
(13:10; 14:9); indeed, not until the Parousia of Jesus in his role as the
Son of Man will it have run its course (13:10–13, 24–27). But although the time of the gospel does span a succession of ministries,
what is decisive is the ministry of Jesus. The ministry of John is
preparatory to it (1:2–3, 7–8), the ministry of the pre-Easter disciples
is an extension of it (3:13–16; 6:7, 12–13, 30), and the ministry of
the post-Easter disciples is founded upon it (14:9). Hence, in Mark's
conception of things the time of the gospel coincides with the end-
phase of the history of salvation, and pivotal to the time of the gospel
is the action God undertakes in the ministry of Jesus. For Mark, then,
Jesus is the decisive figure in the whole of God's history of salvation,
and he alerts the reader to this as early as, again, the first verse of the
Gospel: "[The] beginning of the gospel of Jesus Messiah, the Son of
God."

The Figure and Ministry of John

In line with God's prophetic decree, Mark portrays the sending of
John as inaugurating the eschatological time of the gospel ("Behold,
I [God] send *my messenger* before you"; 1:2b). As Mark tells of John,
he describes his person, his ministry to Israel, and his relationship to
Jesus (1:2–8).

John is, to be sure, the "forerunner" the prophets have foretold
(above all, "Isaiah"; 1:2–3, 7–8). In his ministry and fate, he typifies
the ministry and fate of the one who will come after him.[55] The food
of locusts and wild honey he eats links him with the desert (1:6),[56]
and the clothing he wears (especially the leather belt) is meant to

---

53. Cf. Mark 1:1, 14–15; 8:35; 10:29; 13:10; 14:9.
54. Cf. Mark 1:14–15; 3:13–16; 6:7, 12–13, 30.
55. Cf. Marxsen, *Markus,* pp. 19, 23–25 (ET, *Mark,* pp. 33, 40, 42–43).
56. Cf. Vielhauer, "Tracht und Speise," pp. 53–54.

identify him with the prophet Elijah (1:6; cf. 2 Kgs. 1:8).[57] Because
2 Kings does not tell of the death of Elijah but of his ascension iŋ a
"chariot of fire" into heaven (2:11), Malachi prophesies that before
the "day of the Lord" comes, God will send Elijah to earth to effect
reconciliation in Israel and thus enable it to persevere in the judgment
that will accompany that day (Mal. 4:5–6; LXX 3:22–23). Mark draws
on this Jewish expectation associated with Elijah (9:12), but omits the
note of judgment and presents a "christianized" version of it. Elijah
who is to come is John the Baptizer who has come (9:13), and John
is the forerunner, not of God, but of Jesus (1:7–8; 9:12–13). So that
there is no confusion about the latter, Mark quotes the OT passages
that lie behind 1:2–3 in such a form and context that the four genitives
of the pronouns "you" and "he" and of the noun "Lord" refer
exclusively to "Jesus Messiah, the Son of God" (1:1, 11) and not,
as originally, to "God" (Isa. 40:3; Mal. 3:1).[58] In Mark's story, John
the Baptizer is Elijah redịvivus, the forerunner of Jesus Messiah.

John discharges his ministry in the "desert" of Judea near the
Jordan river (1:4–5),[59] fulfilling the hope of a new exodus (1:3; cf.
Isa. 40:1–11).[60] He proclaims a "baptism of repentance for the forgiveness of sins" (1:4, RSV),[61] and the people of all Judea and all
the Jerusalemites respond by going out to him, submitting to his bap-

---

57. So also Hengel (*Nachfolge,* p. 39 esp. n. 71) and Wink (*John the Baptist,*
pp. 2–4), who are to be preferred on this point to Vielhauer ("Tracht und Speise,"
pp. 53–54). The latter argues that although the clothing and leather belt of John
mark him as an eschatological figure who resides in the desert, they do not associate him with Elijah. But at the level of his story, Mark shows by the "flash-
back" of 9:13 that the reader is indeed to identify John both in 1:2–8 and 6:14–29
with Elijah.

58. In Exod. 23:20 (LXX), which also lies behind Mark 1:2–3 but which has
been subordinated to Mal. 3:1, the genitive of the pronoun "you" refers to "Israel" ("And behold, I send my angel [messenger] before you [Israel]").

59. On the geographical significance of "the desert" in the NT, cf. Funk, "The
Wilderness," pp. 205–14.

60. Cf. Gnilka, *Markus,* I, 44–45.

61. By and large, commentators (cf., e.g., Pesch, *Markusevangelium,* I, 79)
associate the "forgiveness of sins" with "repentance" and regard "being baptized" as constituting the seal that God has in fact granted forgiveness. By contrast,
Feneberg (*Markusprolog,* pp. 171–72) insists that it is the "baptism" John ad-
ministers which effects "repentance" and hence results in the "forgiveness of
sins." The difficulty in deciding on any interpretation of 1:4 is that the evidence
is too scanty to permit one to make any judgment with confidence.

tism, and confessing their sins (1:5). In this way, John "restores all things," even as Elijah was to do (9:12), and he readies Israel for the one who is to follow him (1:7).

As a prophetic and eschatological figure whose own appearance in history had been prophesied (1:2–3), John closes out his ministry in Mark by himself prophesying the coming of the one mightier than he (1:7–8). In the words of John, so exalted will this mightier one be in comparison with him that he will not be worthy to perform for him even the most menial task of the slave: that of bending down and loosing the thong of his master's sandals (1:7). If his own baptism with water effected preparation through repentance and forgiveness (1:8a), the "baptism with the Spirit" that the mightier one will administer through his ministry will effect final, or eschatological, salvation (1:8b).

The Baptism of Jesus

The baptismal scene (1:9–11) is the centerpiece of the first main part of Mark's story. Here God, himself participating as "actor" in the story, formally identifies for the reader "who Jesus is." Hence, the baptismal scene elaborates such frame-passages as 1:1 ("Jesus Messiah, the Son of God") and 1:2–3 ("Behold, I [God] send my messenger before you [the Lord]"). The unit itself falls neatly into two sections: the event of the baptism itself (1:9); and the two revelatory events that follow (1:10–11).

No sooner has John uttered the prophecy that "after me *comes* he who is mightier than I" (1:7) than Mark records the fulfillment of this prophecy: "In those days Jesus *came*." (1:9). Unlike Matthew in his account of the baptism, Mark is not concerned to explain why it is that Jesus should even submit to baptism by John (Matt. 3:14–15). Instead, Mark is content simply to assert that John does in fact baptize Jesus (1:9). By the same token, Mark does something in his baptismal account Matthew does not, namely, he makes prominent reference to "Nazareth" of Galilee (1:9). The reason Mark refers to "Nazareth" is patent: he employs the expressions "Jesus from Nazareth" (1:9) and "Jesus the Nazarene" (16:6) at the beginning and end of his story in order to "enclose" it and consequently to affirm that the Jesus whom God raises from the dead is the same Jesus from Galilean Nazareth whom John at the outset baptized and about whom he has been speaking throughout his narrative.[62] Or, to put it differently, Mark skillfully employs this "inclusion" in order to identify "Jesus the Nazarene" whom God raises from the dead with "Jesus from Nazareth" whom God declares at his baptism to be "his Son." The resurrected Jesus and the baptized Jesus are one, namely, the Son of God.

Immediately following his baptism, Jesus goes up from the water and two revelatory events occur, one of sight and one of sound (1:10–11). Jesus' "going up from the water" (1:10a) removes him from the presence of John. No tie, therefore, exists between Jesus' being baptized by John and these revelatory events. Jesus alone experiences them, and they bear the stamp of apocalyptic eschatology.[63]

Mark writes of the first revelatory event: "he saw the heavens split apart and the Spirit descending upon him as a dove" (1:10). For scholars who advocate a divine-man christology in Mark, this passage assumes critical importance.[64] In their opinion, it is here that the divine substance of the Spirit penetrates Jesus so that he ceases to be a mere human being and is transformed instead into a supernatural being, or divine man.[65] To lend support to this thesis, these scholars lay emphasis on the supposed Hellenistic tenor of 1:10. The arguments they advance in this connection are basically four, two of which are specious and can be dismissed[66] but two of which merit consideration.

---

62. Cf. also Mark 1:24; 10:47; 14:67.

63. Cf., e.g., Rev. 4:1; 10:4; 11:19; 14:13; 18:4; 19:11; 21:3; Acts 7:56; *2 Apoc. Bar.* 22:1–2; *T. Levi* 2:6; 5:1; also Lohmeyer, *Markus,* pp. 21–22; J. M. Robinson, *History in Mark,* pp. 26–28; Pesch, "Anfang des Evangeliums," pp. 124–30.

64. Cf., e.g., Hahn, *Hoheitstitel,* p. 343.

65. Cf. Hahn, *Hoheitstitel,* pp. 342–45; Schulz, *Stunde der Botschaft,* p. 55; Bultmann, *Geschichte der synoptischen Tradition,* pp. 266–68 (ET, *History of the Synoptic Tradition,* pp. 249–51, 253); also Wrede, *Messiasgeheimnis,* p. 73 (ET, *Messianic Secret,* pp. 73–74).

66. For instance, it is specious to argue that the symbol of the "dove" or the apparent absence of a baptismal pericope in Q are indicative of the Hellenistic cast of 1:10 (cf. Schulz [*Stunde der Botschaft,* p. 54] on the first point and Bultmann [*Geschichte der synoptischen Tradition,* pp. 266, 268 (ET, *History of the Synoptic Tradition,* pp. 250–51)] on both points). As a symbol, the dove was, of course, not confined to Greek traditions (cf., e.g., Greeven, *"Peristera,"* pp. 64–70; Keck, "Spirit and Dove," pp. 46–57; Lentzen-Deis, *Taufe Jesu,* pp. 170–83), and the length and exact contents of Q can only be surmised.

For example, Bultmann contends, on appeal to Gustaf Dalman, that the "decisive pointer" to the Hellenistic origin of 1:10 is the absolute use of the term "the Spirit." This is the case because in Palestinian tradition one does not find the word "spirit," used absolutely, serving as a reference to the Spirit of God.[67] And second, Ferdinand Hahn believes that the use of the prepositional phrase *eis auton* ("into him") betrays Hellenistic thought, for the Spirit is not portrayed as "coming upon" Jesus but as "entering into" him.[68] In consideration of these and other factors, then, the respective elements of 1:10 are made to yield the following meaning: the "splitting apart of the heavens" is the necessary presupposition for the incarnate epiphany of the Spirit; the "dove" is the hypostasis of the Spirit; and the descent of the dove "into Jesus" connotes the physical union of the transcendent Spirit with the man Jesus.[69]

This interpretation of Mark 1:10 is tenuous at best. For one thing, Bultmann's "pointer" proves not to be "decisive," for Leander Keck has shown that the absolute expression "the Spirit," referring specifically to God's Spirit, turns up in such thoroughly Palestinian literature as that of Qumran.[70] For another thing, Hahn's argument concerning the prepositional phrase *eis auton* is likewise debatable. On this score, both Nigel Turner and A. T. Robertson deserve to be heard. Turner observes that, in Mark, the preposition *eis* ("into") frequently appears in places where one would expect to find some other preposition (e.g., *pros* ["to," "towards"]), so that "the full meaning of *eis* . . . cannot be insisted on."[71] And Robertson, expressing a more pointed opinion, cites Mark 1:10 as an example of the use of the preposition *eis* "where *epi* would have been used in earlier Greek."[72] In other words, grammatically it is as legitimate to translate *eis auton* in 1:10 as "towards him" or "upon him" as it is to translate it "into him," and if Rob-

---

67. Bultmann, *Geschichte der synoptischen Tradition*, pp. 267–68 (ET, *History of the Synoptic Tradition*, pp. 250–51).

68. Hahn, *Hoheitstitel*, p. 342.

69. Cf. esp. Hahn, *Hoheitstitel*, pp. 342–45; Schulz, *Stunde der Botschaft*, pp. 54–55; also Wrede, *Messiasgeheimnis* (ET, *Messianic Secret*, p. 73).

70. Keck, "Spirit and Dove," p. 59.

71. N. Turner, *Syntax*, p. 256.

72. Robertson, *Grammar*, p. 1393.

ertson is followed, the preferred translation is "upon him."[73] Interestingly, although it has become unfashionable to look at Matthew or Luke when dealing with Mark, both Matthew (3:16) and Luke (3:22) read "upon him" (*epi* + *auton*) in their respective pericopes on the baptism.

In the third place, the Hellenistic, divine-man interpretation of 1:10 is the product of a tradition-critical approach, that is, an approach to 1:10 from "outside" Mark. For such an interpretation to be credible, it must square itself with the role that 1:10 seems to play when examined literary-critically, that is, from within Mark's story. Now Mark makes no mention of the preexistence of Jesus, as do Paul and John. Nor does he have a narrative that tells of the virginal conception of Jesus, as do Matthew and Luke. As far as his story goes, therefore, Mark appears to concern himself even less than these others do with the question of the "nature" of Jesus. In point of fact, Mark is "functional" in his approach to christology, and Hahn, for one, acknowledges this.[74] But as Hahn must also acknowledge, in the divine-man interpretation of 1:10 the emphasis is exactly the reverse: the descent of the Spirit is not interpreted "functionally" to mean that God empowers Jesus, but it is interpreted "ontically" to mean that Jesus becomes infused with the Spirit so that he acquires a supernatural nature and is changed into a divine man.[75] The pericope on the transfiguration notwithstanding,[76] this interpretation of 1:10 appears to spring from a logic that is external to, and not internal to, the story Mark narrates.

Other observations support this conclusion. Mark begins his story by making reference to "Jesus Christ, the Son of God" (1:1). With respect to the term "Christ" *(christos)*, Mark employs it titularly in his story to mean "Messiah" ("Anointed One").[77] When viewed

---

73. Cf. further Feuillet, "Le Baptême," p. 477; Richter, "Tauferzählungen," p. 50. The expression "upon him" would indicate that the Spirit descends until it actually reaches its goal, namely, Jesus (cf. BAG, p. 288).

74. Hahn, *Hoheitstitel*, pp. 343–45.

75. Cf. ibid., pp. 342–45. Also Fuller, *Christology*, p. 258 n. 3.

76. On Mark's story of the transfiguration of Jesus, cf. the later discussion in this chapter.

77. There are two passages in Mark where *christos* seems to be used as a

from this angle, the name "Jesus Christ," too, can be seen to bear titular overtones: "Jesus [who is] Messiah (Anointed One)" (1:1). But the fact that *christos* is still fundamentally titular in Mark, characterizing Jesus as the "Anointed One," almost inevitably gives rise to the question: Is there not a place within his story where Mark depicts for the reader the "anointing" of Jesus? The answer, of course, is yes, in the descent of the Spirit upon Jesus here in 1:10. But the answer, in turn, gives rise to a further question: What, according to Mark, does the anointing of Jesus effectuate? Again, the answer is plain: as a result of his anointing, Jesus functions during his ministry on the "authority" *(exousia)* of God (11:27–33; cf. 1:22, 27; 2:10; also 6:7). In other words, if one probes the story of Mark itself, the indications are that 1:10 is part and parcel of the same OT and Jewish imagery that is so prominent throughout the whole of the section 1:1–13.[78] Add to this the twin circumstances that Mark does not say in 1:10 that Jesus is physically transformed into a divine man and that the very concept of divine man seems to be an uncertain factor as far as the time when the second evangelist wrote is concerned, and there appears to be no compelling reason for interpreting 1:10 along these lines.[79]

Consequently, to approach 1:10 from the standpoint of the traditions that flow from the OT, the meaning of the two main ideas is readily discernible: the "splitting apart of the heavens" is both a gracious sign that divine revelation is about to occur and the "precondition" for the Spirit to descend (cf. Isa. 64:1 [LXX 63:19b]; also Ezek. 1:1);[80] and the "descent of the Spirit upon Jesus" connotes his empowerment with divine authority for messianic ministry (cf. Isa. 61:1; 42:1; 11:2; Mark 11:27–33).[81] Unclear, because of grammatical ambiguity, is the manner in which "the Spirit" and the "dove" are to

personal name (1:1; 9:41), but even in them it is not devoid of titular overtones. On 9:41, cf. Grundmann, *"Chriō,"* pp. 530–31; Hahn, *Hoheitstitel,* p. 224 n. 1.

78. Cf. Vögtle, "Mk 1,9–11," pp. 134–37.

79. Cf. also Lentzen-Deis, *Taufe Jesu,* pp. 273, 277.

80. Cf. Lentzen-Deis, *Taufe Jesu,* p. 280; Vögtle, "Mk 1,9–11," pp. 135–36; also van Unnik, "Die 'geöffneten Himmel,'" pp. 272–73; Richter, "Tauferzählungen," pp. 148–49.

81. Cf. J. M. Robinson, *History in Mark,* p. 29; Lentzen-Deis, *Taufe Jesu,* p. 278; Vögtle, "Mk 1,9–11," p. 136; Feneberg, *Markusprolog,* pp. 181–83.

be related to each other. Does Jesus see the Spirit descend upon him *in the form of a dove* (cf. Luke 3:22),[82] or does he see the Spirit descend upon him *in a dove-like motion?*[83] Whichever option one chooses, the notion that with the descent of the Spirit Jesus is empowered by God holds firm.

The second revelatory event that occurs following the baptism of Jesus is auditory rather than visual. About it Mark writes: "And a voice came from heaven, 'You are my beloved Son, in you I take delight'" (1:11).[84] Important as the first revelatory event is, this one is more important still, for Mark has accorded it the position of stress. The voice from heaven is the voice of God (cf., e.g., 9:7; Gen. 15:4; Deut. 4:36; Dan. 4:31). God addresses Jesus personally in words that constitute a composite quotation taken from Psalm 2:7 and Isaiah 42:1, and most likely from Genesis 22:2 as well (cf. also Gen. 22:12, 16).[85] In Isaiah 42:1, the servant in whom God delights is one whom God has "chosen" for ministry. In Genesis 22:2, Abraham's beloved son Isaac is his "only" son.[86] And in Psalm 2, God is described as solemnly addressing the words, "My son are you," to the king-

---

82. In this case, the expression "as a dove" is taken to be adjectival and to modify "the Spirit." This is the option most commentators choose (cf., e.g., Pesch, *Markusevangelium*, I, 91–92). But why the Spirit should be compared to a dove and not to some other bird is a question for which commentators seem not to have found a satisfactory answer; on this matter, Keck's comments are still germane ("Spirit and Dove," pp. 66–67).

83. In this case, the expression "as a dove" is taken to be adverbial and to modify the participle "descending." Keck ("Spirit and Dove," p. 63) and Jeremias (*Theologie*, pp. 58–59) argue for this option; Richter ("Tauferzählungen," pp. 43–45), on the other hand, denies that it is even viable.

84. On the translation of Mark 1:11c, cf. Taylor, *St. Mark*, pp. 64, 161–62.

85. Some scholars (e.g., Jeremias, *"Pais Theou,"* pp. 700–705; Lührmann, "Biographie des Gerechten," pp. 28–30) claim that Mark 1:11 is to be derived from Isaiah 42:1 alone. But Lindars (*Apologetic*, pp. 139–40), Marshall ("Mark I. 11," pp. 326–36), and Steichele (*Sohn Gottes*, pp. 123–35) call attention to the difficulties associated with this supposition. For his part, Bretscher ("Voice from Heaven," pp. 301–11) contends that the words of the heavenly voice are to be traced back to the Hebrew text of Deut. 4:22–23. That Mark does not see them in this light is evident from the decidedly "royal" character of his christology.

86. Cf. Judg. 11:34; Amos 8:10; Zech. 12:10; Jer. 6:26. Cf. also C. Turner (*"Agapētos,"* pp. 113–29), who states that *agapētos* ("only") in Mark 1:11; 9:7; and 12:6 also has the connotation of "unique" (cf. Judg. 11:34 LXX; also Feuillet, "Le Baptême," p. 480).

designate from the house of David, "his anointed" ("messiah"), who on the day of his coronation assumes the throne of Judah.[87]

As incorporated into Mark's story, the several emphases of these OT quotations combine to form a statement in which God "names" Jesus,[88] that is, declares "who Jesus is" from his "evaluative point of view" (how he "thinks" about Jesus). The passage 1:11, then, is a divine asseveration whereby God solemnly affirms that Jesus, the Anointed One (Messiah-King)[89] from the line of David,[90] is his only, or unique,[91] Son whom he has chosen for eschatological ministry.

Christologically, 1:11 is the central passage in the section 1:1–13. Because it is none other than God who names Jesus "my Son," 1:11 informs the reader that "Son of God" will be the "normative" title for Jesus in Mark's story. What this title highlights, more than any other single factor, is the unique filial relationship that Jesus has to God, though along the lines just described. In addition, through the passage 1:11 the other designations for Jesus in 1:1–13 also receive qualification or elaboration. By means of 1:11 the reader learns, for example, that the "mightier one" to whom John refers in 1:7, the "Lord" about whom Isaiah prophesies in 1:3, and the "you" whom God addresses in the words of OT scripture in 1:2, are all Jesus in his capacity as the Son of God. Indeed, 1:11 even elaborates Mark's own words in 1:1. Text-critically, if the correct reading in 1:1 is simply "Jesus Messiah," then 1:11 explains that this "Messiah," or "Anointed One," is to be understood to be the royal Son of God. But if, as most scholars believe, the correct reading is "Jesus Messiah, Son of God," then 1:11 shows that Mark's own "evaluative point of view" concerning the identity of Jesus coincides with that of God. God's understanding of Jesus is normative in Mark's story, and Mark,

---

87. Whereas von Rad ("Königsritual," pp. 205–13) understands Psalm 2 to refer to the single coronation ceremony that inaugurates the reign of the king, Kraus (*Psalmen,* I, 14) entertains the notion that Psalm 2 may have had its *Sitz im Leben* in a yearly celebration of the king's coronation.

88. On the literary-critical significance of "naming," cf. Uspensky, *Poetics of Composition,* pp. 20–32.

89. Cf. Ps. 2:2, 6 LXX; Mark 1:10; 15:32.

90. Cf. Mark 10:47–48; 11:9–10; 12:35–37.

91. Cf. above, n. 86.

a "reliable narrator," aligns his understanding of Jesus with that of God.

Mark 1:11 was just characterized as a "divine asseveration" (cf., e.g., Pss. 109:4; 21:10; 43:5 LXX). It could just as easily be labeled a "predication-formula."[92] In principle, the term by which 1:11 is described is not unimportant, for it involves the exegetical decision as to whether Jesus is to be regarded as "becoming" the Son of God through the words God speaks, or whether these words are to be understood as affirming what is already the case, namely, that Jesus "is" the Son of God. Scholars who espouse the first view think of 1:11 as a declaration of "investiture"[93] or of "adoption"[94] or "legitimation."[95] Mark himself provides no clear-cut answer to this issue. Still, the purpose of 1:1–13 is to introduce the reader to John in the one instance and to Jesus in the other. In presenting John, the focus of Mark's attention is not on his "becoming" Jesus' forerunner but on his "being" Jesus' forerunner. If this can be taken as guide, then with Jesus, too, the focus of Mark's attention is on who he is.[96] Hence, at the level of Mark's story the purpose of 1:11 is that God himself, at that juncture where Jesus is about to embark upon his public ministry, should solemnly affirm both his station and call.

To sum up, Mark utilizes the baptismal pericope to assert the baptism of Jesus by John (1:9) but especially to tell of the two revelatory events that follow (1:10–11). These revelatory events, the first of sight and the second of sound, are experienced by Jesus alone. In the one,

---

92. The idea behind this term is that God, in uttering the expression "you are" in 1:11, "predicates" to Jesus the royal status of being "my Son." Cf. Norden, *Agnostos Theos*, pp. 177–85; Gnilka, *Markus*, I, 53.

93. Cf. Hahn, *Hoheitstitel*, pp. 343–44.

94. Cf., e.g., Bultmann, *Geschichte der synoptischen Tradition*, pp. 263–64 (ET, *History of the Synoptic Tradition*, pp. 247–48); Dibelius, *Formgeschichte*, p. 271 (ET, *Tradition to Gospel*, pp. 271–72); Vielhauer, "Christologie des Markusevangeliums," p. 213. Steichele (*Sohn Gottes*, pp. 149, 157–59) toys with this idea but finally dismisses it.

95. In Psalm 2, v. 7 is, of course, just such a declaration of adoption or legitimation (cf. Kraus, *Psalmen*, I, 18–19).

96. Lindars (*Apologetic*, pp. 144, 146) speaks of the baptismal saying as expressing the "manifestation" of Jesus as the Messiah. Cf. further Lohmeyer, *Markus*, p. 23; Marshall, "Mark I. 11," pp. 333, 335; Lentzen-Deis, *Taufe Jesu*, p. 270; Vögtle, "Mk 1,9–11," pp. 126, 135–37.

God empowers Jesus with his Spirit for the eschatological (messianic) ministry he is about to undertake. In the other, God discloses how he "thinks" about Jesus—that is, who he conceives Jesus to be—by solemnly affirming both his station as the royal Son of God and his call. The extreme importance that Mark attaches to the baptismal scene is evident from the fact that here he depicts God as entering his story as "actor"; it is thus God himself who sets forth the understanding of Jesus which is normative for Mark's story.

The Temptation of Jesus

As Mark portrays it the temptation, or testing, of Jesus (1:12–13) follows hard on the event of his baptism ("And immediately"; 1:12). The pronominal reference to Jesus ("him"; 1:12) indicates that he stands forth in this pericope in the same capacity as in the baptismal scene: as the royal Son of God. That the Spirit should drive, or lead, Jesus out into the desert reveals that it is God who wills that Jesus should confront Satan (1:12). Once more, then, Mark points to God as the ultimate "author" of the action he will describe in his story.

The "desert" is the abode of Satan (1:13).[97] The reference to "forty days" is reminiscent of the forty years Israel spent in the desert, during which time it, too, was tested (Deut. 8:2).[98] "Satan" is figuratively named the "strong man" (3:27) in Mark; he is the cosmic antagonist of Jesus (3:23–27; 4:15). The Marcan notion of "being tested (tempted)" *(peirazomenos)* is uniformly negative, suggesting that Satan entices Jesus to act in a fashion that would undermine his fealty to God.[99] The image of "being with the wild beasts" is best interpreted as an allusion to the eschatological age of salvation when humankind and wild animals will once again dwell in peace with one another (Isa. 11:6–9; 65:25; 2 Apoc. Bar. 73:6).[100] And the notation that "angels were ministering to him [Jesus]" connotes that these heavenly beings sustain Jesus, either literally, by feeding him (cf.

---

97. Best, *Temptation*, p. 5.

98. Hartman, "Taufe," p. 105; Barrett, *Holy Spirit*, p. 51.

99. Cf. Mark 8:11–12; 10:2–12; 12:13–17; also Gnilka, *Markus*, I, 57.

100. Cf. Leder, "Versuchungsgeschichte," pp. 205–6, 211.

1:31), or, more generally, by serving him in some undefined manner (cf. 10:45).[101]

These definitions point to the meaning of the pericope on the temptation. God impels Jesus, whom he has just declared to be his Son, into the desert to confront Satan in the place of his abode. For forty days Jesus, sustained by angels, is put to the test by Satan. But far from succumbing to Satan's assault, which would have alienated him from God, Jesus Son of God proves himself to be stronger than the "strong man." Thus, he overcomes Satan and "binds" him (cf. 3:27),[102] and so inaugurates the eschatological age of salvation.

Contextually, the purpose of the pericope on the temptation is to complement that on the baptism. In the baptismal scene, the reader is told by God who Jesus is: he is God's royal Son whom God has chosen and empowered for eschatological ministry. In the temptation, the reader learns what Jesus is about: he overthrows the rule of Satan and hence inaugurates the eschatological age of salvation.

Summary

In his caption-summary (1:1), Mark informs the reader that the entire story he is about to narrate is the "beginning of the gospel." The protagonist, he says, will be Jesus ("Jesus Christ [Messiah]"), and the reader is to understand him to be the Messiah, the Son of God ("Jesus [who is] Messiah, Son of God").

But although Jesus is the protagonist of his story, Mark hastens to point out in an epigraph (1:2–3) that neither he nor the messenger who will precede him, John, are to be seen as acting autonomously (1:2). On the contrary, it is under divine auspices that they will act, which is to say that what is normative in the story to be told is "God's evaluative point of view," his will.

Temporally, Mark shows that the context in which his story unfolds is God's history of salvation. Through the sending of John the Baptizer (1:2–3, 4–8) and Jesus (12:6), God has brought to an end the "time of prophecy" (1:2–3) and inaugurated the "time of fulfillment" (1:2–3, 15), which is the "time of the gospel" (1:1, 14–15; 13:10).

---

101. Cf. further Barrett, *Holy Spirit,* pp. 50–51.
102. Cf. Grundmann, *"Ischyō,"* p. 401.

John is Elijah redivivus (1:2, 6; 9:13), the forerunner of Jesus Messiah (1:1–3, 7). The mission he performs is one of summoning Israel to baptism and hence to repentance and the reception of the forgiveness of sins (1:4–5, 8). In this manner, he readies Israel for the "mightier one," whose coming he prophesies (1:7–8).

True to John's prophecy, Jesus comes from Nazareth of Galilee and is himself baptized by John (1:9). Immediately after his baptism, Jesus goes up from the water (1:10) where, removed from John, he becomes the recipient of two revelatory events (1:10–11). In these events, the one visual and the other auditory, God himself enters the realm of Mark's story as "actor." He empowers Jesus with his Spirit (1:10), and he solemnly asseverates both his station and call: Jesus is God's only, or unique, Son (the Davidic Messiah, the royal Son of God), whom God has chosen for messianic ministry (1:11). In witnessing the baptismal scene, the reader thus hears from God himself how he "thinks" about Jesus. And because Mark has already explained that the evaluative point of view which is normative in his story is that of God (1:2), the reader knows that God's understanding of Jesus will likewise be the normative understanding, the one with which Mark's own understanding, too, tallies (cf. 1:1 to 1:11).

Hard on the heels of these revelatory events, God brings Jesus out into the desert (1:12). There, sustained by angels, he submits to temptation by Satan for forty days (1:13). Stronger than the "strong man," Jesus Son of God overcomes Satan and "binds" him (3:27), thus inaugurating the eschatological age of salvation (1:13; cf. 1:8).

The key pericope in this first main part of Mark's story (1:1–13) is plainly the baptismal scene (1:9–11), which goes to the heart of Mark's christology. As we saw especially in Chapter 2, the dominant way in which scholars have interpreted Mark's christology in the last quarter century is in terms of a "corrective approach." The idea is that Mark first presents Jesus as Son of God and divine man, that is, as a figure that epitomizes a theology of glory, and then "corrects" this picture in the course of his narrative by means of his own theology of the cross and, according to some, the use of the title the Son of Man. As applied to the pericope on the baptism, the corrective approach in its "stronger" form pinpoints 1:10 as the place where Jesus is physically transformed into the Son of God, or divine man, and, in its "weaker" form, insists that, however 1:10 is to be interpreted, the title Son of God is inaccurate or ambiguous in Mark's story until it has been reinterpreted by means of the title the Son of Man.

With respect to this approach, two points need to be made. The first point is that it is important to draw a distinction between "elaboration" and "correction." There can be no question but that the reader, having perused only the first main part of Mark's story, is in no position to know all that Mark would have him know about what it means for Jesus to be the Messiah Son of God. Clearly, having presented Jesus as the Messiah Son of God in 1:1–13, Mark can be expected to employ the rest of his story to "elaborate," which is not at all to say "correct," this picture.

The second point to be made is that the notion of "correction," as generally understood by scholars who espouse the corrective approach, runs afoul of literary-critical considerations. It does so because to claim that Mark, after having first depicted God in the baptismal account as transforming Jesus into a divine man or at least as ascribing to him the title Son of God ("my Son"), then "corrects" this baptismal understanding of divine man or the title Son of God in the course of his narrative is to allege, in effect, that Mark characterizes none other than God himself as being "unreliable." In a literary-critical light, such a position clashes frontally with the position that Mark himself, who is a "reliable narrator," takes, namely, that it is, from the outset of his story (1:2–3; cf. 1:14–15; 8:33d), "God's evaluative point of view" that is "normative." In Mark's perspective, the reader, on "seeing" God empower Jesus with the Spirit in 1:10 and on hearing God's asseveration that Jesus is his beloved Son in 1:11, is to regard the resultant estimate of Jesus to be the correct one and the standard against which all other estimates of Jesus are to be measured.

THE MINISTRY OF JESUS IN AND
AROUND GALILEE, (1:14—8:26)

Mark devotes the second main part of his Gospel to the public ministry of Jesus in and around Galilee (1:14—8:26). As the reader henceforth observes Jesus carry out his ministry, he knows how he is to conceive of him: Jesus is the Davidic Messiah, the royal Son of God, whom God has empowered for eschatological ministry. But be that as it may, if the reader, and transcendent beings such as God or also Satan (1:11, 12–13), know the identity of Jesus, the human characters in Mark's story, such as the Jewish people (1:5) or even John, do not. Accordingly, as Mark narrates the second main part of his story, the reader can anticipate that one theme certain to occupy him is that regarding the identity of Jesus.

The Public Activity of Jesus

The beginning of a segment of a story often plays a critical role in alerting the reader to what that segment is about. This is particularly true in the case of Mark 1:14—8:26. Mark begins this section by reporting, in rapid succession, that Jesus comes into the region of Galilee (1:14), makes his way to the Sea of Galilee and passes by along the lake (1:16, 19), and then travels on to Capernaum, where he spends the sabbath day (1:24–34). Important as this geography may be, the striking thing about this initial journey of Jesus in Galilee is that it serves to bind together a series of four summary-passages. Together, these summary-passages inform the reader in a programmatic way of the kinds of activity that Jesus will undertake during his Galilean ministry: he will preach (1:14–15), call disciples (1:16–20), teach (1:21–22), and heal and exorcize demons (1:32–34). And to make certain that the reader does not lose sight of the fact that it is just such activity that occupies Jesus during this phase of his ministry, Mark dots the pages of 1:14—8:26 with additional summary-passages: Jesus continues to preach (1:38–39), to call disciples (2:14; 3:13–19), to teach (2:13; 6:6b, 30–34; cf. 4:1–2; 10:1), and to heal and to exorcize demons (1:39; 3:7–12; 6:53–56).

To begin with, then, Mark focuses on the preaching of Jesus. In the summary-passage 1:14–15, he presents Jesus as proclaiming: "The time is fulfilled and the Kingdom of God is at hand; repent and believe in the gospel!" Not until John has been handed over to the authorities, thus typifying in his own fate the fate of the "Lord" for whom he has prepared the way (1:3; 9:11–13), does Jesus commence preaching (1:14). By the same token, "preaching" *(kēryssein)* is the activity that conspicuously binds together the several ministries that comprise for Mark the "time of the gospel": John, Jesus, and the pre-Easter and post-Easter disciples all "preach" (1:4, 14; 6:12; 13:10).

The burden of Jesus' message to Israel is "the gospel of God"

(1:14), that is, the good news about God which Jesus proclaims in 1:15.[103] This good news consists of a double announcement and a double summons. Jesus announces that "the time is fulfilled" (1:15), which in Marcan parlance alludes to the circumstance that God has brought the OT "time of prophecy" to its close (1:2–3) and has inaugurated the end-phase of history, the "time of the gospel" (1:1; 8:35; 10:29; 13:10; 14:9). And Jesus furthermore announces wherein the peculiarity of this fullness of time lies, namely, in the fact that "the Kingdom of God is at hand" (1:15). In Marcan thought, the Kingdom of God is, of course, the kingly Rule of God. So near has God drawn that his kingly Rule is already determinative of the present and hence is a present, albeit hidden, reality; and it is likewise a future reality, for it is rapidly tending towards its consummation in splendor at the end of time (4:26–29, 30–32). As the royal Son of God, Jesus is not only the herald of the kingly Rule of God, but he is its bearer as well (4:26–29, 30–32).

In the face of the nearness of God's kingly Rule, Jesus summons Israel to "repent and believe in the gospel!" (1:15). "Repentance" and "faith" are two sides of the same coin. Repentance connotes radical conversion: an unconditional turning away from evil ways and all that is contrary to God.[104] Faith connotes radical confidence, an unconditional turning towards the gospel in complete trust. For Mark, however, to place one's trust in the gospel is at the same time to place one's trust in the one in whom God in his kingly Rule has graciously drawn near, namely, in Jesus. In preaching to Israel, therefore, Jesus is calling Israel to decision. Those who heed his summons will become his disciples (8:34), live in the sphere of God's eschatological Rule (1:15; 4:26–32; 10:15), and at the latter day be saved (13:26–27). Those who refuse his summons will align themselves with "this adulterous and sinful generation" and at the latter day incur judgment (8:38).

Having announced the message he proclaims in Israel, the Marcan

---

103. Keck ("Introduction to Mark's Gospel," p. 359 n. 1) construes the genitive "of God" in the expression "the gospel of God" as being both subjective and objective: "the God-given message about God." While this is correct from the standpoint of Mark's overall theology, in 1:14–15 in particular the genitive appears to be objective: "the message about God."

104. Cf. Behm, *"Metanoeō,"* p. 1002.

Jesus calls his first disciples (1:16–20).[105] The calling of disciples, too, is a major aspect of the public activity of the royal Son of God. The portrait Mark sketches of the disciples casts them in both a positive and negative light.[106]

The initiative in calling disciples Mark places squarely with Jesus ("he saw"; 1:16, 19; 2:14), in this way highlighting his authority. Indeed, it is only "those whom he himself wants" that Jesus invites into the circle of the twelve (3:13). Those called by Jesus respond "immediately" to his summons by leaving behind their former mode of life (10:28–30) and going after him (1:18, 20; 2:14; 3:13).

In the case of the twelve, the call Jesus gives is to be "with him" and to be "sent" by him (3:14). As those who are "with him," the twelve become the close followers of Jesus,[107] the eye- and ear-witnesses of his ministry, whom he also charges with living out in their own existence the "way of the cross" (8:34–35). As those who are "sent" by him, the twelve are given to share in Jesus' own authority (3:16; 6:7). In extension of his ministry, they go first to Israel, preaching repentance and exorcizing demons and healing (3:14–15; 6:6b–13, 30). After Easter, they will go to all the nations, proclaiming the gospel that tells of "Jesus Messiah, the Son of God" (1:1, 17; 13:10; 14:9).

This is the positive side of Mark's presentation of the disciples. The negative side is that, despite their call and privileged status, the disciples prove themselves to be "hard of heart" (6:52; 8:17), that is to say, without understanding (8:17, 21). In the three boat-scenes, for example, the disciples show that they comprehend neither the secret of Jesus' identity (4:35–41) nor the sustaining power that is his (6:45–51; 8:14–21). Similarly, neither do they evince any ability to perceive the nature of Jesus' ministry: three times they counter Jesus' predictions of his passion either by repudiating the notion that he should suffer (8:32) or by embroiling themselves in quarrels over matters of personal privilege (9:33–35; 10:35–41). At the last, so perversely blind are the disciples that they commit "apostasy": Judas

105. The scholarly literature on the subject of the disciples in Mark is voluminous. For a recent study which can also serve as a guide to the secondary sources, cf. Best, *Following Jesus,* passim.

106. Cf. Tannehill, "Disciples in Mark," pp. 393, 395, 396–405.

107. Cf. Mark 1:17–18, 20; 6:1; 10:28; also 2:14.

betrays Jesus (14:43–46), all forsake him (14:50), and Peter denies him (14:66–72). Still, this is not the final word on the disciples, for Mark holds out the prospect that the resurrected Jesus reconciles them to himself at his meeting with them in Galilee (16:6–7).

The third aspect of the public activity of the royal Son of God which Mark mentions at the beginning of his Galilean ministry is "teaching" *(didaskein)*. Of all that Jesus undertakes during his ministry in Mark, teaching is what is most typical of him (2:13; 6:34; 10:1; 14:49). Whether it be disciples, individual strangers, a friendly scribe, or opponents, "teacher" (or "rabbi") is the appellation of respect by which he is addressed.[108] In his frequent encounters with the crowd, whether it be beside the sea (2:7, 13; 4:1–2; 5:21) or in the villages (6:6b), it is the "custom" of Jesus that he teach (10:1). And if Mark depicts the disciples as "preaching" and "exorcizing demons" (3:15; 6:7, 12–13), he reserves the task of teaching, with but one exception (6:30), to Jesus alone.

The content of Jesus' teaching in Israel, irrespective of audience, turns on a wide variety of topics: the Kingdom of God (chap. 4), Jesus' impending passion (8:31; 9:31), matters pertaining to discipleship (9:38–50), specific questions having to do with the will of God as expressed in scripture, religion, tradition, law, and ethics,[109] and pressing issues that concern the time before the end (chap. 13).

But apart from such particulars, what Mark emphasizes most about the teaching of Jesus is its divine origin and character. This is the emphasis, in fact, that distinguishes Mark's first, and most important, summary-passage on teaching in 1:21–22. As Jesus teaches in the synagogue in Capernaum, the people react with amazement (1:21–22). The reason, Mark explains, is that Jesus teaches them as one who has authority, and not as the scribes (1:22). Elsewhere in his story, Mark portrays the scribes as legalists who "teach as doctrines the precepts of men" (7:7). Conversely, Mark portrays Jesus in the baptismal scene as the royal Son of God whom God has empowered with the Spirit for messianic ministry (1:10–11). Given these contrasting portrayals, we see, therefore, that what Mark wants to convey to the reader in

---

108. Mark 4:38; 9:17, 38; 10:17, 20, 35; 12:14, 19, 32; 13:1; 9:5; 10:51; 11:21; 14:45.

109. Cf. Mark 2:18–22, 23–27; chap. 7; 10:1–12; 12:13–40.

1:21–22 is that the teaching of Jesus is no mere questionable word of human derivation but is the word of the Messiah Son of God, that is, of the one who, empowered with the Spirit, is the mouthpiece of God. Or, to put it differently, the teaching of Jesus can also be said to be "new" (1:27), that is, it is itself to Mark's way of thinking a manifestation of the fact that in Jesus Son of God the eschatological Rule of God is a present reality.[110]

The final aspect of the public activity of the royal Son of God which Mark underscores throughout 1:14—8:26 is "healing" *(therapeuein)* and "exorcizing demons" *(ekballein daimonia)* (1:34). Concerning the whole topic of Jesus as miracle-worker, because it is none other than God who is at work in Jesus (1:11) and because it is both his words and his deeds that are "Spirit wrought" (1:10) or "from heaven" (11:27–33), the attitude Mark invites the reader to adopt towards the miraculous activity of Jesus is one that is positive and not one that is fraught with reservations about a false theology of glory.[111] Throughout 1:14—8:26, the reader looks on as Jesus preaches, calls disciples, teaches, and heals and exorcizes demons, all on the authority of God. Certainly, Mark's story does not end at 8:26. Necessarily, therefore, the reader's knowledge of Jesus is as yet incomplete. Hence, for the reader to understand Jesus as preacher, gatherer of disciples, teacher, and healer and exorcist is, on the one hand, "correct," but, on the other hand, "insufficient." Still, this is true both of any and of all of these aspects of Mark's portrait of Jesus, and not just of that aspect which has to do with his activity as miracle-worker.

---

110. Cf. also Kertelge, *Wunder Jesu,* pp. 57–58, 87; Behm, *"Kainos,"* pp. 447–50.

111. Perhaps the best clue Mark gives as to the overall impression he would convey of the miraculous activity of Jesus is to be found in his use of the term *dynamis* ("power"). *Dynamis* (pl.: *dynameis*) is, as is well known, Mark's designation for a miracle of Jesus and characterizes it as a "deed of power" (cf. 6:2, 5, 14; BAG, p. 208). On Mark's view, "power" is of God (12:24). Not only this, but the term "power" itself can be used, as Jesus does in the words of the psalmist, as a metaphor for God (14:62). Contrariwise, "power" in the sense of *dynamis* is not something that is ever predicated to Satan, demons, or the opponents of Jesus. When the Marcan Jesus predicts that false messiahs and false prophets will arise and work miracles, he does not say that they will perform "deeds of power" but that they will perform "signs and wonders" (13:22). Mark's logic, then, is clear: God, the source of "power," has empowered Jesus with the Spirit; in consequence of this, the miracles Jesus performs are "deeds of power" but not (false) "signs and wonders."

The first thing to take note of in Mark's presentation of the miraculous activity of Jesus is the "categories" of miracles to which Mark
does (and does not) make reference. In the summary-passages devoted
to Jesus' "deeds of power,"[112] Mark speaks of what are termed "ther-
apeutic miracles" on the one hand and "exorcisms" on the other but
not of miracles in which Jesus displays mastery over the forces of
nature.[113] What this indicates is that it is squarely on the liberation,
or "salvation," of persons whose bondage to sin and evil manifests
itself as physical affliction that Mark places the accent in depicting the
miraculous activity of Jesus.

More specifically, Mark conceives of Jesus, in his exorcisms,[114] as
engaged in eschatological conflict with Satan (3:22–27). He, the royal
Son of God, "plunders thoroughly the house of the strong man" Satan
by releasing persons, not only Jews but also Gentiles,[115] from the
dominion of Satan and bringing them into the sphere of the Reign of
God (1:12–13; 3:24–27). In his miracles of healing,[116] Jesus stands
forth as the savior of the sick (6:56). Empowered with the Spirit
(1:10), the royal Son of God is "power-ladened."[117] The ill, the
afflicted, and the infirm throng, or are brought, to him in order that
they might touch him, and he, in turn, heals, or "saves," them (1:32,
34; 3:10; 6:54–56). Individuals, too, come, or are brought, to him in
the belief that he can cure them, and these he heals, or "saves," as
well.[118] In point of fact, not even is death able to place one beyond
the reach of Jesus' life-giving power (5:22–24, 35–43).

But however remarkable Jesus' deeds of power may be, they, no
more than his acts of preaching and teaching, are naked revelations
of his divine sonship and the circumstance that in him God's Rule is
a present reality. The demons about to be cast out know to their dread
that Jesus is the Son of God, but he suppresses their knowledge of

---

112. Cf. Mark 1:32–34, 39; 3:7–12; 6:53–56; also 6:13.

113. Apart from the cursing of the fig tree (11:12–14, 20–21), Theissen (*Wundergeschichten*, pp. 318–19) categorizes the "nature miracles" of Mark as a
"miracle of deliverance" (4:35–41), an "epiphany" (6:45–52), and "gift-mira-
cles" (6:35–44; 8:1–10).

114. Cf. Mark 1:21–28; 5:1–20; 7:24–30; 9:14–29.

115. Cf. Mark 5:1–20; 7:24–30.

116. Cf. Mark 1:29–31, 40–45; 2:1–12; 3:1–6; 5:21–43; 7:31–37; 8:22–26;
10:46–52.

117. Cf. Mark 3:10; 5:27–34; 6:56.

118. Cf. Mark 2:3–5; 5:22–24 and 35–43, 25–34; 10:46–52.

him (1:24–25, 34; 3:11–12). The leaders of the Jews witness the
miracles of Jesus, but the scribes conclude from his exorcisms that he
is in collusion with Satan (3:22, 30) and the Pharisees demand of him
that he have God perform a sign on his behalf to attest to them that
he is God's chosen agent (8:11–12). Twice the disciples are the ben-
eficiaries of Jesus' power over nature (4:35–41; 6:45–52) and twice
they even participate in his feeding of the crowds (6:35–44; 8:1–10),
but these experiences lead them to perceive neither who Jesus is (4:41;
6:45–52) nor that they have in him the "bread of life" (8:14–21).
And the townspeople of Nazareth hear of the miracles he has performed, but the notion that these could be deeds that God is working
"through his hands" causes them to react by taking offense at him
and hence thwarting his ability to heal there (6:2–6).

The Itinerancy and Fame of Jesus

The public ministry of the royal Son of God in Mark is one of
"divine favor" towards especially Israel. Jesus is the pivotal figure
in what is the "time of the gospel" (1:1); John the Baptizer predicts
of Jesus that he will baptize Israel "with the Holy Spirit" (1:8); and
it is in view of the fact that the nearness of God's Rule is "good
news" that Jesus summons Israel to repentance (1:14–15; cf. 6:12).

Jesus' ministry to Israel is marked by itinerancy. If it can be said
that he is "at home" anywhere, then perhaps it is in Capernaum,[119]
in the house that seemingly belongs to Simon and Andrew.[120] Typically, however, the Marcan Jesus discharges his ministry by wandering from place to place. He traverses the whole of Galilee (1:39) and
also visits briefly the regions beyond (7:24, 30). It is in the synagogues
of all Galilee, for example, that he preaches his gospel of the Kingdom
(1:39). Wherever his travels take him, he teaches the people: in the
synagogues of Capernaum (1:21–22) and of Nazareth (6:1–2), beside
the sea (2:13; 4:1–2), going about among the villages (6:6), or even
in a lonely place (6:33–34). And whether it be in synagogues,[121]
cities,[122] at the sea (3:7–12), in villages or fields (6:56), or beyond

---

119. Cf. Mark 1:21; 2:1; 9:33.

120. Cf. Mark 1:29, 33; 2:1; also 3:20 (?); 7:17 (?); 2:15 (Levi's house? or
Jesus' house?).

121. Cf. Mark 1:23–27, 39; 3:1–5; 6:5.

122. Cf. Mark 1:32–34, 38; 6:56.

Galilee in Gentile territory,[123] he likewise heals the sick or exorcizes demons.

Regardless of the locale, Jesus' acts of teaching or of healing or exorcizing demons create no little stir among the people. Characteristically, he "amazes" or "astounds" the hearers or onlookers.[124] Thus, he teaches in the synagogue at Capernaum, and of the reaction of the people Mark writes, "And they were amazed at his teaching" (1:21–22). And following Jesus' healing of the paralytic in the house in Capernaum, Mark reports of the crowd, ". . . they were all amazed and glorified God, saying, 'We never saw anything like this!' " (2:12).

As a result of his authoritative teaching and powerful deeds, the fame of Jesus spreads far and wide. Indeed, from the outset of his ministry news of him begins to circulate. No sooner has Jesus taught and exorcized an unclean spirit in the synagogue at Capernaum than Mark records of him: "And at once his fame spread everywhere throughout all the surrounding region of Galilee" (1:28). Nor is this the whole of it. At 3:7–8, Mark emphasizes that all parts of Palestine and Gentile lands as well hear the word of Jesus' activity: Galilee, Judea, Jerusalem, Idumea, Trans-Jordan, and Tyre and Sidon. In the Decapolis, too, people are told of him (5:20). In fact, as Mark narrates it the truth of the matter is that the fame of Jesus is such that it cannot be suppressed. Jesus himself, for example, can command silence concerning a miracle he has performed, and yet even his command can be ignored and the news of him proclaimed (1:44–45; 7:36).

The fame of Jesus in Mark's story causes people to flock to him. From all over Palestine and also from Tyre and Sidon, they come to him (3:7–8). He can be at home in Capernaum, and a crowd will gather (2:1–2; 3:20, 32). In fact, one evening the whole city congregates at his door so that he might heal the sick and cast out demons (1:32–34). What is more, the next day all the people go looking for him again (1:37).

Wherever Mark's Jesus travels in Galilee, the same scenes recur. As soon as the word is out that Jesus is in an area, individuals find their way to him (5:27; 7:25) or a whole crowd runs to him. Even in

---

123. Cf. Mark 5:1–20; 7:24–30.
124. Cf. Mark 1:22, 27; 2:12; 5:42; 6:2, 51; 7:37; also 9:15; 10:24, 26; 11:18.

unpopulated areas, people come to him from everywhere (1:45). When he is beside the sea, the crowd masses to listen to his teaching (2:13; 3:7; 4:1–2; 5:21). On one occasion, he and his disciples, embarking by boat for a deserted location, are spotted by the crowd, the upshot being that when he disembarks, the crowd is already awaiting him and his word of teaching (6:32–34). On another occasion, Jesus no sooner lands at Gennesaret from having journeyed across the sea when he is recognized, and the people of the whole area round up their sick and bring them to him for healing (6:53–55). Throughout 1:14—8:26, therefore, it is commonplace that Jesus should either have a crowd following him as he conducts his ministry[125] or that he should summon a crowd to himself for instruction (7:14; cf. 8:34). In one instance, Mark does not even shrink from having a crowd remain with Jesus for three days (8:1–2).

To impress the reader with the extraordinary popularity of Jesus, Mark even employs what we may call "negative indicators." Twice, for example, Mark states that the crowd about Jesus is so great that it prevents him and his disciples from eating (3:20; 6:31). Indeed, in the ears of Jesus' family, his fame becomes notoriety; to their way of thinking, he has gone mad (3:21). Again, the crowd is sometimes so large or the people so intent upon touching him in order that they might be healed that they press against him (3:10) and threaten to crush him (3:9; 5:24, 31). In other respects, news of a deed of Jesus can create such intense anticipation in the minds of the populace that Jesus is not able to enter into a city openly (1:45). Even in the region of Tyre, Jesus is unable to remain incognito, although that is his wish (7:24). And on occasion the crowd becomes such a burden that Jesus attempts to escape from it, usually by boat (3:9; 4:35–36; 6:31–32, 45–46).

Questions about the Identity of Jesus

Why should Mark go to such great lengths in 1:14—8:26 to emphasize the enormous impact the activity of Jesus has upon people and the widespread fame that is his? A major reason is that these twin factors play a key role in the development of the motif of the identity of Jesus. In selected pericopes, for example, the striking nature of

---

125. Cf. Mark 2:15; 3:7; 5:24.

Jesus' activity prompts those who witness it to ask themselves who he is. And the widespread fame of Jesus generates various "guesses" in the mind of the Jewish public as to who, conceivably, he could be.

To such questions and such notions regarding the identity of Jesus Mark attaches immense significance, as is evident from the following observations. To begin with, it is precisely a question touching on the identity of Jesus which is the central feature in the first pericope of Mark's story which is not a summary-passage and in which Mark describes public reaction to the teaching of Jesus and to a miraculous deed he performs (1:27). Second, the groups of characters who pose the several questions about Jesus' identity in 1:14—8:26 either constitute, or are representative of, the principal characters in Mark's story: the Jewish people (1:27), the Jewish authorities (2:7), the disciples (4:41), and the family, relatives, and acquaintances of Jesus (6:3). Third, Mark's concern that the reader should not be ignorant of the various conceptions that the Jewish public has of Jesus reflects itself in the fact that he broaches this subject not once but twice (6:14–16; 8:27–28). And last, the profound importance these questions and notions about Jesus' identity have for Mark can also be seen in the circumstance that this entire series of passages to which we have just referred, namely, 1:27; 2:7; 4:41; 6:3, 14–16; and 8:27–28, connects like a red thread with 8:29, which is the first passage in Mark's story in which a human character gives a correct, even if insufficient, estimate of who Jesus really is.

To consider the several questions about the identity of Jesus, the first of these occurs in the pericope on the healing of the demoniac in the synagogue at Capernaum (1:21–28). Upon encountering a man with an unclean spirit after having taught the people, Jesus demonstrates his power over the spirit by suppressing its recognition of him and exorcizing it (1:23–26). Having attended to Jesus' teaching in amazement, the people now look on in astonishment at this exorcism he has accomplished. Astounded as they are, they both query one another and exclaim, "What is this? A new teaching with authority![?]" (1:27c–d).[126]

---

126. Whether these words constitute the correct reading of 1:27c–d, whether the exclamation should not also be read as a question ("A new teaching with authority?"), and whether the exclamation should form one or two sense units ("A new teaching"; "With authority . . .") are all matters of debate, text-crit-

At first blush, it may appear that these words of the people have little to do with the matter of Jesus' identity. Their question envisages the miracle Jesus has just performed, and this exclamation makes mention of his teaching. Still, operative in the words of 1:27c–d is a literary technique according to which inquiry about what Jesus has done becomes in effect inquiry about Jesus himself. A glance at the rest of 1:27 and 1:28 confirms the truth of this statement, for here the focus shifts abruptly to Jesus: "*He* commands even the unclean spirits, and they obey *him*. And at once the report of *him* spread everywhere . . ." (italics mine). In other words, implicit in the question, "What is this?" in 1:27c is the question, "Who is this?" The people in the synagogue at Capernaum are astonished at the authority with which Jesus teaches (1:21–22) and acts (1:26), and this causes them to wonder who he is.

The second question pertaining to the identity of Jesus follows soon after the first and is posed by "some of the scribes" (2:1–12). Jesus is at home in Capernaum proclaiming the word to a crowd when four men, carrying a paralytic on a pallet but unable to reach Jesus, climb to the roof, dig through the clay, and let down the man on the pallet to him. Seeing the faith of these men, Jesus forgives the paralytic his sins. This act, however, provokes the scribes who are sitting there to reason in their hearts, "Why does this man speak thus? He blasphemes! Who can forgive sins but God alone?" (2:7). Perceiving that these scribes are harboring these thoughts in their hearts, Jesus addresses them openly and replies to their questions by asserting that "the Son of Man has authority on earth to forgive sins" (2:10).

As regards the topic of Jesus' identity, there are two interrelated problems that stand out in this pericope. The one problem concerns the question the scribes pose in 2:7c, "Who can forgive sins but God alone?" Because this question anticipates the answer, "No one," it is plainly rhetorical. But if it is rhetorical, is it legitimate to claim that the words of the scribes in 2:7 even raise the issue of the identity of Jesus? Yet, should it be decided that these words do raise this issue, another problem presents itself. One must ask, namely, what the term "the Son of Man" connotes, since this is the term by means of which Jesus designates himself in giving reply to the scribes (2:10).

---

ically. Here I have followed the 26th edition of Nestle-Aland, *Novum Testamentum Graece*, but have indicated that in my opinion the exclamation, too, should be read as a question.

The words of the scribes in 2:7 do indeed raise the issue of the identity of Jesus, but, as was also the case with 1:27, indirectly so. When the scribes reason, "Why does this man speak thus? He blasphemes! Who can forgive sins but God alone?" the net effect of their questions and exclamation is, as Jesus' answer in 2:10 reveals, to ask who this Jesus is who dares to arrogate to himself the prerogative of God and to forgive sins.[127]

Jesus' reply to the thoughts of the scribes is that "the Son of Man has authority on earth to forgive sins" (2:10).[128] Mark's use of the title "the Son of Man" is a matter we shall explore next chapter. To understand what it signifies here, suffice it to say that it functions neither as a circumlocution for the pronoun "I"[129] nor as a synonym, whether explicit[130] or veiled,[131] for "Messiah" or "Son of God." Instead, "the Son of Man" is a title by means of which Jesus refers to himself in public in order to point to himself as "the man," or "the human being" (this man, or this human being), and to assert his divine authority in the face of opposition.

---

127. Interestingly, Luke shows that he, too, has understood Mark 2:7 to be an inquiry about the identity of Jesus, for he has recast Mark 2:7a–b to make this clear. Luke's rendition of Mark 2:7 is: "Who is this who speaks blasphemies? Who can forgive sins but God only?" (Luke 5:21).

128. One approach to Mark 2:1–12 (cf., e.g., Boobyer, "Secrecy Motif," pp. 228–29; Cranfield, *Mark,* p. 100; Hay, "Son of Man," pp. 71–73;.Perrin, "Christology of Mark," pp. 112, 116 n. 24; idem, "High Priest's Question," p. 92; Fowler, *Loaves and Fishes,* pp. 161–62) construes 2:10a ("But that you may know that the Son of Man has authority on earth to forgive sins") as an "aside" that Mark is himself directing to the reader of the Gospel and not as a remark that Jesus directs to the scribes. Obviously, what is attractive about this approach is that if it can be claimed that "the Son of Man" in 2:10a, and in 2:28 as well, is not uttered by Jesus "in public" but instead appears in "private comments" Mark directs to the reader, then one is absolved from asking what impact the "public use" of "the Son of Man" would have upon Mark's motif of the secret of Jesus' identity at this early stage in his story. But to take this view of 2:10a (and 2:28) remains problematical, for there are no firm criteria for demonstrating that it is in fact correct. Vague appeals to a change in style or to a disruption of syntax are elusive, and the alleged parallels often cited (e.g., 7:19b; 13:14) are too distant in grammar or wording to decide the case.

129. Cf., e.g., Bultmann, *Geschichte der synoptischen Tradition,* p. 13 (ET, *History of the Synoptic Tradition,* p. 15); Martin, *Mark,* p. 191; Vermes, *Jesus the Jew,* p. 180.

130. Cf., e.g., Sjöberg, *Menschensohn,* p. 105; Kertelge, *Wunder Jesu,* p. 82; Räisänen, *Messiasgeheimnis,* pp. 144–45.

131. Cf., e.g., Theissen, *Wundergeschichten,* p. 212.

Thus, "the Son of Man" is a title, and one indication of this in 2:10 is the circumstance that Mark has Jesus designate himself as *"the* Son of Man."[132] But "the Son of Man," title though it may be, functions in 2:1–12 to describe Jesus as "the man," or "the human being" (this man, or this human being).[133] With a view to the scribes' charge of blasphemy, Jesus, in speaking of himself as the Son of Man, boldly advances the claim that he is the man who possesses the divine authority to do what otherwise only God can do, namely, to forgive sins. But if "the Son of Man," while being a title, is nonetheless used by Jesus in 2:10 to point to himself as the (this) man, it becomes clear that Jesus, in availing himself of this self-designation in responding to the scribes' indirect inquiry as to his identity, is not telling them "who he is." Accordingly, Jesus' utterance in public of the title of the Son of Man, not only here in 2:10 but in other passages as well,[134] results neither in the premature disclosure of the secret of Jesus' identity[135] nor in rendering further questions about his identity superfluous (cf. 4:41; 6:3).

The third question concerning the identity of Jesus stems from the disciples (4:35–41). Following the parable discourse he delivers from the boat (4:1), Jesus commands the disciples towards evening to cross over to the other side of the sea (4:35–41). On the way, as Jesus is asleep in the stern of the boat, the disciples become caught in a storm. With the waves beating against the boat and filling it, the disciples arouse Jesus and call on him to show his concern for them by rescuing them from the peril of the storm. In response to their sense of imminent doom, Jesus rebukes the wind and commands the sea to silence. At

---

132. On the distinctiveness of the expression " 'the' Son of Man," cf. Moule, "Neglected Features," pp. 419–21.

133. Whereas my contention is that "the Son of Man" in 2:10 is titular and describes Jesus as "the man" (this man), some scholars hold that "the Son of Man" is non-titular and simply describes Jesus as "a man." For example, Colpe (*"Ho Hyios tou Anthrōpou,"* p. 430) would paraphrase 2:10a as follows: "But that you may know that not only God may forgive, but in the case of me, Jesus, also a man." Cf. further T. W. Manson, *Teaching,* p. 214; Hay, "Son of Man," pp. 71–73. For his part, Moule ("Neglected Features," p. 421) does not argue that "the Son of Man" is titular, but construes it as preserving something which is "more distinctive than simply an Aramaic phrase meaning 'a man.' . . ."

134. Cf. Mark 2:24, 28; 8:34a, 38.

135. Cf., e.g., Sjöberg, *Menschensohn,* p. 105; Kertelge, *Wunder Jesu,* p. 82; Räisänen, *Messiasgeheimnis,* pp. 144–45.

once a great calm ensues. Overwhelmed, the disciples, cowardly, bereft of faith, and filled with great fear, ask one another, "Who then is this, that even wind and sea obey him?" (4:41, RSV).

The fourth question that touches on the identity of Jesus occurs in the mouths of the villagers of Nazareth (6:1–6). Accompanied by his disciples, Jesus travels to his home town. On the day of the sabbath, he enters the synagogue and teaches (6:2), with acquaintances, relatives, and family in attendance (6:4). When the many people assembled there hear him, they become amazed and fall to asking one another about this wisdom that is his and about the great miracles it is reported he performs. The motive sparking their questions, however, is unbelief, for they find it incredible that one whose origins they know should be able to do such astonishing things. Taking offense at Jesus, they ask themselves, "Is not this the carpenter, the son of Mary?" (6:3, RSV).

Public Opinion on the Identity of Jesus

With this question from the villagers of Nazareth, Mark suddenly breaks off the string of inquiries about the identity of Jesus which has stretched from the beginning of Jesus' ministry in Capernaum to his rejection by the people in the synagogue of Nazareth (1:27; 2:7; 4:41; 6:3). Abruptly, Mark exploits instead the theme of the fame of Jesus in order to apprise the reader of the particular ways in which the Jewish public has come to think of him (6:14–16).[136] Wondering who he is, the various segments of the Jewish public have formed their "evaluative points of view" concerning his identity.

As Mark tells it, Jesus, having left Nazareth, sends the disciples out on their ministry to Israel (6:7–13). While they are "away," Mark interrupts his story of Jesus in order to recount for the reader the fate that has already befallen John the Baptizer (6:14–29). As something of a preface to this account, Mark presents a "survey" of Jewish public opinion on Jesus (6:14–16). Because his "name had become known" (6:14), news of Jesus has reached the court of King Herod. The reports Herod hears about who Jesus is, however, are mixed. There are some, for example, who claim that Jesus is "John the

---

136. On the syntax, translation, and meaning of Mark 6:14–16, cf. Ljungvik, "6:14," pp. 90–92; Blinzler, "6, 14–16," pp. 119–31; Hoehner, *Herod Antipas*, pp. 184–87; Theissen, *Wundergeschichten*, pp. 171–72.

Baptizer raised from the dead'' (6:14). There are others who insist
that he is "Elijah" (6:15). And there are others who contend that he
is a "prophet," like one of the prophets of old (6:15). Herod for his
part opts for the first view: "John, whom I beheaded, has been raised"
(6:16, RSV).

The Identity of Jesus:
Demonic Knowledge and Human Ignorance

Thus far, we have said almost nothing about the cries of the unclean
spirits, or demons. Yet these cries play no small role in Mark's treatment of the motif of Jesus' identity in 1:14—8:26. At selected inter-
vals, Mark depicts demons as shouting aloud that Jesus is the Son of
God (1:24; 3:11; 5:7; cf. 1:34). Moreover, the fact that Mark twice
refers to such demonic cries in summary-passages (1:34; 3:11) has the
"generalizing effect" of making Jesus' encounters with demons a
typical feature of his public ministry. By the same token, Mark is also
at pains to show that these cries are systematically suppressed by Jesus
(1:25, 34; 3:12) or occur, as in one instance, in private confrontation
between Jesus and the demoniac (5:2–13). The end result is that the
demons' knowledge of Jesus' identity does not get out.

But this notwithstanding, the demons' knowledge that Jesus is the
Son of God plainly coincides with God's "evaluative point of view"
regarding Jesus' identity expressed at the baptism (1:11). Does this
mean, then, that Mark ascribes veracity to the cries of demons? Although scholars have often denied it, the answer is affirmative. The
"hermeneutical key" for assessing the reliability of the demonic cries
is the passage 1:34. Here Mark, himself a "reliable narrator," unequivocally states that "they [the demons] knew him [Jesus]." Hence,
although it is demons who identify Jesus as the Son of God in 1:14—
8:26 and although the "revelatory content" of their cries does not get
out, the knowledge they possess of Jesus is "correct." Demonic utterance of the title Son of God, therefore, not only does not bring
discredit upon this title but serves the positive purpose of reminding
the reader throughout 1:14—8:26 of who Jesus truly is.

In terms of the dynamics of Mark's story, how do the cries of the
demons relate to the questions the human characters ask concerning
the identity of Jesus? Schematically, the relationship between the cries
and the questions is "contrapuntal." Counting 1:34, which is a neg-

ative reference to the cries of demons, the pattern runs like this: demonic cry (1:24), question (1:27), demonic cries (1:34), question (2:7), demonic cries (3:11), question (4:41), demonic cry (5:7), question (6:3). Also, it should be noted that the first demonic cry and the first question both occur in the first pericope that is not a summary-passage in which Mark portrays Jesus as being active in public (1:23–28 [vv. 24, 27]).

Literarily and theologically, the effect of this pattern is that it exposes the reader, from the beginning of Jesus' public ministry, to a sustained sequence of utterances in which cries revealing the identity of Jesus alternate with questions about who he is. Now we know that the cries of the demons, though suppressed, are correct and in accord with God's estimate of Jesus (1:11). But what is the underlying sense of the questions posed by the human characters?

Mark reveals this in the pericopes in which these questions are embedded. The first question, for example, is asked in "amazement" (1:27). Whatever the positive value of "amazement," Mark shows elsewhere in his story that it masks an inability to understand (6:51–52). For their part, the next three questions are asked in a spirit of utter disapprobation (2:7), or of fear born of cowardice and lack of faith (4:40–41), or of repudiation rooted in unbelief (6:3, 6). In other words, all four of these questions bring to expression an "ignorance" that is reflective of an inability to understand who Jesus is. Accordingly, the literary and theological function of the contrapuntal pattern outlined above is to juxtapose "knowledge" and "ignorance": as the reader takes note of the cries of the demons alternating with the questions of the human characters, he is continually being reminded that Jesus is the Son of God even as he observes the Jewish people, the Jewish authorities, the disciples, and the family, relatives, and acquaintances of Jesus wonder uncomprehendingly who he is.

But this contrapuntal pattern of demonic cry and human question, of (suppressed) knowledge and ignorance, also provides the avenue of approach for interpreting the passage 6:14–16. In this passage, Mark presents the reader, we recall, with the "evaluative points of view" concerning Jesus' identity of the Jewish public and Herod: some, including Herod, take Jesus to be John the Baptizer raised from the dead; others take him to be Elijah; and yet others take him to be a prophet. But all three of these judgments the reader can quickly dismiss as being false. They are false, on the one hand, because they do not square with what the reader knows is the "normative" understanding of Jesus in Mark's story: Jesus is the royal Son of God, as God himself has asseverated (1:11), as the "reliable narrator" Mark has stated (1:1), and as the demons, who "know Jesus," have repeatedly said (1:24, 34; 3:11; 5:7). On the other hand, these judgments are also false because they spring from the cogitations of human characters, and Mark has made it plain that thus far in his story no human character has any inkling as to who Jesus is. Then, too, it must furthermore be kept in mind that the Jewish public and Herod are not just any characters in Mark's story. They are representative of "those who are outside" (4:11). As such, the judgments they make about Jesus will necessarily be false because they cannot do otherwise than confound the truth. Ironically, in this case they confound the truth by attributing to Jesus, the royal Son of God, the kinds of claims that Mark otherwise makes on behalf of John. To Mark, "John the Baptizer" is himself a "prophet" (11:32) and, what is more, "Elijah" redivivus (1:6; 9:11–13). Inevitably, therefore, the end result of this confusion about both John and Jesus, the two agents whom God has sent to Israel (1:2), is that neither the one nor the other ever comes to be understood by the Jewish public or Herod for what he truly is. Herod, in fact, has already put the seal to his ignorance, for he did not shrink from beheading John, the "forerunner" of Jesus (6:16).

Summary

Mark, then, devotes the second main part of his Gospel (1:14—8:26) to the public ministry of Jesus. Affirmed by God to be his royal Son and empowered with the Spirit (1:10–11), Jesus preaches the gospel of God (1:14–15), calls disciples (1:16–20), teaches with authority (1:21–22), and heals the sick and exorcizes demons (1:32–34). In discharging his ministry, he traverses the whole of Galilee and also visits Gentile lands. Through his teaching and the powerful deeds he performs, his fame spreads everywhere. People from all parts of Palestine and from as far away as Trans-Jordan and Tyre and Sidon stream to him (3:7–8). Wherever he goes, the crowds tend to gather and the disciples follow. Such teaching as he imparts and such miracles as he works stir people who hear and see him to wonder who he is. Whether out of astonishment (1:27), disapprobation (2:7), fear

(4:41), or unbelief (6:3, 6), the people, their leaders, the disciples, and the acquaintances, relatives, and family of Jesus, respectively, raise the question as to his identity. King Herod, too, hears of Jesus (6:14), and through the reports he receives learns of the public's perceptions of him: whereas some, like Herod himself, hold Jesus to be John the Baptizer raised from the dead (6:14, 16), others hold him to be Elijah (6:15), and still others hold him to be a prophet after the fashion of the great prophets of old (6:15). But if these are the popular "evaluative points of view" Jesus has evoked, the reader of Mark's story knows better: the demons, whose knowledge of Jesus has not got out, have nevertheless steadily reminded him that Jesus is in truth the royal Son of God (1:24–25, 34; 3:11–12; 5:7).

THE JOURNEY OF JESUS TO JERUSALEM AND HIS SUFFERING, DEATH, AND RESURRECTION (8:27—16:8)

The purpose of the first main part of Mark's story (1:1–13) is to present John and especially Jesus to the reader. The purpose of the second main part (1:14—8:26) is to depict the public ministry of Jesus in and around Galilee. Here in the third main part of his story (8:27—16:8), Mark portrays the journey of Jesus to Jerusalem and his suffering, death, and resurrection.

The three passion-predictions of Jesus control the plot of Mark's story in this last main part (8:31; 9:31; 10:33–34). But the theme of suffering and death they strike runs the length of the story. At the beginning of Jesus' ministry Mark twice raises the specter of his "betrayal," once when he reports that John, the forerunner of Jesus, is "handed over" into the custody of the authorities (1:14), and once when he identifies Judas, in citing the names of the twelve, as the one "who also betrayed him" (3:19). Early in this story, Mark also twice adumbrates the death of Jesus, once when he has Jesus speak of the days "when the bridegroom is taken away" (2:20), and once when he himself says of the Jewish leaders, following their initial debates with Jesus, that they "began to take counsel against him, how to destroy him" (3:6). In other respects, Mark likewise calls attention in the early part of Jesus' ministry to his progressive alienation from Israel: the family of Jesus thinks him mad (3:20–21), the Jewish crowd receives his teaching in parables as people who are blind, deaf, and without understanding (4:1–2, 10–12), and in Nazareth the neighbors and relations of Jesus take offense at him (6:3–4).

The passion-predictions in Mark 8—10, therefore, highlight a central theme Mark has steadily been developing from the beginning of his story. Indeed, in chapter 11 Mark echoes the passage 3:6 and thus both plays on this theme yet another time and reminds the reader of "how long" he has been pursuing it: ". . . and they were considering how to destroy him" (11:18). With chapter 12, Mark moves his story to the point where the chief priests and the scribes and the elders "tried to arrest him but feared the crowd" (12:12). Then, following the apocalyptic discourse of Jesus (chap. 13), Mark begins the narration of precisely those events that Jesus has foretold in his three passion-predictions.

Intertwined with this motif of the suffering and death of Jesus is the motif that is of special interest to us, namely, that of the secret of Jesus' identity. Beginning with the third main part of his story (8:27—16:8), Mark dramatically alters the way in which he deals with this motif. Up to this point (1:14—8:26), he has been following a pattern according to which the human characters in his story have not broached the question of Jesus' identity as such. Instead, it has been a powerful word or deed of Jesus or his fame that has prompted persons to wonder who he is. In fact, the ones on whom the reader has had to rely to be reminded of Jesus' identity have been the demons. The upshot is that throughout 1:14—8:26 the human characters have exhibited no insight into Jesus' identity. Indicative of this are the "guesses" that the Jewish public and Herod have made in view of him.

In 8:27—16:8, by contrast, a different pattern emerges. No longer do demons shout aloud the identity of Jesus. On the contrary, Jesus' identity becomes a focal issue for the human characters, and some evince insight into it. Indeed, Mark seems to proceed in "stages," depicting a progressive disclosure of Jesus' identity. At the same time, he does not proceed "linearly," portraying a single human character or group of human characters as advancing from insight to insight until finally penetrating completely the secret of Jesus' identity. Instead, it is more accurate to say that it is from the standpoint of the reader that Mark depicts the progressive disclosure of Jesus' identity throughout 8:27—16:8. Thus, as the reader follows along, Mark guides him through a series of scenes in which he observes Peter confess Jesus to be the Messiah (8:29), Bartimaeus appeal to him as the Son of David (10:47–48), the Roman centurion declare him to be the Son of God (15:39), and the disciples receive the promise that they will see him in Galilee following his resurrection (14:28; 16:6–7).

The notion that some human characters evince insight into Jesus' identity prior to the centurion's declaration (15:39) or the resurrection (16:6–7) if indeed at all touches on a hotly debated issue in Marcan studies. For one of two reasons, any number of scholars contest this notion. Some contest it because they believe that it makes of Mark an inept writer who allows for the secret of Jesus' identity to be "broken" and hence undermined as a motif. Others contest this notion because they believe that Mark's concern to highlight the gross "ignorance" of the principal human characters in his story rules it out. But regardless of the reason, the result is that many scholars deny, for example, that Peter's confession of Jesus as the Messiah is valid or that Bartimaeus's appeal to Jesus as the Son of David is of positive christological relevance. Such interpretations of these passages, however, miss the mark. In what follows, I shall argue that Mark's motif of human "ignorance" does not preclude him from ascribing to the disciples and certain others "correct," even if "insufficient," insight into the identity of Jesus prior to 15:39 and also that such insight does not result in the "breaking" of the secret of Jesus' identity.

The Confession of Peter and
the Transfiguration

The pericope on the confession of Peter (8:27–30) represents the first stage in the progressive disclosure of Jesus' identity. Contextually it is followed, first, by a section in which Jesus speaks of himself as the Son of Man in foretelling his passion and Parousia (8:31—9:1) and, second, by the pericope on the transfiguration and the ensuing discussion between Jesus and the three disciples (9:2–13).

In form, style, and thought, the confession of Peter (8:27–30) comprises a well-rounded unit.[137] It begins the third main part of Mark's

---

137. Cf., e.g., Pesch, "Messiasbekenntnis," I, 179–88; idem, *Markusevangelium,* II, 27–30; Lane, *Mark,* pp. 287–92; Haenchen, *Weg Jesu,* p. 292; Lohmeyer, *Markus,* p. 161 (but without 8:30); Percy, *Botschaft Jesu,* pp. 227–31;

story (8:27—16:8) by treating the topic of Jesus' identity against the
background of his public ministry in and around Galilee (8:27c–28;
6:14–15). Its purpose is to contrast sharply the "evaluative points of
view" according to which Jesus is John the Baptist, Elijah, or a
prophet (8:28) with the "evaluative point of view" Peter expresses on
behalf of the disciples according to which Jesus is the "Messiah"
("Christ," "Anointed One"; 8:29).

Peter's confession, "You are the Messiah," is correct and not false.
This is apparent from considerations of both a positive and negative
nature. Negatively, Peter's confession can be seen to be correct because it is itself the antithesis to views about Jesus which the reader
knows to be false by virtue of both their source and substance. Recall
that the source of the views that Jesus is John the Baptist (raised from
the dead) or Elijah or a prophet is the Jewish public (6:14–16), that
is, "those outside" (4:11–12). And recall that the substance of these
views constitutes confusion about the identity of both John and Jesus.
Hence, by making Peter's confession the antithesis to these views,
Mark invites the reader to accept it as true.

But from a positive standpoint, too, Peter's confession can be seen
to be correct. By having Jesus ask the disciples who the Jewish public
imagines him to be and by having the disciples repeat the rumors

---

Schmidt, *Rahmen,* pp. 215–17; Lagrange, *Marc,* p. 214; Swete, *Mark,* pp.
175–78; C. H. Turner, *Mark,* pp. 39–40.

Many commentators prefer to combine 8:31–33 with 8:27–30 to form the unit
8:27–33 (cf., e.g., Hahn, *Hoheitstitel,* pp. 226–30; Cranfield, *Mark,* pp. 266–81;
Weeden, *Mark,* pp. 64–68; Kelber, *Kingdom in Mark,* pp. 82–83; Schweizer,
Markus, pp. 88–93; Gnilka, *Markus,* II, 10–17). The reason, of course, is transparent: it is not predicated so much on formal considerations as on the desire to
draw "Messiah" into the orbit of "the Son of Man" so that the former can be
interpreted in terms of the latter. In a careful analysis of 8:27–30 and 8:31–33,
Pesch ("Messiasbekenntnis," I, 181–82) shows that even the "catch-words" the
two units share do not function in the same way or bear the same meaning. And
equally important, Mark also calls attention to a division between the two by
beginning 8:31a with the words, "And he began to teach them . . ." (*ērxato
didaskein*). While the verb *archomai* can be used pleonastically in Mark, this is
not the case here. Instead, it is being used in its literal sense to signal the start of
a new action, as can be seen from the fact that the passion-prediction of 8:31
constitutes "new teaching" within the framework of Mark's story (cf. also Lagrange, *Marc,* pp. XCIII, 216; Grundmann, *Markus,* p. 167; Meye, *The Twelve,*
p. 74; Müller, "Absicht des Markusevangeliums," pp. 163–64; Pesch, *Markusevangelium,* II, 47; Ernst, "Petrusbekenntnis," pp. 47–48; and Taylor's reluctant
admission, *St. Mark,* p. 377).

about Jesus previously enumerated in 6:14–15, Mark alerts the reader to the circumstance that it is against the backdrop of the second larger part of his story (1:14—8:26) that the question of Jesus' identity is being broached. Therefore, when Peter states, in contradistinction to the erroneous notions of the Jewish public, that Jesus is the Messiah, Mark is presenting Peter as declaring how the disciples have come to know Jesus thus far in his ministry. As the summary-passages have revealed, the Jesus of 1:14—8:26 is the Jesus who preaches, teaches, heals, and exorcizes demons. As those called by Jesus to be "with him" (1:16–20; 3:13–14), the disciples view Jesus at the point of 8:27–30 in this light.[138] Mark, in fact, leaves no doubt about this irrespective of whatever lack of understanding the disciples may have evinced prior to 8:27, for he has depicted the disciples as having engaged, in extension of Jesus' own ministry, in the selfsame activities as he: they have preached (3:15; 6:12), taught (6:30), healed (6:13), and exorcized demons (3:15; 6:7, 13). In terms of the contours of Mark's story, therefore, the "Messiah" of Peter's confession is, to reiterate, the Jesus who preaches, teaches, heals, and exorcizes demons, and who has done all this on the authority, and therefore with the "approval," of God (1:10, 22, 27; 11:27–33). Hence, for Peter to confess Jesus to be the Messiah in 8:29 is for Peter, in Mark's perspective, to confess Jesus aright.

In addition to the preceding, there are yet other indicators in Mark's story which also point to the correctness of Peter's confession. To begin with, Mark himself comments "reliably" as early as the first verse of his Gospel that the Jesus of his story is the "Messiah." Moreover, Jesus, too, lends credibility to Peter's confession when, in a slightly later conversation with the disciples, he designates himself as the "Christ," or "Messiah":[139] "For whoever gives you a cup of

---

138. Cf., e.g., Mark 1:16–20 to 1:21–22, 32–34, 38–39.

139. It might be objected that Jesus' use of "Christ," or "Messiah," in 9:41 cannot be understood as lending credibility to Peter's use of "Messiah" in 8:29 because one can always argue that the term "Messiah" does not mean the same thing in the mouth of each. It is true, of course, that "Messiah" is defined variously in Mark's story. To cite but three obvious examples, in 12:35 it denotes "Son of David," in 14:61 it denotes the "Son of the Blessed [God]," and in 15:32 it denotes the "King of Israel." The point to observe, however, is that regardless of the several connotations "Messiah" may bear in Mark's story, whenever it is applied to Jesus, it is applied "correctly" and never "falsely," even

water to drink because you belong to Christ (Messiah)." (9:41). And third, the command to silence which Jesus issues on the heels of Peter's confession (8:30) likewise attests to the correctness of this confession. This is clear from the "reliable" comment Mark makes in connection with Jesus' suppression of the cries of the demons. Mark states, "And he [Jesus] . . . cast out many demons; and he would not permit the demons to speak, because they knew him" (1:34, RSV). Here it is exactly knowledge of Jesus' identity which Mark cites as the factor that impels Jesus to suppress the shouts of the demons (cf. 1:24–25; 3:11–12). Consequently, in Mark's scheme the suppression of Peter's confession by Jesus betokens, again, its correctness.

But Peter's confession, correct as it is, is only correct as far as it goes. To the extent that it does not mesh with the total understanding of Jesus Mark projects in his story, it is "insufficient." In what it connotes, it does full justice to neither the identity nor the mission of Jesus.

Peter's confession does not do justice to Mark's total conception of the mission of Jesus because it does not envisage the passion of Jesus. The Jesus whom Peter declares to be the Messiah is, as we said, the Jesus of 1:14—8:26. When Jesus now teaches the disciples in 8:31 that it is God's will that he suffer, die, and rise, what he speaks for them in Mark's story is a "new word."[140] Insofar as this new word lies beyond the purview of Peter's confession in 8:29, that confession

---

when uttered "ironically" in mockery or blasphemy (cf. 1:1; 8:29; 9:41; [12:35]; 13:21; 14:61; 15:32). When Mark does want to cast the term *christos* in a false light, he makes this eminently clear and speaks of "false christs," or "false messiahs" (13:22). Hence, the circumstance that Jesus does use the term "Messiah" in 9:41 to refer to himself can in fact be seen as lending further credibility to Peter's use of this term in 8:29.

140. If we judge from the story-line of his narrative, Mark does indeed seem to regard 8:31 as the first time the disciples confront the fact of Jesus' suffering and death. In 1:14 and 3:19, the "betrayal" of John and of Jesus is mentioned in commentary Mark gives to the reader alone, and the same is true of the notation in 3:6 that the Pharisees and Herodians take counsel to destroy Jesus. And in the pericope 2:18–22, where Jesus speaks of the "days whenever the bridegroom is taken away from them [the disciples]," Mark makes no mention of the disciples as being in the audience and has Jesus address these words to the anonymous "them." Accordingly, Jesus' passion-prediction of 8:31 constitutes "new teaching" for the disciples.

can be seen to be insufficient. Insufficient, but not false. Indeed, even the completely negative reaction of Peter to Jesus' new word, described in 8:32, does not put the lie to what Peter has said in 8:29. When Peter, at the behest of Jesus, confesses Jesus to be the Messiah in 8:29, he speaks the truth.

But this now brings us face to face with one of the celebrated problems of interpretation as regards the title of "Messiah" in 8:29. We just stated that Peter's confession is "correct" and not "false" but, insofar as it does not envisage the passion of Jesus, it is also "insufficient." Still, there are many Marcan scholars who stoutly maintain that Peter's confession is indeed to be construed as being false.[141] It is false because, as Mark tells his story, the notion of "Messiah" that Peter and the disciples harbor must be judged to be erroneous. It is erroneous because it denotes, say most of these scholars, a national, political king[142] or, say others, a divine man.[143] But this latter difference of opinion aside, all of these scholars agree that the way Mark counters Peter's erroneous notion of Messiah is by debunking it through Jesus' use of the title of "the Son of Man" in 8:31. Far from being the national, political king or the divine man Peter and the disciples conceive him to be (8:29), Jesus declares that he is instead the suffering Son of Man (8:31).

To relate these titles to each other in this fashion, however, is wrong on two counts. In the first place, "Messiah" in 8:29 characterizes Jesus neither as a national ruler of political stripe nor as the exponent of an errant theology of glory but as the Anointed One who heretofore in Mark's story has been authoritatively preaching, teaching, healing, and exorcizing demons (1:14—8:26). What Mark is concerned to

---

141. Cf., e.g., Petersen, *Literary Criticism for New Testament Critics,* pp. 61, 63, 67–68; Schweizer, *Markus,* pp. 92–93; Kelber, *Kingdom in Mark,* pp. 82–83; Perrin, "Christology of Mark," pp. 114; Weeden, *Mark,* pp. 64–69; Burkill, *Mysterious Revelation,* p. 152; Nineham, *Mark,* pp. 224–25; Grundmann, *Markus,* pp. 167, 169; Tyson, "Blindness of the Disciples," pp. 261–68.

142. Cf., e.g., Petersen, *Literary Criticism for New Testament Critics,* pp. 61, 63, 67; Schweizer, *Markus,* pp. 92–93; Cranfield, *Mark,* p. 271; Nineham, *Mark,* pp. 224–25; Burkill, *Mysterious Revelation,* p. 152; Grundmann, *Markus,* p. 168; Taylor, *St. Mark,* p. 377.

143. Cf., e.g., Weeden, *Mark,* pp. 54–58, 64–69; also Perrin, "Christology of Mark," pp. 110–11, 113; Müller, "Absicht des Markusevangeliums," pp. 170–75, 181.

debunk, as the contrasting questions of 8:27c and 8:29b reveal, is not the title "Messiah" but the notions of the Jewish public that Jesus is John the Baptist or Elijah or a prophet. Hence, it is exegetically inadmissible to pit against each other the title of "the Son of Man" in 8:31 and the title of "Messiah" in 8:29. Plainly, each must be given its due.

But to pit these titles against each other is also wrong for a second reason. Behind the claim that Jesus disavows Peter's title of "Messiah" in favor of his own title of "the Son of Man" is the assumption that both titles are being used by Mark as alternative answers to a single question about Jesus' identity. What is being alleged, in effect, is that Jesus makes the disciples the butt of an exchange he himself initiates with them: he asks them to tell him who they think he is (8:29) only to demolish Peter's answer, "You are the Messiah" (8:29), by countering that, on the contrary, he is the suffering Son of Man (8:31).

It is beyond dispute, of course, that Mark does employ the title "Messiah" in 8:29 to address the issue of Jesus' identity. Jesus asks the disciples, "Who do you say that I am?" and Peter replies, "You are the Messiah." At the same time, however, Mark gives no indication that he is employing the title "the Son of Man" in 8:31 to address this same issue of Jesus' identity. In point of fact, whenever the issue of "who Jesus is" does arise in Mark's story, it is never by drawing on the title of "the Son of Man" that Mark settles it. Never, for example, do God, the demons, or any human character ever declare to Jesus, or say with reference to him, "You are (he is) the Son of Man." And by the same token, the one time that Jesus himself gives an unequivocal answer to a direct query as to his identity, he replies "I am," not to the question "Are you the Son of Man?" but to the question "Are you the Messiah, the Son of the Blessed [God]?" (14:61–62). Clearly, the purpose for which Mark employs the title of "the Son of Man" in 8:31 is to have Jesus refer to himself, not in relation to the matter of his identity, but in relation to the matter of his fate or destiny. But if the title of "the Son of Man" in 8:31 is associated with the destiny of Jesus whereas the title of "Messiah" in 8:29 is associated with his identity, it follows that the two titles are not functioning in the same way. The focus of the one is on "who Jesus is"; the focus of the other is on "Jesus in relation to his opponents and what he must endure from them." The two titles, then, are in no wise mutually exclusive replies to the one question concerning the identity of Jesus, and the purpose of the title of "the Son of Man" in 8:31 is not to serve as Jesus' "replacement" for Peter's title of "Messiah."

But can we go a step further in explaining Mark's use of the title "the Son of Man" in 8:31? Without unrolling here our later discussion of this title, we may permit ourselves perhaps one observation. If we consider the four Son-of-Man passages we have met thus far in Mark's story, we will notice that they differ in at least one striking manner from the way in which "Messiah" is used in 8:29. In 8:31, the setting in which Jesus delivers his Son-of-Man saying is that of teaching the disciples. Nevertheless, the humans in view of whom Jesus refers to himself as the Son of Man are quite plainly the Jewish authorities: at the hands of the "elders," the "chief priests," and the "scribes," the Son of Man is going to suffer many things and be rejected. At 8:38, it is in the audience, not just of the disciples, but of the Jewish "crowd" (8:34) that Jesus refers to himself as the Son of Man. And at 2:10 and 2:28, it is in the audience of the Jewish "crowd" (2:4) and of "some of the scribes" (2:6) in the one case and in the audience of the "Pharisees" (2:24) in the other that Jesus likewise refers to himself as the Son of Man. The point is, what these passages show is that "the Son of Man" is a "public" title in Mark's story in the sense that it is the title by which Jesus refers to himself when he is in public or tells his disciples what the Jewish public in the persons of the Jewish authorities is going to do to him. But if the title of "the Son of Man" is of the nature of a public title, can the same be said of the title of "Messiah" in 8:29? Obviously not. A glance at 8:29 shows that "Messiah" is being used as a "confessional" title. Hence, the markedly different nature of these two titles is further reason why it is improper exegetically to play off the title of "the Son of Man" in 8:31 against the title of "Messiah" in 8:29.

My argument is that Peter's use of the title "Messiah" in 8:29 is "correct" but "insufficient." On the one hand, it correctly identifies Jesus in terms of the Marcan narrative of 1:14—8:26. On the other hand, because it does not take account of his passion (cf. 8:31), it is insufficient. Still, Peter's use of "Messiah" in 8:29 is furthermore insufficient because, even in terms of stipulating "who Jesus is," it falls short. In what way?

"Christ," or "Messiah," denominates Jesus as the "Anointed One."[144] Correct though this title is in Mark's story, it tends to be unspecific in what it denotes.[145] As a result, Mark continually explicates it throughout his story. He does this by means of the context, wider or immediate. Here in 8:29, Mark draws on the whole of 1:14—8:26 to show that "Messiah" describes Jesus as preacher, teacher, healer, and exorcist. At 12:35, Mark uses a simple statement, embedded in a question, to explicate "Messiah": "the Messiah is the Son of David." And in three instances Mark explicates "Messiah" by placing another title in apposition to it: "Jesus Messiah, the Son of God" (1:1); "the Messiah, the Son of the Blessed [God]" (14:61); and "the Messiah, the King of Israel" (15:32).

Through this process of explicating "Messiah," or "Anointed One," Mark reveals in great measure how he wants the reader to understand Jesus. He indicates, more generally, that Jesus is a "royal" figure. He indicates, more particularly, that the title that most adequately defines his conception of "Messiah" is that of "Son of God." Indeed, this is evident already from the opening verse of the Gospel.

But the surest evidence that "Son of God" defines "Messiah" most adequately comes from the use of this title by God. Only twice does God appear in Mark's story as one of the "actors." On both occasions, however, he does so in order to affirm, that is, express his "evaluative point of view," that Jesus is his Son (1:11; 9:7). Also, on both occasions God's affirmation either confirms or elaborates a use of "Messiah" in the preceding context. At the baptismal scene, God's affirmation that Jesus is his Son confirms Mark's own reference in the caption-summary of his Gospel to Jesus as the "Messiah, the Son of God" (cf. 1:11 to 1:1). And at the scene of the transfiguration, God's affirmation of Jesus' divine sonship elaborates Peter's confession of Jesus as the "Messiah" (cf. 9:7 to 8:29). It is this elaboration of Peter's confession by God at the transfiguration which we now want to examine more closely.

---

144. Cf. BAG, p. 887.

145. Horstmann (*Christologie*, p. 18) characterizes *christos* in Mark as "vague."

Scholars who find in the baptism of Jesus an account of his transformation by the Spirit into a divine man tend to interpret the transfiguration as the epiphany par excellence of the divine-man Jesus.[146] But the text itself does not require this interpretation, and can even be seen to resist it. It is not Jesus, for instance, who "withdraws the veil of the flesh" to manifest the glory of a supernatural being; instead, it is God who causes Jesus to "be transfigured" (cf. the "divine passive" in 9:3: *metemorphōtē*).[147] Moreover, the heavenly glory Jesus radiates is not depicted as a quality he "presently" possesses;[148] rather, it is anticipatory of the existence he will enter upon when he rises from the dead (cf. 9:9–10).[149] And following the revelatory events that occur on the mountain things return to "normal" (9:8), for not until Jesus has first "suffered many things and been treated with contempt" will he attain permanently to the eschatological glory of his resurrection (9:12). In sum, God clothes Jesus in the transfiguration in the transcendent glory of heaven, and this glory is "proleptic" of the splendor that will attend his resurrection.[150]

Of critical importance is the dual fact that God reveals to the three disciples atop the mountain of the transfiguration the divine sonship of Jesus but that they do not comprehend this. Not only are the disciples eye-witnesses of the event of transfiguration itself (9:3), but they are also ear-witnesses of God's declaration (9:7). With the latter, God states a second time in Mark's story his "evaluative point of view" regarding Jesus' identity: if in the first instance he did so to Jesus alone (1:11), this time, of course, he does so to the three disciples. Accordingly, the words God speaks echo for the reader the baptismal asseveration, and describe Jesus (the royal Messiah from the house of David) as being God's only Son (cf. LXX Ps. 2:2, 6–7;

---

146. Cf., e.g., Georgi, *Gegner des Paulus*, pp. 215–16; Betz, "Divine Man," pp. 122–23; Schulz, *Stunde der Botschaft*, p. 74; also Burkill, *Mysterious Revelation*, pp. 156–59.

147. Cf. also Pesch, *Markusevangelium*, II, 72.

148. Cf. Stein, "Transfiguration," p. 94.

149. Cf. Baltensweiler, *Verklärung*, p. 116; Nützel, *Verklärungserzählung*, pp. 241, 255.

150. Cf., e.g., Pesch, *Markusevangelium*, II, 75–76; also Carlston, "Transfiguration," pp. 233–40.

Gen. 22:2).[151] The injunction God adds, ". . . hear him!" (9:7), plays on Deuteronomy 18:15 (LXX). It attests to his divine resolve that in the present "time of the gospel" his Son Jesus has superseded Moses as the one through whom he makes his will known. While this injunction is comprehensive and encompasses all that Jesus says, it is no accident that the first words Jesus utters following God's giving of it touch on his impending passion (9:9–13; cf. 8:31). In like manner as John (Elijah), his "forerunner," the royal Son of God will, as the Son of Man whom the Jewish authorities oppose and in keeping with the will of God, suffer many things, be rejected, but also rise from the dead (9:9–13).

Despite this extraordinary revelation of sight and sound, the disciples remain uncomprehending. The three exhibit great "fear" (9:6), which in Mark is the opposite of "faith" and "understanding."[152] When, therefore, Peter speaks foolishly because "he did not know what to say" (9:6), he acts as spokesman for the disciples, just as he also did earlier when he confessed Jesus aright (8:29). Then, too, the incomprehension of the disciples extends not only to the vision they see (9:3–4) but also to the voice they hear (9:7). This is apparent for two reasons. In the first place, both vision and voice have to do with the matter of Jesus' identity. And in the second place, circumstances do not suddenly return to normal for the disciples until after God has spoken and the cloud has disappeared (9:8).

Not until after Jesus' resurrection do the three disciples finally grasp the revelation concerning his identity which eludes them atop the mountain. Jesus commands the disciples to tell no one about "the things they have seen" (9:9), and the disciples hold to this command. Nor would Mark have it otherwise in his story. In his perspective, for the disciples to be able to "think" about Jesus as God "thinks" about him, namely, as the royal Son of God, they must, to be sure, see him as preacher, teacher, healer, and exorcist (1:14—8:26) but, beyond this, they must also see him as the one who submits to crucifixion and whom God raises to glory (12:6–11; 14:27–28; 15:39; 16:6–7). Destiny and identity are inextricably bound together. One cannot com-

---

151. Cf. also Norden, *Agnostos Theos*, pp. 185, 188; Horstmann, *Christologie*, pp. 96, 103; Steichele, *Sohn Gottes*, pp. 185–87, 189–90.

152. Cf. Mark 4:40–41; 6:50–52; 9:32.

prehend who Jesus is without at the same time comprehending what it is that God accomplishes in him.

But this is not to suggest that the transfiguration is therefore an idle experience as far as the three disciples are concerned. Mark is laying the groundwork for the projected meeting in Galilee which all the disciples will have with Jesus following his resurrection (14:27–28; 16:6–7). On that occasion, the disciples will at last see Jesus for what he is, the crucified and resurrected Son of God (12:6–11; 15:39; 16:6–7). At that moment, the time will have arrived when the three can recall and "recount" (9:9) their experience of the transfiguration, for as they do all the disciples will be able to comprehend the secret of Jesus' identity and to "think" about him as God "thinks" about him (1:11; 9:7).

It remains for me to retrace the lines of the discussion we have been pursuing. The pericope on Peter's confession (8:27–30) begins the third main part of Mark's story (8:27—16:8). It does so, however, by calling to the reader's mind the sweep of the second main part of the story (1:14—8:26). Jesus and his disciples have traveled in and around Galilee, and the fame of Jesus, owing to the authority on which he acts, has spread. Jesus' fame, in turn, has caused the Jewish public to wonder who he is. Whereas some guess that he is John the Baptist raised from the dead, others guess that he is Elijah, and still others that he is a prophet (8:28; 6:14–15). These notions, however, are all false. Still, they form the backdrop against which Jesus asks the disciples who they think he is. On behalf of the disciples, Peter announces that Jesus is the Messiah (8:29). In terms of the christology of Mark's story, Peter's confession signals a change of direction in the plot. For the first time, a human character evinces insight into the identity of Jesus. This insight, however, is at once "correct" but "insufficient." It is correct because it declares Jesus to be the Anointed One who preaches, teaches, heals, and exorcizes demons on the authority of God (1:14—8:26). It is insufficient because it envisages neither the passion of Jesus nor the secret of his divine sonship. In the section 8:31—9:1, Jesus teaches the disciples the "new word" of the divine necessity of his passion, and in the section that focuses on the transfiguration (9:2–13), three of his disciples are exposed to the secret of his divine sonship. But neither in the one section nor in the other do the disciples comprehend what they are taught or what is revealed to them. Nor could they in Mark's conception of reality. For according to Mark, Jesus' identity as the royal Son of God is inseparably bound up with Jesus' destiny of the cross. Not until one sees the cross to be the ultimate goal of Jesus' ministry can one see Jesus to be the royal Son of God (15:39). And not until one sees Jesus to be the royal Son of God can one "think" about him normatively, that is, as God "thinks" about him (1:11; 9:7; 15:39). Hence, Peter's confession in 8:29, correct though it is, does not constitute a "break" in the secret of Jesus' identity. And as far as the divine revelation which the three disciples do not comprehend atop the mountain of the transfiguration is concerned, this is not "lost." When the disciples shall have seen Jesus in Galilee following his resurrection, this revelation of sight and sound will be recounted and understood (9:9–10). Then the disciples will be able to do what they cannot do prior to that time: "think" about Jesus as God "thinks" about him (1:11; 9:7).

The Healing of Bartimaeus,
the Triumphal Entry, and the Question
about David's Son

We have seen that Mark deals with the question of Jesus' identity differently in the first half of Jesus' ministry (1:14—8:26) as compared with the second half (8:27—16:8). In the second half, Mark describes, from the standpoint of the reader, the disclosure of Jesus' identity in stages. If the first stage is Peter's correct but insufficient confession of Jesus to be the Messiah (8:29), the second stage is Bartimaeus's appeal to Jesus as the Son of David (10:46–52). And if "Messiah" in 8:29 constitutes the "evaluative point of view" concerning Jesus' identity of Peter and the disciples, "Son of David" constitutes the "evaluative point of view" concerning Jesus' identity of Bartimaeus.

The setting for the story of Jesus' healing of Bartimaeus is the outskirts of Jericho: Bartimaeus, a blind beggar, is sitting beside the road as Jesus, in the company of his disciples and a great crowd, journeys towards Jerusalem (10:32, 46; 11:1). The nub of the story is that Bartimaeus insistently appeals to Jesus as the Son of David to have mercy on him, and Jesus responds to his appeal by restoring his sight (10:47–52).

Many scholars find this text difficult to incorporate into Mark's christology. To those who hold that the motif of the secret of Jesus' identity is central to Mark this text appears to portray Bartimaeus as "breaking" this secret.[153] To others, who want to claim either that "Son of David" is of little or no importance to Mark's christology[154] or that Mark outright rejects the idea that Jesus is the Son of David,[155] this text is troublesome because it confronts them with the clear use of the title Son of David. In what follows, I shall argue that Bartimaeus's use of "Son of David" does not result in the breaking of the secret of Jesus' identity and that Mark is not at pains to discount or indeed to reject a Son-of-David christology.

The main emphasis in this miracle-story is on the great faith of Bartimaeus.[156] Faith is understood as fervent trust that Jesus can heal, and the various elements of the story call attention to this trust. Thus, it is an expression of Bartimaeus's trust in Jesus that he initially appeals to him to have mercy on him, that is, to heal him (10:47, 51). Moreover, although many in the crowd rebuke Bartimaeus and order him to keep silent, he persists in crying out to Jesus (10:48).[157] Again, when Jesus stops and the bystanders tell Bartimaeus that Jesus has summoned him, the alacrity with which Bartimaeus responds to Jesus' summons also attests to his trust in Jesus: he throws off his mantle,

---

153. Thus, Schniewind (*Markus*, p. 111) and Nineham (*Mark*, p. 292) assert that this story is the first one in Mark in which the "messianic secret" is explicitly lifted. For his part, Boobyer ("Secrecy Motif," p. 231), while acknowledging that "evidently the narrative signifies that the messianic secret has got abroad," tries to blunt the force of this acknowledgment by insisting that the secret in reality remains intact both because the crowd, in ordering Bartimaeus to be silent, rejects the truth that Jesus is the Son of David and because Bartimaeus himself is treated by Mark as one who becomes a disciple of Jesus. Again, Burkill (*Mysterious Revelation*, p. 192) takes much the same position, contending that although Bartimaeus presents the multitude with an opportunity to apprehend and acknowledge the fact that Jesus is the Son of David, "the opportunity is not taken." Somewhat ingenuously, Sjöberg (*Menschensohn*, pp. 101–2) states simply that Mark himself would most likely not have regarded the secret as having been broken because he probably drew no connection between the cries of Bartimaeus and his motif of the messianic secret. For further comment on this matter of "breaking" the secret, cf. Räisänen, *Messiasgeheimnis*, pp. 148–51.

154. Cf. Achtemeier, "Mark 10:46–52," pp. 115, 130–31; Best, *Following Jesus*, p. 140.

155. Cf. Kelber, *Kingdom in Mark*, p. 95; Suhl, *Funktion der alttestamentlichen Zitate*, p. 93.

156. Cf. Kertelge, *Wunder Jesu*, p. 180; Schenke, *Wundererzählungen*, pp. 356–58, 368; Koch, *Wundererzählungen*, p. 129.

157. Cf. Achtemeier, "Mark 10:46–52," pp. 118–19, 122, 124.

he jumps up, and he comes to Jesus (10:49–50). Fourth, after Jesus has asked what he wants him to do for him, Bartimaeus replies with a prayer-like request that likewise gives evidence of his trust in Jesus: "Rabboni, I want to regain my sight"[158] (10:51). Fifth, with the declaration, "your faith has made you well" (10:52, RSV), Jesus himself attests to the fervent trust of Bartimaeus. And last, the comment Mark makes authenticating the miracle (10:52) authenticates as well the trust of Bartimaeus, for the healing that takes place corresponds exactly to the request Bartimaeus had made: "I want to regain my sight . . . and immediately he regained his sight" (10:51–52).

But prominent as the theme of faith is in this miracle-story, it is not the sole theme.[159] The certain object of Bartimaeus's great faith

---

158. Cf. BAG, p. 51.

159. A panoply of scholarly opinion notwithstanding, this pericope is not a "call story" and Bartimaeus is not depicted as becoming a disciple of Jesus (cf., e.g., Boobyer, "Secrecy Motif," p. 231; Kertelge, *Wunder Jesu,* p. 181; Burger, *Davidssohn,* p. 46; Robbins, "Blind Bartimaeus," pp. 226–27, 230, 239–41; Schenke, *Wundererzählungen,* pp. 367–69; Koch, *Wundererzählungen,* pp. 129–32; Achtemeier, "Mark 10:46–52," pp. 115, 132–36; Johnson, "Blind Bartimaeus," p. 201; in this connection, Reploh [*Lehrer,* p. 224] even contends that Bartimaeus becomes a disciple of Jesus "against the express will of Jesus"). The confusion over this stems from a misreading of the Marcan notation, ". . . and he [Bartimaeus] began following him [Jesus] on the way" (10:52). Mark uses the verb "to follow" *(akolouthein)* both in its literal sense ("to come or go after a person in place, time, or sequence"; cf., e.g., 3:7; 5:24; 11:9; 14:13, 54) and in its metaphorical sense ("to come or go after a person as his disciple"; cf., e.g., 1:18; 2:14; 8:34; 10:21, 28). In "call stories," where "to follow" is used metaphorically to connote discipleship, the pattern is that Jesus "calls" the persons and they go away after him (1:20) or that he commands them to "come after me" or to "follow me" and they do so or refuse to do so (cf. 1:17–18; 2:14; 10:21–22; also 3:13; 8:34). In this pericope on Bartimaeus, however, Jesus not only does not command Bartimaeus to follow him, he orders him instead to "go" (10:52). This imperative "go" *(hypage)* appears in several miracle-stories in Mark, where it functions as a quasi-technical term by which Jesus "dismisses" the afflicted person he has just healed (cf. 1:44; 2:11; 5:19, 34; also 7:29; Theissen, *Wundergeschichten,* p. 77). When, therefore, the notation in 10:52, ". . . and he began following him on the way," is construed in conjunction with Jesus' command to Bartimaeus to "go," it becomes evident that Mark is not employing the verb "to follow" metaphorically to connote discipleship but that he is employing it literally. That is to say, the point Mark is making is that Bartimaeus, whom Jesus dismisses even as he restores his sight (10:52), uses this gift of sight to join the crowd of people which is accompanying ("following") Jesus as he journeys on his way to Jerusalem (= "proof" of cure; 10:46, 52; 11:1, 8–9). Consequently, Mark deftly utilizes the figure of Bartimaeus to link this pericope on his healing with that on

is, of course, Jesus. The theme of "christology," therefore, also stands out in this text.[160] Twice Bartimaeus appeals to Jesus, as the "Son of David," to "have mercy on him" (10:47–48). The second of these appeals exemplifies best both the fervor and the greatness of Bartimaeus's faith, for with it he surmounts the obstacle of the crowd's ill will and induces Jesus to stop, to have him summoned, and to ask him what he wants him to do for him (10:48–51). Accordingly, when Jesus at last grants Bartimaeus his request for sight and hence does "have mercy on him," the reader can only conclude that Jesus has in fact healed Bartimaeus in his capacity as the Son of David.

There are some scholars, however, who would resist this conclusion on the grounds that Bartimaeus's use of "rabboni" in his final word to Jesus ("Rabboni, I want to regain my sight"; 10:51) mitigates the force of his earlier use of "Son of David."[161] Is there any evidence

---

the entry of Jesus into Jerusalem (10:52; 11:1, 8–9a).

But although Mark does not make of Bartimaeus a disciple of Jesus, he does make of him a "model of faith" (cf. 7:24–30; esp. 7:29). At this juncture in his story, Mark has already pictured the disciples, for example, as exhibiting ignorance, fear, and amazement in the face of Jesus' predictions of his passion (8:31–33; 9:31–32; 10:32–34). Later, the disciples will also fail to persevere in faith, and will abandon Jesus and flee (14:27, 50). Given this example of "unfaith" on the part of the disciples, the reader finds in Bartimaeus one whose faith is both fervent and persevering (cf. also Achtemeier, "Mark 10:46–52," pp. 115, 135). Telling his story sets the tone for the joyful acclamation Jesus will receive upon his approach to the gates of Jerusalem (11:8–10).

160. Robbins ("Blind Bartimaeus," pp. 225–27, 242) is one of the few commentators in recent years who does not attempt to minimize the christological relevance of this text but to give it its due. Cf. further Hahn, *Hoheitstitel*, pp. 262–63; Burger, *Davidssohn*, pp. 45–46, 62–63.

161. Cf., e.g., Boobyer, "Secrecy Motif," p. 231; Schreiber, "Christologie," p. 164; Achtemeier, "Mark 10:46–52," pp. 115, 131; also Bultmann, *Geschichte der synoptischen Tradition*, p. 228 (ET, *History of the Synoptic Tradition*, p. 213). The argument advanced by Kelber (*Kingdom in Mark*, p. 95; cf. also Johnson, "Blind Bartimaeus," p. 197; Best, *Following Jesus*, p. 140) to the effect that Mark alludes to the unimportance of the title Son of David by the very fact that it occurs on the lips of one who is "blind" is beside the point. Unless one rejects the text as it stands, when else, except while blind, could Bartimaeus have uttered the title? Then, too, this argument does not come to grips with the central issue of the text: Bartimaeus appeals to Jesus in his capacity as the Son of David to have mercy on him, and Jesus, by restoring the sight of Bartimaeus, does have mercy on him. Hence, Jesus responds "positively" to one who has appealed to him precisely as the Son of David.

in Mark to prove the truth of this contention? None whatever. "Rabboni" is essentially the equivalent of "rabbi" and "teacher" *(didaskalos)*.[162] The use to which Mark puts these terms, when they occur in the vocative case, is readily discernible: they serve as terms of human respect by which unknown persons,[163] a "friendly" scribe (12:32), disciples,[164] opponents,[165] and Judas (14:45) alike address Jesus.[166] Nowhere in Mark's story is there any indication that he employs "rabbi" or "teacher" to "relativize" a christological title.

Mark, therefore, is not concerned in this pericope on the healing of Bartimaeus to de-emphasize the title Son of David but to apply it to Jesus in a fully positive sense.[167] Because Jesus has not heretofore appeared in Mark's story as the Son of David, this pericope plays a pivotal role in conveying to the reader Mark's sense of this title. To begin with, Mark affirms with it that Jesus is indeed of the lineage of David. Unlike Matthew and Luke, Mark has no genealogy that links Jesus with the line of David (Matt. 1:2–17, 18–25; Luke 3:23, 31). But it appears that it is exactly the Davidic descent of Jesus which is being attested to when Bartimaeus addresses "Jesus, the man from Nazareth," as "Jesus, Son of David" (10:47).[168] In addition, Mark also affirms, in attributing "Son of David" to Jesus, that the eschatological expectations associated with David are being fulfilled in Jesus. In this connection, however, Mark's characterization of the Son of David is radically different from that found, for example, in Psalms of Solomon 17. There the Son of David is made out to be a warrior king, who will place his royal authority in the service of political and military struggle in order to vindicate Israel and crush its Gentile enemies. Here, by contrast, Jesus wields his Davidic authority in order

---

162. Cf. Lohse, *"Rabbi,"* p. 964.

163. Cf. Mark 9:17; 10:17, 20.

164. Cf. Mark 4:38; 9:5, 38; 10:35; 11:21; 13:1.

165. Cf. Mark 12:14, 19.

166. Cf. also Lohse, *"Rabbi,"* p. 964. In other respects, Kelber (*Kingdom in Mark,* p. 95) asserts that "rabbi" is a "title clearly rejected by Mark." This claim, however, is without foundation unless it can be shown that Mark likewise casts the equivalent term of "teacher" *(didaskalos)* in a negative light.

167. Cf. also Hahn, *Hoheitstitel,* pp. 262–63; Koch, *Wundererzählungen,* p. 128.

168. Cf. Schneider, "Davidssohnfrage," p. 88.

to have mercy on one who is afflicted (10:47–48, 52), to heal and in this fashion to "save" (10:52).[169]

Does Mark, in narrating this pericope on the healing of Bartimaeus, allow for the secret of Jesus' identity to be broken? Before answering this question, we shall treat first the pericopes on the triumphal entry and on the question about David's son.

The pericope on the triumphal entry (11:1–10) follows immediately that on the healing of Bartimaeus. Mark prepares for the triumphal entry by having Bartimaeus, his sight restored, join the throng accompanying Jesus to Jerusalem (10:32, 46, 52; 11:1). Publicly identified by Bartimaeus as the Son of David, Jesus approaches Jerusalem under the auspices of this title. The entire narrative on the triumphal entry, in fact, is redolent of messianic allusions that Mark associates with David.[170] Thus, the whole of it is informed by such messianically interpreted passages as Zechariah 9:9 and Genesis 49:11.[171] In sending his disciples to bring the "colt"[172] on which he will ride (11:1–7), Jesus makes use of the royal prerogative by which a king can requisition an animal for his use (cf. 1 Sam. 8:10–11, 17).[173] The colt on which Jesus sits (11:2–7) is the symbol par excellence for the messianic mount,[174] and Jesus is its "true owner" (". . . its lord is in need"; 11:3).[175] The spreading of garments and of leafy branches on the way (11:8) are gestures of adoration that befit a king (cf. 2 Kings 9:13).[176] And in the antiphonal acclamation of those who accompany Jesus, he is hailed with shouts to God that assume the form of a petition for salvation ("Hosanna" [cf. Ps. 118:25]) and is praised as the one who comes on the authority of God and is therefore the bearer of "the Kingdom of our father David" (11:9–10).[177] In short, although

---

169. Cf. also Hahn, *Hoheitstitel,* pp. 262–63.

170. Cf. Kuhn, "Reittier Jesu," pp. 87, 90; Hahn, *Hoheitstitel,* pp. 264–67; Burger, *Davidssohn,* pp. 63–64.

171. Cf. Kuhn, "Reittier Jesu," pp. 86–91.

172. Cf. ibid., p. 83.

173. Cf. Derrett, "Colt," pp. 243–49.

174. Cf. Kuhn, "Reittier Jesu," pp. 86–91.

175. Cf. Derrett, "Colt," pp. 246, 249–57; Pesch, *Markusevangelium,* II, 180.

176. Pesch, *Markusevangelium,* II, 182–83.

177. Cf. Hahn, *Hoheitstitel,* pp. 266–67; Burger, *Davidssohn,* p. 64. Crossan ("Mark 11:9–10," pp. 40, 49–50) and Kelber (*Kingdom in Mark,* pp. 96–97)

Jesus is not explicitly named the Son of David in this narrative, there can be no mistake but that he is being so presented. Israel's peculiar hope is in him who is, among other things, David's Son.[178]

Mark, then, raises the claim on behalf of Jesus that he is in truth the Son of David who exercises the eschatological rule of David. At the same time, Mark has also shown that Jesus exercises such Davidic rule, not in an imperial manner, but by having mercy on the afflicted, as he did in the case of Bartimaeus. Nevertheless, Mark furthermore shows that, "correct" as it is to apply the title Son of David to Jesus, it, like the title Messiah in 8:29, only "insufficiently" describes him. Mark brings to light the insufficiency of the title Son of David in the pericope on the question about David's son (12:35–37).

A proper assessment of the form of this pericope (12:35–37) is crucial to a proper interpretation of its message. It is essential, for example, to observe that this pericope is not of the nature of a "debate." In the preceding context Jesus has, to be sure, been engaged in debate with the leaders of the Jews.[179] But Mark's notation at 12:34 (RSV) reveals that such debate is now over: "And after that no one dared to ask him any question." With debate closed, Mark effects a change in both the audience Jesus addresses and the rhetorical style he adopts: his audience is the "great crowd,"[180] which hears him gladly (12:37), and no longer the Jewish leaders, who would entrap him in his speech (11:27; 12:13, 18); and instead of reacting to questions put to him, whereby he bests his opponents, Jesus reverses the process and "teaches" the people by himself posing questions (12:35–37).

Since Mark indicates that Jesus is not involved in debate in

---

contend that the reader of Mark's story is to construe the acclamation "Blessed be the coming Kingdom of our father David" (11:10) as being false, for it is part and parcel of the Davidic messianism Mark rejects. On our reading of Mark's story, however, it appears, not that Mark rejects Davidic messianism, but that he accepts it even as he also casts it in a particular light: Jesus is indeed the Son of David, but as such he is not a warrior king but one who heals (10:46–52).

178. Cf. Lohse, "Hosianna," p. 117.

179. Cf. Mark 11:27–28; 12:13, 18. The exchange with the scribe in 12:28–34d, however, is "friendly" and not hostile; on the significance of this, cf. the body of the discussion.

180. Cf. also Schneider, "Davidssohnfrage," p. 87; Pesch, *Markusevangelium*, II, 251; Gnilka, *Markus*, II, 170.

12:35–37, the interpreter errs if he casts Jesus in the role of striking down a false understanding of the Messiah.[181] In his initial question to the crowd, Jesus does, of course, take up the "evaluative point of view" regarding the identity of the Messiah held by the scribes (12:35). But "scribal" though this viewpoint is, it is not on this account false. Mark has, in fact, already had occasion to depict Jesus as being positively disposed towards the opinion of a scribe. A glance at the series of debates which precedes 12:35–37 (11:11—12:34d) shows that the last one differs from the others (12:28–34d). While it possesses the form of an exchange, the dialogue is friendly, with Jesus receiving approval from, and giving approval to, a scribe (12:28, 32, 34a–d). The question on David's son is unlike this last "debate" because it does not have the form of an exchange. But it also resembles it in the positive attitude Jesus displays towards scribal opinion.

The two questions Jesus poses to the crowd have to do with the problem of "antinomy" (12:35, 37).[182] In this case, however, the ostensible contradiction is not between two verses of scripture but between two views about the Messiah. The resolution of the problem lies, not in choosing one view over the other, but in giving both views their due.

The first view Jesus cites is that of the scribes. "With what right,"[183] Jesus asks the crowd, "do the scribes say that the Messiah is the Son of David?"[184] The second view is one Jesus derives from the inspired speech of David[185] recorded in OT scripture (Ps. 110:1

---

181. The position many scholars have taken over the years is that Mark presents Jesus in 12:35–37 as denying that the Messiah must be of Davidic lineage. Cf., e.g., Wrede, *Vorträge*, pp. 168, 175; Klausner, *Jesus*, p. 320; Suhl, *Funktion der alttestamentlichen Zitate*, pp. 91–94; Kelber, *Kingdom in Mark*, pp. 95–96; Achtemeier, "Mark 10:46–52," pp. 126–30.

182. Cf. Daube, *Rabbinic Judaism*, pp. 162–63.

183. Cf. BAG, p. 732.

184. Inexplicably, Schneider ("Davidssohnfrage," pp. 82–83) and Gnilka (*Markus*, II, 172) contend that, because "Son of David" does not have the article in 12:35, it is indefinite and not used as a christological title ("a son of David"). "Son of David," however, is a predicate nominative, and when the predicate nominative precedes the copula, as here, it is to be construed as definite unless there is some overriding reason dictating otherwise (cf. Colwell, "Use of the Article," pp. 12–21; Zerwick, *Biblical Greek*, p. 56). Hence, the proper translation of this designation is "the Son of David," and it is titular in character.

185. The argument of Neugebauer ("Davidssohnfrage," p. 89; also Pesch,

[LXX 109:1]): "David himself calls him lord; so in what way[186] is he his [David's] son?" (12:37). The conundrum, then, is this: How is it possible for the Messiah to be both the "son" of David and the "lord" of David?

Since the solution to the problem of antinomy lies in giving both factors their due, Jesus can be seen to affirm that the Messiah is the Son of David (12:35). But Jesus also affirms that the Messiah is the "lord" of David (12:37). What does this mean? To all intents and purposes, there are three options from which to choose: Jesus is at once Son of David and (a) "Lord," or (b) "the Son of Man," or (c) "Son of God."

The first option, that Jesus is not only Son of David but also "Lord" (kyrios),[187] is attractive only at first sight. The reason is that kyrios proves, upon scrutiny, not to be a major christological title in Mark. On the contrary, it exhibits a wide range of meanings, and the most one can say is that it functions in some few passages as an auxiliary christological title.

Kyrios occurs approximately sixteen times in Mark. Nine times it refers to God,[188] and seven times it is used of Jesus. Of the latter, it appears once in the vocative case (7:28) and may connote no more than the equivalent of "sir"; if translated as "Lord," it imputes to Jesus the divine authority to heal (cf. 7:26, 29–30). In another case, kyrios again attributes divine authority to Jesus, this time to regulate the sabbath in his role as the Son of Man (2:28). In three other instances, kyrios may be termed an auxiliary christological title: in 1:3, it constitutes the transfer to Jesus of the name for God found in

---

Markusevangelium, II, 253), according to which "in the Holy Spirit" is an "apocalyptic formula" that denotes that David was "translated" in the Spirit to heaven, where he heard what "the Lord said to his lord," is without foundation in Marcan thought. Even in the pericope on the transfiguration (9:2–8), Elijah and Moses come from heaven and make their appearance with Jesus in the sight of the disciples on the top of the mountain. Mark shows no affinity in his Gospel for translation stories that tell of events that transpire in heaven. For a discussion of the phrase "speaking in the Holy Spirit," cf. Barrett, Holy Spirit, pp. 107–12.

186. Cf. BAG, p. 680.

187. Cf. Lohmeyer, Davidsohn, p. 75; Lohse, "Hyios Dayid," pp. 484–85; also Schreiber, "Christologie," p. 164; Schneider, "Davidssohnfrage," pp. 89–90; Loader, "Right Hand," p. 215; Gnilka, Markus, II, 171.

188. Cf. Mark 5:19; 11:9; 12:9, 11, 29a–b, 30, 36; 13:20 (cf. "Father" in 13:32).

the Septuagint and points to Jesus as the Messiah, the Son of God (cf. 1:3 to 1:1); in 13:35, it points to Jesus as bearer of the title of the Son of Man (cf. 13:24–27); and in 12:36, in this pericope on the question about David's son, it once again points to Jesus as the Messiah (cf. 12:35, 37). In 11:3, *kyrios* may simply mean "master," or "owner," or it may be that we have here yet a fourth instance in which it serves as an auxiliary christological title, pointing to Jesus as, in effect, the Son of David (cf. 11:9–10). Finally, in 12:37, which likewise belongs to this pericope on the question about David's son, we have a use of *kyrios* which parallels what we found in 2:28 and perhaps 7:28 as well. That is to say, the purpose of the term *kyrios* in the words, "David himself calls him [the Messiah] lord, so in what way is he [the Messiah] his [David's] son?" (12:37), is to attribute to the "Messiah" a station and an authority that are superior to the station and authority of "David." Hence, as in 2:28, *kyrios* does not function in 12:37 as a christological title.[189]

On balance, then, the designation *kyrios,* which occurs three times in 12:35–37, refers in the first instance to "God" (12:36) and in the second instance to the "Messiah" (12:36) and is, in the third instance, used to attribute to the Messiah a station and an authority that surpass those of David of old (12:37). Because this use of *kyrios* in 12:35–37 reveals that it is not in its own right a christological title, we can set aside the postulate that the counterpart to the title Son of David in this pericope is the title "Lord."

The second option, that the counterpart to "Son of David" is "the Son of Man,"[190] can also be set aside. It does not commend itself because the title "the Son of Man" does not lie within the orbit of the titles Mark directly associates with "Messiah." For example, while Mark writes, respectively, "Jesus Messiah, the Son of God" (1:1; 14:61), "the Messiah, the King of Israel (the Jews)" (15:32), and "the Messiah is the Son of David" (12:35), never does he write "the Messiah, the Son of Man" or that "the Messiah is the Son of

---

189. Van Iersel (*Der Sohn,* p. 172) comes to this same conclusion, but for different reasons.

190. Advocates of this option are, e.g.: Neugebauer, "Davidssohnfrage," pp. 89–95; Pesch, *Markusevangelium,* II, 254, 256; Schniewind, *Markus,* p. 129; also Bultmann, *Geschichte der synoptischen Tradition,* pp. 145–46 (ET, *History of the Synoptic Tradition,* pp. 136–37).

Man." Then, too, had Mark wanted to associate the title of "the Son of Man" with the title of "Messiah," there is one passage in which he would have had an excellent opportunity to do so, namely, in 14:61. Thus, although Jesus openly refers to himself as "the Son of Man" in the audience of the Jewish "crowd" (2:2, 4, 10; 8:34, 38), of "some of the scribes" (2:6, 10), and of the "Pharisees" (2:24, 28), so that his being "the Son of Man" cannot be presumed to be a secret to the Sanhedrin, the high priest does not ask Jesus at his trial whether he is "the Messiah, the Son of Man" but whether he is "the Messiah, the Son of the Blessed [God]" (14:61). Accordingly, the twin circumstances that, on the one hand, Mark never directly associates "the Son of Man" with "Messiah" and that, on the other hand, he does directly associate "King of Israel (the Jews)," "Son of David," and "Son of God" with "Messiah" combine to preclude the notion that Mark would have the reader infer in 12:35–37 that the Messiah is not only the Son of David but also the Son of Man.

The title that Mark does want the reader to infer is the counterpart to "Son of David" in 12:35–37 is "Son of God."[191] This is apparent on three counts. For one thing, Mark directly associates, as we noted above, the title "Son of God" with the title "Messiah" (14:61; 1:1). For another thing, on the textual-critical assumption that "Son of God" is the proper reading at 1:1, this is the title Mark himself employs in the caption-summary of his Gospel in order to explain to the reader who Jesus Messiah, about whom he will narrate, truly is (1:1). And third, of decisive significance is the fact that "Son of God" ("my Son") is the title by which God knows Jesus Messiah (1:11; 9:7). Because in Mark's story God's "evaluative point of view" is normative, it stands to reason that the title God gives to Jesus Messiah will be the one Mark would have the reader infer.

If we accept the title "Son of God" as being the counterpart to "Son of David" in 12:35–37, what is the message of this pericope? The conundrum Jesus puts to the crowd is, we recall, this: How is it possible for the Messiah to be both the "son" of David and the "lord" of David? The answer this question anticipates is this: The Messiah is the "son" of David because he is descended from David; by the

---

191. Cf. also Burger, *Davidssohn*, pp. 64–70; Schneider, "Davidssohnfrage," pp. 89–90.

same token, the Messiah is also the "lord" of David because, as the Son of God, he is of higher station and authority than David.

We are pursuing the larger topic of the "correctness" yet "insufficiency" of the title Son of David as a description of the Marcan Jesus. Like the title of "Messiah" that Peter predicates to Jesus in 8:29, the title "Son of David" also "correctly" applies to Jesus. It characterizes him both as the descendant of David (10:47; 12:35) and as the one in whom the eschatological expectations associated with David come to fulfillment (11:9–10). In fulfilling such expectations, however, Jesus does not engage in military and political conflict but instead exercises his Davidic authority in mercy to heal and hence to save (10:47–48, 51–52).

Again, like the title of "Messiah" in 8:29, the title "Son of David" is also "insufficient." It, too, does not encompass the notion of Jesus' passion. Although the section 10:46—11:10 presents Jesus as journeying towards Jerusalem (10:46; 11:1) and the pericope 12:35–37 presents him as teaching in the temple, the specter of the cross (and resurrection) is not immediately apparent in them. Apart from the event(s) of the cross (and resurrection), however, one cannot "think" about Jesus as God "thinks" about him (1:11; 9:7; 8:33d), which is to say that one cannot penetrate the secret of his identity (15:39). The upshot, therefore, is that Bartimaeus can publicly appeal to Jesus as the Son of David (10:47–48), the throng about Jesus can publicly hail him as the bearer of "the kingdom of our father David that comes" (11:9–10), and Jesus, teaching in public, can ask how the Messiah can at once be the "son" and "lord" of David (12:35–37), and yet none of these occurrences results in the "breaking" of the secret of Jesus' identity.

In stark juxtaposition, both the "correctness" and the "insufficiency" of the title Son of David come to the fore in the pericope on the question about David's son (12:35–37). On the one hand, Jesus affirms that the Messiah, descended from David, is the "son" of David (12:35). On the other hand, Jesus likewise affirms that the Messiah, of higher station and authority than David, is the "lord" of David (12:37).

Projected onto the background of Mark's story, this pericope not only does not deny but asserts the Davidic sonship of Jesus Messiah. At the same time, it calls on the reader to infer that Jesus Messiah is

"more" than merely the Son of David: he is also the Son of God.
What it means to be the Son of David Jesus shows by saving one such
as Bartimaeus in that he has mercy on him and heals his affliction.
What it means to be the Son of God Jesus shows by saving humankind
in that he dies on the cross and is raised. While Mark stoutly maintains
that Jesus is in truth the Son of David, he binds the secret of his
identity neither to his descendence from David nor to the healing he
performs in his capacity as the Son of David, but to his death and
resurrection as the Son of God (15:39; 16:6). Or, to put it differently,
Mark binds the secret of Jesus' identity not to the "evaluative point
of view" that Jesus is the Son of David expressed by Bartimaeus but
to the "evaluative point of view" that Jesus is the Son of God expressed by God. Hence, in narrating three pericopes that pertain to
Jesus as the Son of David, Mark plainly takes a step beyond 8:29 in
permitting the human characters of his story to know who Jesus is,
but still the secret of Jesus' identity remains intact.

The Parable of the Wicked Husbandmen,
Jesus before the Sanhedrin,
Jesus before Pilate, Jesus on the Cross

In the third main part of his Gospel (8:27—16:8), Mark leads the
reader through a series of three stages in the gradual disclosure of the
identity of Jesus. The first stage focuses on the confession of Peter
(8:29) and the second stage on the appeal of Bartimaeus (10:47–48)
and on the acclamation of those who accompany Jesus to Jerusalem
(11:9–10). In the third stage, the Roman centurion, seeing Jesus expire
on the cross, affirms that he truly was the Son of God (15:39). Because
Mark preserves unbroken the secret of Jesus' divine sonship until the
event(s) of the cross (and resurrection), it is only with the centurion's
expression of his "evaluative point of view" regarding Jesus' identity
that Mark finally lifts this secret. Our concern in this segment of our
discussion, therefore, is to trace the movement in the plot of Mark's
story which culminates at last in the disclosure of the secret of the
divine sonship of Jesus.

The first pericope that adumbrates the cross and resurrection and
prepares for the centurion's declaration is the parable of the wicked
husbandmen (12:1–12). This parable has aptly been characterized as

a "parable of judgment":[192] it describes God's dealings with Israel in the history of salvation. Because the key event in the story the parable narrates is the "sending of the son" (12:6–8), the accent is on "christology," or better, on God's action in his Son Jesus.[193] Within the context of Mark's Gospel, a number of the parable's traits assume allegorical significance, as follows: the vineyard is Israel (Isa. 5:1–7); the "man," or owner of the vineyard, is God (12:1, 9); the tenant-farmers are (the leaders of) Israel (11:27; 12:1, 12); the slaves sent by the owner are the prophets (12:2–5); the son and heir, sent last, is Jesus (12:6); the killing of the son is the crucifixion (12:8; 15:37, 39);[194] the "destroying" of the tenant-farmers, whether or not this refers to the destruction of Jerusalem,[195] expresses the conviction that Israel has lost its privileged place in the history of salvation; and, concomitantly, the "giving of the vineyard to others" alludes to the belief that the "church" has assumed Israel's place in the history of salvation.[196] In addition, it also appears that, in the reference to the "stone" in the quotation of Ps. 118:22 at 12:10, there is the evocation of the "stone(s)-son(s)" imagery found in the OT.[197] If so, then the rejection-elevation of the "stone" is an allusion to the crucifixion-vindication of God's "son" Jesus.

---

192. Blank, "Sendung des Sohnes," pp. 14–18; Carlston, *Parables,* p. 179.

193. Cf. also Carlston, *Parables,* p. 178.

194. The insistence of many commentators (cf., e.g., Weder, *Gleichnisse,* p. 149; J. A. T. Robinson, "Wicked Husbandmen," p. 449) that, because the owner's son in Mark's parable is first killed and then thrown out of the vineyard (12:8), his death does not allude to the crucifixion is misplaced. Jesus tells this parable to the chief priests, the scribes, and the elders (11:27; 12:1). In 8:31, Jesus has already told his disciples that these three groups will "kill" him, and in 14:53–65 it is these same three groups who condemn him to death. Add to these two observations the fact that the counterpart to the "killing of the son" in the scriptural quotation at the end of the parable is the "rejection of the stone" (12:8, 10), which is itself an allusion to the crucifixion, and the conclusion is compelling: Mark would indeed have the reader associate the "killing of the son" in the parable with the "crucifixion of the Son" in his story. Cf. also Hubaut, *Vignerons homicides,* pp. 50–51; Drury, "Vineyard," p. 372.

195. Cf. Klauck, "Weinberg," p. 125.

196. Cf. also Blank, "Sendung des Sohnes," p. 19; Weder, *Gleichnisse,* pp. 159–60.

197. Cf. 1 Kgs. 18:31; Isa. 54:11–13; Lam. 4:1–2; Black, "Christological Use of the OT," p. 12.

Translated thusly, these metaphors combine to project a reasonably coherent picture of the history of salvation[198] as viewed by Mark from the standpoint within this history which he adopts for himself, namely, somewhere around the event of the destruction of Jerusalem (cf. Mark 13). Having chosen Israel to be his people, God made its leaders responsible for it. Throughout the "time of the OT," God repeatedly sent to Israel the prophets, who summoned it to obedience and faithfulness. Continually, however, the prophets God sent were repudiated. Now in these "last times,"[199] God has sent his only son to Israel. But instead of receiving him, Israel has repudiated him as well. Because of this, God has punished Israel, and the "church" has acceded to its place in the history of salvation. For indeed, God has most assuredly kept the word he has spoken in scripture: the son ("stone") whom Israel rejected in the crucifixion, he it is whom God has vindicated by raising him to glory.

At this point in his story (chap. 12), Mark has Jesus address the parable of the wicked husbandmen to "the chief priests and the scribes and the elders" (11:27; 12:1). They are the ones with whom Jesus identifies the murderous tenant-farmers, even as he is the one with whom he identifies the owner's son. It is these two features of the parable which are of immediate interest.

Jesus so narrates this parable that the initiator of the action in the story, as opposed to the "responders," is the owner of the vineyard. It is the owner who plants the vineyard (12:1), sends the slaves (12:2–5), sends at the last his son (12:6–8), punishes the tenant-farmers (12:9), and entrusts his vineyard to others (12:9). As the owner is in the act of dispatching his son to the tenant-farmers, he speaks of him, designating his "one, beloved son" as "my son": "*he* sent him to them, *saying,* 'They will respect *my son*' " (12:6). Now this "owner," we know, is "God." Accordingly, when Jesus, in narrating this parable, has the owner utter the words "my son," he is depicting God as uttering the words "my son." In effect, therefore, what Jesus does in this parable is to bring to expression God's own "evaluative point of view" regarding him. He has God, as the owner of the

---

198. Cf. Carlston, *Parables,* pp. 185–90; Klauck, *Allegorie,* pp. 310–11; Weder, *Gleichnisse,* pp. 158–60.

199. On the eschatological overtones of the adverb *eschaton* ("last [of all]," "finally"), cf. Klauck, *Allegorie,* p. 307.

vineyard, repeat the words he had earlier spoken in the baptismal scene and at the transfiguration ("my [beloved] Son"; 1:11; 9:7). For the third time in Mark's story, therefore, the reader "hears" the very "thoughts" of God concerning Jesus' identity (cf. 8:33d). As in the other two instances, Jesus again stands forth as the royal Son of God. Additionally, Jesus Son of God is also shown to be the decisive figure in the whole of God's history of salvation, the one who, though rejected and crucified, will be raised by God and vindicated.

Upon hearing Jesus' parable, the chief priests, scribes, and elders try to arrest him (12:12). "They knew," Mark writes, "that he had told this parable against them" (12:12). As is obvious, the Jewish leaders comprehend perfectly well that Jesus has made them out to be the tenant-farmers and himself the owner's beloved son. Does this mean, then, that the secret of Jesus' identity has been lifted? Not in Mark's eyes. As Mark tells it, "those outside" are unable to understand Jesus' parabolic speech (4:11–12), for to do so means not only grasping it intellectually but also appropriating it existentially.[200] By attempting to arrest Jesus, the Jewish leaders demonstrate that, whereas they have in fact grasped with their minds the message of his parable, they have repudiated the truth-claim with which it confronts them. Consequently, theirs is, as I said in Chapter 1, an "obdurate understanding";[201] having heard the truth, they cannot receive it and so reject it and are in turn condemned by it. Hence, to Mark's way of thinking the secret of Jesus' identity continues unbroken, for the Jewish leaders, in repudiating this secret, remain "ignorant" of it.

One further word begs to be said. Insofar as it is Jesus in Mark who speaks this parable, the "evaluative point of view" according to which the history of salvation is assessed may be said to be his. But as we mentioned above in discussing the phrase "my son" in 12:6, Mark in reality has Jesus bring to expression, in this sketch of the history of salvation, "God's evaluative point of view." This comes to light not only in the direct speech Jesus attributes to the owner of the vineyard, or to God ("he sent him . . . saying, 'They will respect my son' " [12:6, RSV]), but also in the heavy use the parable makes

---

200. Cf. Boucher, *Mysterious Parable*, pp. 24–25, 82–84.

201. Cf. Pesch, *Markusevangelium*, II, 223; Boucher, *Mysterious Parable*, p. 60.

of OT quotations and allusions and in the circumstance that the owner of the vineyard is throughout the initiator and, ultimately, controller of the action. This parable, then, is an excellent example of how Mark makes Jesus' "evaluative point of view" coincide with God's "evaluative point of view." Not only this, but if it is indeed God's evaluative point of view Jesus is espousing, then it furthermore becomes apparent that when the chief priests, scribes, and elders reject the truth-claim of this parable, they are to be sure rejecting the evaluative point of view of Jesus but, what is more, they are likewise rejecting the evaluative point of view of God himself. In repudiating the notion that Jesus is the "beloved son" of the owner of the vineyard, the Jewish leaders are repudiating the substance of the declarations God had made at the baptism and transfiguration.

The parable of the wicked husbandmen points ahead to the pericope on the trial of Jesus before the Sanhedrin (14:53–65). Of concern is the exchange between the high priest and Jesus in 14:61–62. Unable to secure agreement in the testimony of the witnesses against Jesus (14:55–59), the high priest himself suddenly seizes the word and poses two questions to Jesus. In the second, critical question he asks, "Are you the Messiah, the Son of the Blessed [God]?" (14:61). To this, Jesus replies "I am!" (14:62a), and then adds, "and you will see the Son of Man sitting on the right hand of power and coming with the clouds of heaven!" (14:62).

The question the high priest poses in 14:61 obviously has to do with the identity of Jesus. But in terms of the development of Mark's story, how is one to explain that the thought even occurs to the high priest to ask Jesus whether he is the Messiah, the Son of the Blessed? The one responsible for this is Jesus himself. In narrating the parable of the wicked husbandmen, Jesus was addressing "the chief priests and the scribes and the elders" (11:27; 12:1). These are the same three groups who comprise the Sanhedrin and before whom Jesus now stands trial (14:53, 55). The meaning of Jesus' allegorical statement about the owner's "beloved son" ("my son"; 12:6) was not lost on the ears of these Jewish leaders, and they had wanted to arrest Jesus but feared the crowd (12:12). Against the background of this confrontation, it is apparent that what the high priest is doing in his question at the trial is taking up the claim Jesus had previously made in his parable and casting it in non-allegorical, literal terms: "Are you the Messiah, the Son of the Blessed [God]?'' (14:61). It is the aim of the high priest in Mark's narrative to use Jesus' own claim to destroy him.

If the high priest derives the substance of his question in 14:61 from Jesus' parable of the wicked husbandmen, what role does this question play within the flow of Mark's story? To get at this, it is important to observe that the word order of this question in the Greek is such that, when it is translated literally, it reads: "You are the Messiah, the Son of the Blessed [God]?'' So written, these words, although they constitute a question, nevertheless resemble an affirmation. As such, they call to mind previous affirmations concerning Jesus in Mark's story: that of Mark as narrator (1:1); of God (1:11); of the demons (3:11; cf. 1:24; 5:7; 1:34d); of Peter, which is supplemented by that of God (8:29; 9:7); and of Jesus himself in his parable (12:6).

To return to the trial, the high priest levels his question of 14:61 at Jesus. From his own standpoint, the high priest proposes to bring Jesus to fall by turning against him the claim of his parable (12:6). From the perspective of the reader of Mark's story, however, what the high priest is unwittingly doing is "gathering up" into his question, "Are you the Messiah, the Son of the Blessed [God]?'' all the affirmations concerning Jesus cited above, with the result that Jesus is given the opportunity, at this crucial juncture of his ministry, to reply to them and hence to state openly how he stands to them. Then, too, because all of these affirmations have validity in Mark's story only to the extent that they comply with God's affirmations, that is, with "God's evaluative point of view" concerning Jesus' identity (1:11; 9:7), what Jesus in reality does at his trial is give reply to God's evaluative point of view regarding him. Heretofore in Mark's story, Jesus has been the "object" of these several affirmations. At his trial, he responds directly to them despite, or perhaps precisely because of, the circumstance that they come together in the question of the high priest.

Jesus breaks the silence he has maintained during his trial in order to answer the high priest. His reply corresponds perfectly to the question he has been asked: "Are you . . .?'' . . . "I am!''[202]

---

202. *Ego eimi* is best construed, not as a divine "revelation formula," but as meaning, "Yes, I am!" (cf. Howard, *Das Ego Jesu,* pp. 144, 146).

(14:61–62a). Unequivocally, therefore, Jesus accepts as true the imputation to him of the claim that he is the Messiah, the Son of God.
Indeed, Jesus' acceptance of this claim, his uttering of "I am," is the
pivotal feature on which this entire pericope turns: the false testimony
of the witnesses and the questions of the high priest lead up to it
(14:55–61); and it, in turn, provokes the high priest to tear his clothes,
to dispense with the calling of further witnesses, to charge Jesus with
blasphemy, and to induce the Sanhedrin to sentence him to death
(14:63–65).

Why should it be of such importance to Mark that Jesus should
acknowledge at his trial that he is the Messiah Son of God and on
this account be condemned to death? We have seen that, because it
is "God's evaluative point of view" concerning Jesus' identity which
in reality comes to expression in the question of the high priest, Jesus
is, in giving answer to the high priest, also taking a public stand at
his trial on God's understanding of him. In saying "I am" to the high
priest, Jesus is daring to "think" about himself the way God "thinks"
about him (1:11; 9:7; 12:6; 8:33d). What Mark is after, then, is this:
he desires to show that Jesus is condemned to death by the Sanhedrin
for being exactly who he is, namely, the royal Son of God whom God
has sent to die on the cross and be vindicated in his resurrection (12:6,
10–11; 15:39; 16:6).

This pericope on the trial is, as the discussion thus far has plainly
indicated, "ironic" to the core.[203] Specifically, we have had occasion
to touch on three great ironies. The one irony concerns the question
of the high priest in 14:61. In asking Jesus whether he is the Messiah,
the Son of the Blessed, the high priest unwittingly calls upon Jesus
to acknowledge in public who he really is. The second irony concerns
Jesus. Although he is made to die for committing blasphemy against
God (14:64), his one deed has been to dare to "think" about himself
as God has revealed, at his baptism and transfiguration, that he does
indeed "think" about him (1:11; 9:7; 8:33d). And the third irony
concerns the high priest and the Sanhedrin. In charging Jesus with
blaspheming God, they are alleging, in effect, that they know the

---

203. It is the credit of Juel (*Messiah and Temple,* pp. 47–48) to have forcefully
called attention to Mark's use of "irony" in this pericope and in the passion
account in general.

"thinking" of God. But even while alleging knowledge of God's "thinking," they are, in fact, repudiating his "thinking."

We have observed repeatedly that the high priest, in posing his question of 14:61, names Jesus "the Messiah, the Son of the Blessed." Because these titles are spoken openly, it is commonplace for scholars to adjudge that the pericope on the trial is the place where Mark lifts the secret of Jesus' identity.[204]

A probe of Mark's story, however, does not support this judgment. On the matter of the secret of Jesus' identity, what occurs at the trial is not unlike what occurs when Jesus narrates the parable of the wicked husbandmen. In both cases, Jesus has to do with the same three groups of Jewish leaders (11:27; 12:1; 14:53, 55). As for the parable, the Jewish leaders hear it in a manner that Mark characterizes as "obdurate understanding." Although they grasp the message of the parable (12:12c), they reject the existential claim it makes upon them (12:12a) and consequently remain "ignorant" of its truth (cf. 4:12). At the trial, a similar phenomenon occurs. The high priest, in putting his question to Jesus on behalf of the Sanhedrin, utters the titles that properly convey the secret of Jesus' identity (cf. 14:61 to 1:1, 11; 9:7 12:6). Still, the high priest speaks these titles, not in "faith," but in order to bring Jesus under the sentence of death (14:55). Hence, both he and the Sanhedrin remain "ignorant" of the truth of these titles as they pertain to Jesus, and the secret of Jesus' divine sonship holds firm.

So far we have said nothing about the latter part of Jesus' reply to the high priest: ". . . and you will see the Son of Man sitting on the right hand of power and coming with the clouds of heaven" (14:62b). One of the most debated problems in Marcan interpretation is how the title of "the Son of Man" in 14:62 is to be related to the titles of "the Messiah, the Son of the Blessed [God]" in 14:61.

Prominent in the last years has been the "corrective" approach to this problem, which assumes a variety of forms. Common to the various forms of the corrective approach, however, is the conviction

204. Cf., more recently, Conzelmann, "Historie und Theologie," p. 47; Perrin, "High Priest's Question," pp. 81–83, 89, 95; Donahue, *Christ*, pp. 91, 93, 95, 181; Juel, *Messiah and Temple*, p. 77; Kazmierski, *Son of God*, p. 188; Steichele, *Sohn Gottes*, p. 286; Lührmann, "Markus 14, 55–64," p. 463; also Weeden, *Mark*, p. 65; Räisänen, *Messiasgeheimnis*, pp. 146–47.

that the titles "Messiah, Son of the Blessed" in 14:61 are in some
sense defective or seriously deficient. This is the case, it is said,
because they connote a false perception of Jesus as "divine man"[205]
or as a national, political "king,"[206] or because they are in need of
definition.[207]

In analyzing the plot of Mark's story, I have argued that the source
from which the high priest derives his question of 14:61 is Jesus
himself, that is, his narration of the parable of the wicked husbandmen.
In putting his question to Jesus, the high priest calls upon Jesus to
take a stand with respect to the "parabolic claim" he has made concerning himself in order thereby to secure his condemnation. Now as
Jesus confronts the high priest at his trial, it is to misread Mark badly
if one supposes that he would have the reader construe the two as
"speaking past" each other. Yet this is the mistake the interpreter
makes if he portrays the high priest, in uttering the designations
"Messiah, Son of the Blessed," as depicting Jesus as a "divine man"
of glorious stripe or as a national, political "king," but portrays Jesus,
in accepting these designations, as thinking of himself in totally different categories or indeed as completely redefining the high priest's
words. Literarily, Mark fashions an exact correspondence between the
high priest's question and Jesus' answer: "Are you . . .?"; "I am!"
Mark is concerned to show in his story that Jesus is sentenced to death
on no lesser grounds than that the high priest and the Sanhedrin repudiate as blasphemous the very claim Jesus affirms to be true. Because the high priest draws the substance of his question from Jesus'
own parable of the wicked husbandmen, it is not that the high priest
and Jesus have no common understanding of what the high priest's
question is to mean. On the contrary, it is because both of them do

---

205. Cf., e.g., Weeden, *Mark*, pp. 66–67. In 1971, Perrin ("Christology of
Mark," pp. 112–15, 118) also vigorously advocated this position, but by 1976
("High Priest's Question," pp. 80–95) he seems to have moved to a "corrective"
approach to 14:61–62 which construed "Messiah, Son of the Blessed" as being
in need of definition, or reinterpretation, but not as projecting a picture of Jesus
as "divine man."

206. Cf., e.g., Vielhauer, "Christologie des Markusevangeliums," pp. 204–5;
Petersen, *Literary Criticism for New Testament Critics*, pp. 74–75, 61–63, esp.
67; Achtemeier, *Mark*, pp. 42–46.

207. Cf. Hahn, *Hoheitstitel*, pp. 182–83; Donahue, "Royal Christology," p.
71; Perrin, "High Priest's Question," pp. 83, 89, 95.

understand this question alike that Jesus affirms to be true what the high priest declares to be blasphemy.

Accordingly, the "corrective" approach to 14:61–62 is misguided, for the "content" of the titles "Messiah, the Son of the Blessed" is sound. Although this content can be elaborated, it is in no wise in need of "redefinition." But if the title of "the Son of Man" in 14:62 does not correct or redefine the titles of 14:61, how does it function?

To elucidate this, we must first establish a negative conclusion. Unlike the titles "Messiah, the Son of the Blessed," Mark does not utilize the title "the Son of Man" to explain to the reader "who Jesus is." Never does Mark, as we have mentioned before, ever describe God, the demons, or any human character as saying of Jesus, "You are (he is) the Son of Man." And as for Jesus, although he refers to himself as "the Son of Man," the one time he utters the words "I am!" in order to address directly the matter of his identity, the intent of his declaration is not to assert that "I am the Son of Man" but that "I am the Messiah, the Son of the Blessed" (14:61–62).

To stay with this line of reasoning, it is striking, if one ponders it, that the title "the Son of Man" does *not* appear in the high priest's question of 14:61. Looking back over Mark's story, the reader could well expect that Mark would have the high priest ask Jesus, "Are you in truth the Son of Man?" Earlier, Mark has depicted Jesus more than once as publicly referring to himself as the Son of Man (2:4, 6, 10, 24, 28; 8:34a, 38). Then, too, on these occasions he has performed such provocative acts as forgiving the paralytic his sins (2:5), setting himself above the sabbath law (2:28), and tacitly picturing himself as exercising judgment at the last day (8:38). In the light of these examples, what could be more probable than that the high priest should seize on the opportunity at Jesus' trial to ask him straight out, "Are you, as you have publicly said, the Son of Man?" The fact that the high priest's question does not read like this—even though the groundwork for this seems to have been well laid—is, again, strong indication that Mark does not define Jesus' identity in terms of the title "the Son of Man."

Accordingly, in contrast to the titles "Messiah, the Son of the Blessed" in 14:61, the title "the Son of Man" in 14:62 functions other than to inform the reader of "who Jesus is." In the next chapter I shall discuss Mark's use of "the Son of Man." For now it is enough to state simply that the Marcan Jesus employs "the Son of Man" here in 14:62 as the designation by which he refers to himself in public as he interacts with his adversaries in order to point to himself as "the man" (this man) whom God will vindicate and to assert his divine authority in the face of their opposition to him. Thus, it is publicly, that is, at his trial, and in view of such adversaries as the high priest and the Sanhedrin ("you [pl.] will see"; 14:62) that Jesus designates himself as "the Son of Man." And the purpose for which he so designates himself is to warn them of the judgment they will incur under his auspices at the end of time because of their condemnation of him. Perhaps Jesus' words in 14:62 may be paraphrased as follows: "Yes, I am the Messiah, the Son of the Blessed; and because you (the high priest) have asked me who I am in order to condemn me to death (cf. 14:55), it will be in my (prophesied) role as the man who will have been vindicated by God by being exalted to universal rule[208] and appointed to exercise final judgment[209] that you (the high priest and Sanhedrin) will see me at the end of time." To put it succinctly, if the titles "the Messiah, the Son of the Blessed" in 14:61 denote "who Jesus is," the title "the Son of Man" in 14:62 ascribes to Jesus, that is, to "the (this) man," the eschatological role that will attend his "public" vindication, that of exercising judgment over his opponents at the end of time.

The death of Jesus in Mark's story does not follow immediately upon his trial. Nevertheless, Mark relates these two events to each other in such a way that the intervening material in chapter 15 becomes, properly understood, "transitional." Thus, it is the Jewish Sanhedrin, led by the chief priests, that pronounces the sentence of death upon Jesus (14:55, 64). Pilate, for his part, utters no such sentence, but hands Jesus over for crucifixion because the Jewish crowd calls for this and because he is desirous of doing the people a favor (15:13–15). Also, the reason Jesus is condemned to death at his trial is that he dares to affirm that he is the "Son of the Blessed [God]" (14:61–62). Correlatively, no sooner does Jesus die on the cross than the centurion affirms that he was in truth the "Son of God" (15:39).

---

208. On the use of Psalm 110:1 in 14:62, cf., e.g., Tödt, *Menschensohn,* p. 36 (ET, *Son of Man,* pp. 39–40); Casey, *Son of Man,* pp. 180–82.

209. On the use of Daniel 7:13 in 14:62, cf., e.g., Lindars, *Apologetic,* p. 49; Juel, *Messiah and Temple,* p. 95; Casey, *Son of Man,* pp. 180–83.

Still, between these two occurrences of the title Son of God, the term by which Jesus is consistently designated is the "King of the Jews (Israel)" (15:2, 9, 12, 18, 26, 32). This term is eminently suited to its "Roman setting" and constitutes the "evaluative point of view" regarding the identity of Jesus on the basis of which both Pilate and the Jewish leaders interact with Jesus in chapter 15 and which Jesus accepts for himself as true.

As Jesus stands before Pilate, Pilate asks him in the presence of the chief priests and the other members of the Sanhedrin, "Are you the King of the Jews?" (15:2). To this Jesus replies, "(So) you say" (*sy legeis*; 15:2, RSV). This reply is affirmative in content and not negative,[210] but it is also circumlocutory, or reserved, in formulation.[211]

Mark indicates already by the way he has Pilate frame his question that the reader is to understand Jesus' reply as an acceptance of the predication the "King of the Jews." Like the question of the high priest in 14:61, Pilate's question, too, has the form of an affirmation: "You are the King of the Jews?" (15:2). As such, it, too, aligns itself with the several affirmations Mark strategically places throughout his story which assume the form of "You are . . ." and which present God (1:11; cf. 9:7; 12:6), the demons (3:11; cf. 1:24, 34d; 5:7), or Peter (8:29) as declaring that Jesus is either the Son of God or the Messiah. Because these affirmations are all "correct," and because Mark has Jesus accept as true the "affirmation-question" the high priest puts to him (14:61–62a), the reader can be certain that Jesus' reply to Pilate is, again, affirmative[212] in nature.

But if Jesus' answer is affirmative in content, it is at the same time circumlocutory in formulation. Jesus does not reply "I am!" to Pilate, as he does to the high priest, and this by design. The source from which the high priest draws his question is Jesus' own parable of the wicked husbandmen. But the case with Pilate's question is not the

---

210. For different reasons, Pesch (*Markusevangelium*, II, 457, 459) and Grundmann (*Markus*, p. 307) both insist that the Marcan Jesus denies that he is the King of the Jews.

211. Cf. Catchpole, "Answer of Jesus," pp. 218, 226; also Matera, *Kingship of Jesus*, pp. 63–65.

212. Cf. also Hahn, *Hoheitstitel*, pp. 195–96; Schneider, *Passion Jesu*, p. 87; Dormeyer, *Passion Jesu*, p. 176; Matera, *Kingship of Jesus*, pp. 63–64.

same. The title "King of the Jews" occurs for the first time in Mark's story here in 15:2. Therefore, to ascertain how Pilate understands this title, the reader cannot turn, say, to an earlier word of Jesus but must look to the immediate context. As 15:26 reveals, the term "King of the Jews" labels Jesus in Pilate's eyes an insurrectionist who aspires to political rule over the Jews. In contradistinction to this, as Jesus accepts this title as one that rightly applies to him, he construes it in a radically different fashion, as I shall shortly demonstrate. In any event, by having Jesus answer Pilate with the words, "(So) you say," and thus accept, but only with reserve, the imputation to him of the title "King of the Jews," Mark is likewise urging the reader to regard this title with reserve[213] until such time as he can determine from the ensuing narrative what it connotes from the standpoint of Pilate on the one hand and of Jesus on the other.

Accordingly, Jesus affirms before Pilate, though with reserve, that he is the "King of the Jews," and what Pilate takes this to mean is that Jesus is an insurrectionist. But this notwithstanding, Mark goes to great lengths to show that Pilate does not believe for a moment that Jesus is in fact the King of the Jews, that is, an insurrectionist. Several factors in Mark's narrative of Jesus' hearing before Pilate demonstrate this well.

For one thing, the way in which Pilate reacts to the many accusations the chief priests make against Jesus betrays already a lack of conviction on his part that Jesus is an insurrectionist. Although the charge that Jesus claims to be the King of the Jews is at the heart of these accusations, Pilate's only response to them is one of surprise, or wonder, that Jesus should remain silent and not defend himself against them (15:2–5). For another thing, although Pilate, in dealing with the Jews, does not hesitate to refer to Jesus by means of the "insurrectionist term" "King of the Jews," he nevertheless employs it so as to leave no doubt that this term is not of his choosing. In the episode involving Barabbas, Pilate twice indicates by his remarks that it is the Jews alone who are making Jesus out to be the King of the Jews. At 15:9, Pilate asks the Jewish crowd as he forces a choice between Barabbas and Jesus: "Do you desire that I release for you the King of the Jews?" The words "for you" are a dative of advan-

---

213. This point is well stated by Matera (*Kingship of Jesus*, p. 64).

tage, and to bring out the intention of Pilate's question one may paraphrase it as follows: "Is it your desire that I do you the favor of releasing your King of the Jews?" And at 15:12, Pilate so phrases his question to the Jews that he clearly reveals that "King of the Jews" is, again, their designation for Jesus: "Then what shall I do with him whom *you call* the King of the Jews?" In the third place, Pilate is little inclined to accept the notion that Jesus is in fact an insurrectionist because he himself has discerned the motives that have prompted the chief priests to deliver Jesus to him. At 15:10 (RSV), Mark writes of Pilate: "For he perceived that it was out of envy that the chief priests had delivered him up." Fourth, at one point Pilate even openly, though in the form of a question, expresses his belief that Jesus is no insurrectionist. In the face of the Jewish shouts to "crucify him," Pilate asks the crowd, "Why, what evil has he done?" (15:12–14). And last, Pilate attests also to himself that Jesus is not an insurrectionist, for what finally impels him to hand Jesus over to be crucified is his private desire to satisfy the wishes of the Jewish crowd (15:15).

In Pilate's ears, then, the term "King of the Jews" connotes insurrection against Rome (15:26), but Pilate gives no credence to the notion that Jesus is an insurrectionist. What is the Jewish understanding of this term as applied to Jesus? Only once in Mark's story do Jews utter it, and in their mouths it becomes "King of Israel" (15:32). Nonetheless, as Jesus hangs upon the cross, the chief priests, together with the scribes, mock him, referring to him among themselves as "the Messiah, the King of Israel" (15:32). In their use of these titles beneath the cross, the Jewish leaders seem to be offering their own rendition of Pilate's inscription of 15:26. Hence, what they appear to be suggesting is that Jesus is the Anointed One God has at last raised up to rule over Israel and be its deliverer. Of course the circumstance that they utter these titles in ridicule proves that they regard the cross as putting the lie to any claim that Jesus is in truth Israel's Messiah-King.

Thus, Mark portrays neither Pilate nor the Jewish leaders as believing that Jesus is in reality the "King of the Jews (Israel)." Still, although it is with reserve, Jesus himself does accept, before Pilate and in the presence of the members of the Jewish Sanhedrin, the title as rightly applying to him (15:1–2). In what sense can this be so? Mark reveals this in the two passages in which the Roman soldiers on the one hand and the Jewish leaders on the other mock Jesus as the "King of the Jews (Israel)."[214] The one passage, featuring the Jewish leaders, we just discussed: as Jesus hangs upon the cross, the chief priests with the scribes refer to him among themselves as the "King of Israel" in order thereby to ridicule his seeming helplessness and disavow the claim this title bears (15:31–32). In the other passage, the Roman soldiers, their whole cohort gathered about Jesus, dress him in purple, place a crown of thorns on him, hail him as "King of the Jews," strike him on the head with a reed, spit upon him, and kneel down and pay him homage (15:16–20b). The meaning of these two scenes is patent: Jesus is indeed the "King of the Jews (Israel)," but neither as one who foments rebellion against Rome nor as one who will restore to Israel its national splendor, but as one who exercises his royal authority by willingly enduring the mockery of his enemies and obediently choosing the way which leads to death (14:35–36; 15:25–26).

In review of the preceding, Mark's use of the title "King of the Jews (Israel)" in chapter 15 is such that, although it crosses the lips of Gentiles (15:2, 9, 12, 18, [26]) and Jews (15:32) alike, its real meaning remains hidden from them and is transparent only to the reader. "King of the Jews (Israel)" correctly applies to Jesus Messiah as one who wields authority by submitting to the ridicule of his enemies and ultimately to crucifixion out of obedience to God (15:16–20b, 25–26, 31–32; 14:35–36), not as one who is an insurrectionist or a national ruler. Mark imbues this title with the quality of irony throughout chapter 15, but nowhere does this come to the fore with greater clarity than in the passages 15:18 and 15:32: what Gentile and Jew say "in mockery" (15:20, 31) is—in Marcan perspective—true, namely, Jesus is in fact the "King of the Jews," or "the Messiah, the King of Israel."

We noted above that whereas Mark consistently refers to Jesus as the "King of the Jews (Israel)" in the scenes that attend Jesus' hearing before Pilate and the crucifixion, he suddenly abandons this title at the climactic moment of the death of Jesus in favor of the title "Son of God" (15:39). One reason for this, we said, is that Mark is concerned

---

214. For a detailed analysis of these two passages, cf. Matera, *Kingship of Jesus,* pp. 21–29.

to link the event of the death of Jesus with the event of his trial: at his trial, it is Jesus' claim to be the "Son of the Blessed [God]" that serves as the grounds on which the Sanhedrin condemns him to death (14:61–64). In keeping with this thematic, then, Mark writes of Jesus at 15:39: "And when the centurion, who stood facing him, saw that he thus expired, he said, 'Truly this man was the Son of God!'"[215]

To ascertain the force of the centurion's acclamation of Jesus, a good place to begin is with the adverb "thus" *(houtōs)*. Here in 15:39, it refers to the "manner" in which Jesus dies.[216] To be clear about Mark's description of this, one must ask what exactly it is that the centurion "sees" when he watches Jesus expire. Is it the stark act itself of Jesus' dying, which is accompanied by a great cry (15:37)?[217] Or is it some series of occurrences surrounding Jesus' death?[218] The latter is the preferable option owing to the fact that the verb "to see" *(horaō)* also stands out prominently in each of the two sections that precede 15:37–39, namely, 15:29–32 (v. 32) and 15:33–36 (v. 36). The upshot is that the verb "to see" functions as a catchword to link these three sections together (15:32, 36, 39). What this means in terms of the flow of Mark's story is that he so guides the action that the centurion "sees" the chain of events attending Jesus' hanging on the cross and leading up to his death (15:29–32, 33–36, 37). The result is that the centurion's "perception" of Jesus is thus made to contrast sharply with the "perceptions" of the characters Mark mentions in the scenes of 15:29–32 and 15:33–36.

---

215. "Colwell's rule," coupled with the theology of Mark, dictates that *hyios theou* in 15:39 be translated as "the Son of God" (cf. Colwell, "Use of the Article," pp. 12–21; Moule, *Idiom Book*, pp. 115–16; Zerwick, *Biblical Greek*, p. 56).

216. Cf., e.g., Lohmeyer, *Markus*, p. 348; Weeden, *Mark*, p. 167 n. 8; Schneider, *Passion Jesu*, pp. 124–25; Nickelsburg, "Passion Narrative," p. 175; Matera, *Kingship of Jesus*, p. 136. Contra: Chronis, "Torn Veil," p. 99 n. 8.

217. Cf., e.g., Lohmeyer, *Markus*, p. 348; Nineham, *Mark*, p. 431; Schreiber, *Theologie*, p. 26; Schneider, *Passion Jesu*, pp. 125, 127.

218. Bultmann (*Geschichte der synoptischen Tradition*, pp. 295–96 [ET, *History of the Synoptic Tradition*, pp. 273–74]) speaks for several scholars (cf. Vielhauer, "Christologie des Markusevangeliums," p. 208; Dormeyer, *Passion Jesu*, p. 206; Steichele, *Sohn Gottes*, pp. 269–71) when he argues that the centurion "sees" the events of 15:33–38, especially the "darkness" and the splitting in two of the temple-curtain. Weeden (*Mark*, p. 167 n. 8) contends that the centurion "sees" the "whole drama of suffering and humiliation surrounding Jesus' death."

If we examine these latter two scenes to determine what they tell us of the manner of Jesus' dying, the topic they have in common is that of "deliverance through descent from the cross" (15:30, 31–32, 36). In the scene of 15:29–32, the Jews tempt Jesus by hurling challenges at him to come down from the cross and hence save himself. For his part, Jesus remains passive in the face of these challenges. Had he acted upon them, he would have alienated himself from both himself and God: from himself, because it was he who had affirmed on another occasion that "whoever would save his life will lose it" (8:35 RSV); and from God, because in Gethsemane he had pledged himself to do, not his own will, but God's will (14:35–36). Accordingly, by not capitulating to the challenges of his enemies, Jesus goes to his death as one who, in refusing to save himself, evinces perfect obedience towards God.

But if Jesus will not himself act to come down from the cross, perhaps Elijah will miraculously appear and save him. This is the gist of 15:33–36. At the ninth hour, Jesus cries aloud, "My God, my God, why have you forsaken me?" On hearing this cry, the bystanders misconstrue it to mean that Jesus is appealing to Elijah for deliverance (15:35).[219] Indeed, one of them runs and fills a sponge with sour wine, places it on a reed, and holds it up to Jesus to drink. The idea is to refresh Jesus so that he will live long enough for all to see whether Elijah will in fact come "to take him down" (15:36). Elijah, however, does not suddenly appear to rescue Jesus. Nor, in view of the plot of Mark's story, can he be expected to do so. This is the case first of all because he has already made his appearance, in the person of John the Baptist, now dead (9:13). And second, this is also the case because the bystanders have, as indicated, misunderstood the cry of Jesus. Jesus' cry is to God, not to Elijah, and it expresses continuing trust in God ("my God") in spite of abandonment into death.[220] On balance, therefore, the scene of 15:33–36 is analogous to that of 15:29–32. In it, Jesus is pictured as going to his death as one who places his total trust in God.

This brings us to 15:37, in which Mark tells of the death of Jesus:

---

219. For an explanation of this motif, cf. Str-B, I, 1042; IV, 2, 769–79.

220. On Mark's use of Psalm 22 at 15:34, cf. Matera, *Kingship of Jesus*, pp. 132–35. Concerning the intriguing hypothesis that Jesus' cry of dereliction is viewed by Mark as symptomatic of demonic possession, cf. Danker, "Demonic Secret," pp. 48–69.

uttering a second, wordless cry,[221] Jesus expires. As far as the manner of Jesus' dying is concerned, this verse, by characterizing Jesus' utterance as a "great cry" (*phōnēn megalēn;* also 15:34), reinforces the notion that he embraces death even as he continues to trust in God. In sum, then, if one asks what it is regarding the manner in which Jesus dies that impels the centurion to acclaim him to be the Son of God, the answer is that it is that Jesus dies as one who is utterly obedient to, and places his total trust in, God.

By imputing to the centurion a correct perception of the manner of Jesus' dying, Mark in effect characterizes him as a "convert"[222] and his acclamation of Jesus as being true. By the same token, it is likewise to be noted that the centurion's acclamation is pregnant with meaning beyond his own comprehension as a character confined to a small segment of Mark's story.[223] For one thing, the centurion exclaims that Jesus "truly," or "really," was the Son of God (15:39). In so doing, he is made both to vindicate the claim Jesus raised on his own behalf at his trial ("I am [the Son of the Blessed]!") and to contravene the high priest's contention that this claim was blasphemous (14:61–64).

For another thing, the centurion also declares that Jesus "was" the Son of God (15:39). The verb "was" underlines the circumstances that Jesus has, in his death on the cross, reached the end of his earthly ministry, which is at the same time its culmination. One way in which Mark accounts Jesus' death as the culmination of his ministry he

---

221. Some scholars, e.g., Schneider (*Passion Jesu*, p. 127), Schenke (*Christus,* p. 97), Dormeyer (*Passion Jesu*, p. 204), and Matera (*Kingship of Jesus*, pp. 125–27), contend that, at 15:37, Mark refers a second time to the cry of 15:34, so that the reader is to think of Jesus as uttering, not two cries, but one cry. The difficulty with this position, however, is that one must then assume (a) that the reader, having finished v. 34, can be expected to know that Jesus, in uttering the cry this verse mentions, has now died, (b) that it is of the "dead Jesus" that the bystanders say, "Look, he calls Elijah!" (v. 35), (c) that it is likewise to the mouth of a "dead Jesus" that one places the sponge filled with sour wine and exclaims, "Let us see whether Elijah comes to take him down!" (v. 36), and (d) that, grammatically, the fact that the noun "cry" (*phōnēn*) in v. 37 is without an article of "previous reference" (cf. Dana and Mantey, *Manual Grammar*, p. 141), even though it allegedly denotes no other cry than that of v. 34, is of no consequence. In my judgment, to assume the preceding results in an artificial reading of 15:34–37. It appears rather that Mark's mode of narration in 15:34–37 is that of describing a temporally sequential series of events involving two cries.

222. Cf. also Dormeyer, *Passion Jesu,* p. 213; Schneider, *Passion Jesu,* p. 128.

223. Cf. Vielhauer, "Christologie des Markusevangeliums," p. 209.

indicates in 15:38, a verse the centurion's acclamation "encloses." In 15:38, Mark depicts God as reacting to the death of Jesus by causing the curtain of the temple to be split in two (cf. the "divine passive": *eschisthē*). While it is perhaps not possible to decide whether the curtain in question is that before the holy place[224] or that before the holiest place,[225] the significance of this divine act at the level of Mark's story is that it presages the destruction of the temple (cf. 13:2; 14:58; 15:29).[226] For its part, the destruction of the temple also involves the cessation of the temple cult.[227] This, in turn, points to another dimension of the death of Jesus. At 14:24, Mark has Jesus say at the Passover meal in connection with the giving of the cup, "This is my blood of the covenant which is poured out for many." The reference here is to atonement for the sins of humankind (cf. 10:45), and the place where Jesus does pour out his blood and consequently atone for sins is on the cross.[228] In his death, therefore, Jesus Son of God supersedes the temple and its cult as the "place" where God henceforth grants, to all humankind, the remission of sins. Additionally, Jesus also becomes the "builder" (14:58; 15:29)[229] of the new community that is God's eschatological people (cf. 10:29-30; 14:22-24; 16:7).[230]

And finally, the centurion's acclamation is also of pivotal importance because it constitutes for the first time in Mark's story the open confession of Jesus as the Son of God on the part of a human being and occurs precisely at that point where Jesus does attain to the end and culmination of his ministry. As Jesus was about to embark on his

---

224. So, e.g., Donahue, *Christ*, pp. 201-3; Juel, *Messiah and Temple*, pp. 140-42.

225. So, e.g., Taylor, *St. Mark*, p. 596; Linnemann, *Passionsgeschichte*, p. 159; Schenke, *Christus*, p. 100; cf. also Pesch, *Markusevangelium*, II, 498.

226. Cf. Donahue, *Christ*, p. 203; Juel, *Messiah and Temple*, pp. 137-38, 140-42.

227. Cf. Lohmeyer, *Markus*, p. 347; Schenk, *Passionsbericht*, p. 47; Schenke, *Christus*, p. 100; Schneider, *Passion Jesu*, p. 128; Steichele, *Sohn Gottes*, pp. 256-57; Matera, *Kingship of Jesus*, p. 139.

228. Cf., e.g., Kertelge, "Die soteriologischen Aussagen," pp. 195-99; Gnilka, *Markus*, II, 245-46; Köester, *Einführung*, p. 607.

229. For contrasting views on Mark's treatment of the topic of the "temple," cf. Juel (*Messiah and Temple*, pp. 117-209) and Nickelsburg ("Passion Narrative," pp. 176-82).

230. On Mark's portrayal of his community, cf. Kee, *Community*, pp. 107-16.

ministry, God empowered him with his Spirit and solemnly affirmed him to be his Son (1:10–11). Subsequently, Jesus has, with authority, preached the gospel of God, called disciples to follow him, taught not like the scribes, and healed the sick and exorcized demons (1:14—8:26). He has also journeyed to Jerusalem and suffered and died, thereby atoning for the sins of humankind and laying the foundation for the emergence of the eschatological people of God (8:27—15:39). In the light of these events, Mark for the first time now allows a human character other than Jesus himself to adopt unreservedly God's "evaluative point of view" concerning Jesus' identity and to "think" about Jesus the way God "thinks" about him (1:11; 9:7; 12:6; 15:39; 8:33d). The result is that the centurion becomes the first human being in Mark's story truly to penetrate the secret of Jesus' identity. The narrational and theological significance Mark attaches to this is a matter we shall discuss shortly.

The Resurrected Jesus

The climactic event of the ministry of Jesus Son of God in Mark is his death on the cross (15:37–39), in which he atones for the sins of humankind (15:38; 14:24; 10:45). Obediently, Jesus Son of God embraces death, even as he trusts in God to the end to vindicate him (14:36; 15:34, 37; 8:35). Through the announcement of the angelic young man that God has raised Jesus (16:6), Mark lets it be known that Jesus' trust in God was not in vain. In addition, the young man also delivers a message that pertains to the disciples (16:7). A look at these two sayings of the young man will round out this investigation of the third main part of Mark's story (8:27—16:8).

Strictly speaking, Mark devotes only the one verse 16:6 to the event of Jesus' resurrection. What would Mark have the reader infer from this verse about the identity of the risen Jesus?

The way in which the young man in white both refers to Jesus and describes his resurrection indicates that Mark is alluding to the risen Jesus as the Son of God. The young man designates Jesus as "Jesus the Nazarene" (16:6), an expression that identifies him as one who comes from the city of Nazareth (1:24; 10:47; 14:67; 16:6).[231] Mark makes special mention of the Nazarene background of Jesus both at the beginning and at the end of his story, so that this notation forms

---

231. Cf. BAG, p. 532.

an "inclusion" that brackets the story (1:9; 16:6). In connection with Jesus' initial appearance at his baptism, Mark informs the reader that the "Jesus [who] came from Nazareth of Galilee" is the one whom God likewise declares to be his beloved Son and empowers for messianic ministry (1:9–11). By referring to Jesus as "Jesus the Nazarene (of Nazareth)" here in the pericope on the empty tomb, Mark deftly "gathers up" his entire story and gives the reader to understand that the Jesus whom God has raised from the dead is no other Jesus than the one with whom he began his story, namely, the Jesus who is God's beloved Son. The risen Jesus of Mark, therefore, is the one from Nazareth whom God sent to Israel and has now raised from the dead, his beloved Son.

The young man's further designation of Jesus as "the one who has been crucified and remains the crucified one" (perfect participle: *ton estaurōmenon;* 16:6) also alludes to the risen Jesus as being the Son of God. Except for the one passage 8:34, which has to do with discipleship, Mark employs the terms "cross" and "to crucify" exclusively in chapter 15 and here in 16:6, where they occur no fewer than eleven times.[232] Theologically, the truth Mark underscores by having the risen Jesus designated as the crucified one is that the resurrection does not "undo" the crucifixion but, on the contrary, confirms the fact that Jesus' death on the cross is the decisive event of his ministry. Yet, at that climactic moment when Jesus does die on the cross, his death evokes from the centurion the equally climactic acclamation that he is the Son of God (15:39). Of course the centurion, having just seen Jesus die, says that Jesus "was" the Son of God. But in the resurrection God overturns this "was" so that it becomes "is": the crucified Jesus, who is said upon his death to have been the Son of God, has been raised and so "is" the Son of God.

To describe the event of the resurrection, the young man uses the verb *ēgerthē:* "he has been raised" (16:6). This verb, too, alludes to the risen Jesus as being the Son of God. Cast in the passive voice, *ēgerthē* points to divine activity: it is God, the young man affirms, who has raised Jesus from the dead.[233] In the light of the passion-predictions, the use of *ēgerthē* in 16:6 is surprising, for apart from a

---

232. Cf. Mark 15:13, 14, 15, 20, 24, 25, 27; 16:6; 15:21, 30, 32.

233. Cf., e.g., Fuller, *Resurrection Narratives,* p. 68; Pesch, *Markusevangelium,* II, 533.

passage such as 14:27–28 the verb by which the resurrection is consistently referred to is *anistanai* ("to rise").[234] Within the context of Mark's story, however, the use of *ēgerthē* in 16:6 performs a necessary function: it documents the fulfillment of the OT prophecy Jesus cited in his narration of the parable of the wicked husbandmen (12:10–11). In this word of prophecy, there is, we recall, a play on the "stone-son" imagery. The "stone" which the builders rejected is, in Jesus' parable, the "beloved son" of the owner of the vineyard whom the tenant-farmers kill (12:6–8, 10). But although this "stone—God's beloved Son" is thusly rejected, God has already ordained, Jesus prophesies, that he will place Jesus at "the head of the corner," that is, vindicate him (12:10–11). In terms of the plot of Mark's story, the point at which this prophecy of Jesus reaches fulfillment is in the event of the resurrection. Here the young man proclaims that "God has raised Jesus" (16:6), which is to say that the resurrection is the act whereby God has vindicated the "rejected stone—his beloved Son."

Accordingly, the sheer proximity of 16:6 to 15:39 and the allusive power of the terms by which the young man in white refers to Jesus and describes the event of his resurrection all combine to lead the reader of Mark's story to think of the Jesus of Easter as the crucified Son of God whom God has raised to life. To turn to 16:7, the young man next speaks of the disciples. The word they are to receive is that Jesus precedes[235] them to Galilee, where they will, as he himself told them earlier (14:28), see him.[236]

Norman Petersen has shown that Mark's mention of the women's silence in 16:8 is not to be regarded as frustrating the prediction the young man makes in 16:7 that the disciples will see Jesus in Galilee.[237] On the contrary, Mark makes extensive use of the pattern of prediction-fulfillment throughout his story so as to invite the reader to assume that, because Jesus' predictions do as a matter of course come to pass, this prediction of the young man, which is based on a previous word

234. Cf. Mark 8:31; 9:31; 10:34; also 9:9–10.

235. On the interpretation of *proagein* as "to precede," cf. Fuller, *Resurrection Narratives*, p. 61.

236. I take 16:7 to refer, not to the Parousia, but to a projected resurrection appearance. For a discussion of this, cf. Fuller, *Resurrection Narratives*, pp. 62–64.

237. On Petersen's interpretation of 16:8, cf. "End," pp. 159–63.

of Jesus (14:28), likewise comes to pass despite the fact that Mark presents no account of it.[238] But should this be correct, the reader still must ask himself what it is he is to project as taking place at this meeting of Jesus with his disciples in Galilee.

To begin with, the young man refers to the "disciples and Peter" (16:7). This calls to mind the passages 14:27 and 14:50, in which Jesus first prophesies that the disciples will all fall away from him and then, at his arrest, they do just that, and 14:30 and 14:72, in which Jesus forewarns Peter that he will deny him three times and, subsequently, Peter follows suit. Against this background of failure, Jesus' promise to the disciples that after his resurrection they will see him (14:28; 16:7) means little unless it means first of all that at this meeting he effects a reversal of their failed condition and reconstitutes them as his followers. Accordingly, one thing the reader can project as taking place at this meeting in Galilee is that Jesus reconciles the disciples to himself and gathers the flock that, through the smiting of the shepherd, has been scattered (14:27–28; 16:7).

The second thing the reader can project as taking place is that, in seeing the risen Jesus, the disciples at last penetrate the secret of his identity. At the outset of his ministry, Jesus called the disciples to be "with him" (3:14). As he journeyed about and they followed him, he made of them witnesses to his messianic activity of preaching (1:38–39), teaching (1:21–22), and healing and exorcizing demons (1:32–34). In contrast to the erroneous opinions the Jewish public held of him (6:14–15; 8:28), Jesus elicited from Peter on behalf of the disciples the confession that he is the Messiah (8:29–30). But though correct, this confession was also insufficient, for Jesus had not yet taught the disciples of his passion and Peter's confession did not envisage it. Following Peter's confession, however, Jesus did teach the disciples of his passion (8:31). The disciples, however, again led by Peter, repudiated this teaching, for they preferred to "think the things," not of God, but of men (8:31–33). Nevertheless, atop the mountain of the transfiguration God revealed to Peter and James and John that Jesus is his beloved Son, which is of course the secret of Jesus' identity (9:2–8). But the three disciples did not comprehend this revelation and Jesus suppressed it until after he should have risen

---

238. Cf. Petersen, *Literary Criticism for New Testament Critics,* pp. 76–77; idem, "End," pp. 155–56.

from the dead (9:5–6, 9). Nor are such incomprehension and suppression surprising, for to Mark's way of thinking the sine qua non for humans to be able to penetrate the secret of Jesus' identity and to understand him to be the Son of God is to know him as the crucified Son of God (15:39; 16:6). Indeed, the upshot of the fact that the disciples would have no truck with the notion of suffering and death was that they all forsook Jesus at his arrest (14:50) and Peter denied him (14:72). Still, as Jesus now meets the disciples in Galilee and they see him, he has both suffered death and been raised by God (16:6–7). As at the time of his transfiguration, he stands before the disciples as the exalted Son of God, clothed in the eschatological glory that attends resurrection (9:3–7; 12:10–11; 16:6). But though he is the risen Son of God, he does not cease to be the Son of God who has been crucified (16:6; 15:39; 12:6–8, 10). Hence, in seeing the risen Son of God who is one with the crucified Son of God, the disciples are finally able to appropriate God's "evaluative point of view" concerning his identity (9:7) and to "think" about him aright, that is, as God "thinks" about him (8:33d). At last the disciples comprehend who Jesus has always been: the Son of God whom God sent to die on the cross and be raised to eschatological glory.[239]

The third thing the reader can project about the meeting in Galilee is that the disciples, in seeing the risen Jesus, also gain insight into themselves. In perceiving Jesus aright, the disciples likewise perceive themselves aright, which is to say that they grasp the meaning of true discipleship. The passages 8:34 and 10:43–44 capture well the essence of their new self-understanding: Jesus says, "If anyone desires to come after me, let him deny himself and take up his cross, and let him follow me"; "but whoever would be great among you must be your servant, and whoever would be first among you must be slave of all." Endowed with this new self-understanding, the disciples will henceforth move from the events surrounding the resurrection into the "world" Jesus predicted for them in his discourse of chapter 13.

The "Messiah" and "The Son" in Mark 13

In this discourse (chap. 13) Jesus "transports" the four disciples (13:3) and the reader through the vehicle of prophecy to a place in

---

239. Cf. Mark 1:10–11; 9:7; 8:31; 9:31; 10:32–34; 12:1–11; 15:39; 16:6.

time that lies beyond the resurrection and just short of the Parousia.[240] Temporarily, the reader enters a "future world" that is distinct from the "past world" of the earthly ministry of Jesus. Because the motif of the secret of Jesus' identity has the latter as its frame of reference, it does not extend to Jesus' discourse in chapter 13. Nonetheless, it is not irrelevant, particularly in preparation for our study of "the Son of Man" next chapter, to ask what the titles "Messiah" and "the Son," used in 13:21 and 13:32, connote.

The title "Messiah" in 13:21, construed as a reference to Jesus and not to some other figure, quite simply connotes the "Jesus of Mark's story." It is the Jesus who has preached, called disciples, taught, healed, and exorcized demons (1:14—8:26), who has journeyed to Jerusalem and suffered, died, and been raised (8:27—16:8), and whom his followers, in the time before the Parousia, await with eager anticipation (13:21). Significantly, 13:21 is one of only two passages in which *christos* ("Messiah," "Christ") is, of itself, adequate to describe Jesus. The other passage is 9:41, where it functions as a personal name ("because you are Christ's"). In both cases, the whole of Mark's story is what gives *christos* its definition, which suggests that, shy of this unique circumstance, the title is insufficient to describe Jesus. In other respects, that Mark can designate the Jesus who is awaited as "the Messiah" indicates that "the Son of Man" is not the exclusive term by which he refers to this Jesus.

"The Son" in 13:32 is Jesus' designation for himself. It appears only here, and this alone makes it unlikely in the extreme that Mark would have the reader regard it as introducing a "new christology." At the level of Mark's story, the only question is whether it functions as an alternate to "Son of God" or to "the Son of Man."

"The Son" is a variant form of "Son of God," as is evident from the manner in which it is used. The passage 13:32 stands in a line with such passages as 1:11; 9:7; and 12:6. In 1:11, God says to Jesus, in view of Jesus, "You are my beloved Son." In 9:7, God says to the three disciples, in view of Jesus, "This is my beloved Son." In 12:6, Jesus says to the Jewish leaders, in view of himself, that the owner of the vineyard, that is, God, "had yet one, a beloved son."

---

240. On the relationship of chapter 13 to the rest of Mark's story, cf. Petersen, "End," pp. 157–58, 164, 166.

Noteworthy about 12:6 is the fact that Jesus is, in referring to himself as the owner's "beloved son," employing the "phraseology"[241] God had used with respect to him at the baptism and transfiguration in order that he, in turn, might confront the Jewish leaders with God's "evaluative point of view" concerning his identity. "Phraseologically" and "evaluatively" ("ideologically"), therefore, Jesus is "speaking" and "thinking" about himself in 12:6 the way God "speaks" and "thinks" about him. The same can be said of Jesus' use of "the Son" in 13:32. For one thing, "the Son" is, terminologically, a variation of the expression "beloved Son," as is apparent from the fact that the latter means "only Son" or "unique Son." Also, it is in view of God that Jesus designates himself as "the Son." What these observations add up to is this: just as God, in view of Jesus, speaks of Jesus as "my beloved Son" (1:11; 9:7), so Jesus, in view of God, speaks of himself as "the Son." "Phraseologically" and "evaluatively," Jesus is "speaking" and "thinking" of himself in 13:32 the way God has "spoken" and "thought" of him at the baptism and transfiguration.

But if the titles "the Son" and "Son of God" evince "phraseological" and "evaluative" ("ideological") affinity in Mark, the same is not the case with regard to the titles "the Son" and "the Son of Man." Nowhere in Mark's story does God, in view of Jesus, ever say, "You are (he is) the Son of Man." And correlatively, never does Jesus, where he has specifically God in view, refer to himself as the Son of Man.[242] In Mark's story, "the Son" is, again, a variant form of the title "Son of God." In addition, because Mark applies this title, too, to the Jesus whom his followers await, it, like "Messiah" in 13:21, indicates that "the Son of Man" is not the only term by which Mark points to this Jesus.

Summary

Although this concludes my investigation of the third main part of Mark's story (8:27—16:8), I shall temporarily hold in abeyance a summary of the results. Instead of presenting such a summary, I shall

---

241. On the phraseological aspect of "point of view," cf. Uspensky, *Poetics of Composition*, pp. 17–32.

242. In Mark 8:38, Jesus refers to himself as the Son of Man, not in view of God, but in view of the "crowd" and the "disciples" (cf. 8:34).

consider briefly an important aspect of Mark's use of the major titles
he attributes to Jesus and the narrational and theological purpose the
motif of the secret of Jesus' identity serves. Then I shall combine a
summary of the third main part of Mark's story with a recapitulation
of the whole of the study I have conducted here in this chapter.

CHRISTOLOGY AND SECRECY:
SOME OBSERVATIONS

We have been probing the christology of Mark in consideration of
the motif of the secret of Jesus' identity. The question which has been
put to Mark is, "Who is Jesus?" And the answer which has been
obtained is categorical: he is the Davidic Messiah-King, the Son of
God. Mark's christology, then, is royal in character, and the major
titles it claims for Jesus are "Messiah," "Son of David," "King of
the Jews (Israel)," and "Son of God."

These titles, while they are related and to some extent overlap one
another in meaning, are by no means equivalent terms.[243] Mark draws
distinctions among them which the reader dare not ignore. Easily the
sharpest distinction is that which places the title of the "Son of God"
on a different level from that of the first three of these titles. Whereas
the first three titles constitute, positively or negatively, the "evaluative
point of view" concerning Jesus' identity of human characters only,
the title "Son of God" constitutes, positively or negatively, the
"evaluative point of view" concerning Jesus' identity of such transcendent beings as God and the demons as well as of such human
characters as Jesus, the high priest, the centurion, (and the disciples).
"Son of God" is thus the sole title in Mark's story to be expressly
applied to Jesus by transcendent beings.[244] When observed also from
this angle, therefore, this title can be seen to lie at the heart of the
motif of the secret of Jesus' identity and to dominate the story line of
Mark's Gospel.[245] In content, the distinctiveness of the title "Son of

243. Contrary, e.g., to the opinion of Räisänen, *Messiasgeheimnis*, pp. 105–6;
also Wrede, *Messiasgeheimnis*, pp. 76–77 (ET, *Messianic Secret*, pp. 76–77);
Pesch, *Markusevangelium*, II, 40–41.

244. Cf. Mark 1:11; 3:11; 9:7; also 1:23–24, 34; 5:7.

245. Cf. Mark 1:1, 11, 24, [34]; 3:11; 5:7; 9:7; 12:6; 14:61–62a; 15:39; [16:6];
also 13:32; 8:38 (cf. "his Father").

God'' lies in the fact that, in a way the other titles do not, it highlights the unique filial relationship that Jesus has to God and the soteriological implications associated with this.

But if "Son of God" is the critical term in Mark's motif of the secret of Jesus' identity, and if this motif is the principal vehicle by means of which Mark develops the christology of his story, the question arises as to the purpose this motif serves, both narrationally and theologically. Narrationally, the purpose of this motif is so to guide the action of the story that the way God "thinks" about Jesus, that is, the "evaluative point of view" he enunciates to Jesus in private at the baptismal scene (1:11) and to the three uncomprehending disciples atop the mountain of the transfiguration (9:7), should, despite repudiation on the part of Israel's establishment leading to the death of Jesus (12:12; 14:61–64), nonetheless be espoused at the end by human characters: explicitly by the centurion (15:39), and anticipatively by the disciples at their projected meeting with the resurrected Jesus in Galilee (16:6–7). The motif of the secret is thus a device for showing, in the telling of the story of Jesus, how "human thinking" about Jesus is, under God's direction, brought into alignment with "divine thinking" (cf. 8:33d).

Theologically, the purpose of this motif is to invite readers to appropriate for themselves that "thinking" about Jesus which places them "in alignment" with God's "thinking" about Jesus. This occurs when the readers, in "hearing" Mark's story of Jesus, are brought to the realization that Jesus of Nazareth is of decisive importance as far as their relationship to God is concerned. The reason Jesus is of decisive importance is that it is he whom God affirmed to be his only Son and empowered and chose for messianic ministry (1:1–13). As God's royal Son, Jesus authoritatively preached, called disciples, taught, and healed and exorcized demons (1:14—8:26). Also, in willing obedience he journeyed to Jerusalem, died on the cross and thus atoned for the sins of humankind, and was raised by God, so that he became the founder of the eschatological people of God (8:27—16:8). Should now the readers of Mark be brought to realize the decisive importance of Jesus Son of God, there opens for them the possibility of entering upon, or being confirmed in, a life that is "in alignment" with the will of God because it is "in alignment" with the life of Jesus himself: "If anyone desires to come

after me, let him deny himself and take up his cross, and let him
follow me" (8:34).

RECAPITULATION

It has been the goal of this chapter to explore the christology of
Mark, but to do so in keeping with the way in which Mark develops
the motif of the secret of Jesus' identity. This motif spans the narrated
portion of Mark's story, though not chapter 13, and extends from the
baptism (1:11) on the one hand to the crucifixion (15:39) and resurrection (9:9; 16:6–7) on the other. In fullest measure, Mark identifies
Jesus as the Davidic Messiah-King, the royal Son of God, but he
binds the secret of Jesus' identity more narrowly to the truth of his
divine sonship. Indeed, "Son of God" is the only title in Mark's story
which transcendent beings and human characters alike apply to Jesus.
This is an eloquent attestation to the paramount importance of this title
for Mark's story.

"Jesus," of course, is the personal name of the protagonist of
Mark's story. Of all the characteristics that Mark ascribes to Jesus,
the one that identifies him most typically is "Jesus the Nazarene (of
Nazareth)."[246] By highlighting this characteristic both at the beginning
and at the end of his story (1:9; 16:6), Mark stresses that it is precisely
Jesus, the man from Nazareth of Galilee (1:9), who is affirmed by
God to be his royal Son and chosen for messianic ministry that culminates in his death on the cross and his being raised by God to life
(16:6).

Mark prepares the reader to enter the world of his story through the
use of frame material. Thus, he begins with a caption-summary in
which he, as narrator, informs the reader of his own understanding of
Jesus, that is, of his own "evaluative point of view" concerning his
identity: Jesus (the) Messiah is the Son of God (1:1). Because Mark
honors the reader's trust that he is a reliable narrator, the reader can
rest assured that this understanding of Jesus is "correct" and that it
is the one Mark will elaborate through the medium of his story.

Mark follows his caption-summary with an epigraph, which in this
case is a massive, composite quotation from the OT (1:2–3). In the

---

246. Cf. Mark 1:24; 10:47; 14:67; 16:6; also 1:9.

first half, God ("Behold, *I* send") is depicted as speaking in direct address to Jesus ("before you") about John ("my messenger") (1:2). These references to John and to Jesus can stand as ciphers for their ministries and hence for the substance of Mark's story to follow. Through this OT quotation, Mark presents God as designating himself as the sole initiator and director of the action that will comprise the story Mark has to tell. But if Mark sees in God the supreme arbiter of purpose and meaning, then Mark establishes God's "will," his "evaluative point of view," as normative for his story, and he calls on the reader to regard his own "evaluative point of view" as narrator as being in alignment with that of God. What this means christologically is that it is God's understanding of Jesus which will prove itself to be normative in Mark's story and that Mark will be concerned to show the reader that his own understanding of Jesus is in full accord with that of God. In other respects, since this OT quotation posits God as the "source" of the ministries of John and of Jesus, it characterizes the latter as his agents. Furthermore, with the coming of John and of Jesus, the "time of prophecy" is over and the time of eschatological fulfillment, which is the "time of the gospel," has come (1:1, 14–15). And since God "speaks" to Jesus about John, and John is but the one who precedes Jesus (1:2), it is the ministry of Jesus that will occupy Mark as he narrates his story.

Mark begins his narrative proper by telling of the ministry of John the Baptizer (1:4–8). Appearing in the desert, John proclaims a baptism of repentance for the forgiveness of sins (1:4). As Elijah redivivus, the forerunner, John thus "restores all things" and readies Israel for Jesus, the mightier one, whose "coming" he prophesies (1:5–8; 9:11–13).

Mark introduces the reader to Jesus himself by describing the events surrounding his baptism and temptation (1:9–13). In fulfillment of John's prophecy, Jesus at once "comes" from Nazareth and submits to baptism by John (1:9). In going up from the water, Jesus removes himself from John and, standing before God in private encounter, he becomes the recipient of two revelatory events. In the first event, which is visual, God empowers Jesus with the Spirit and consequently endows him with divine authority (1:10). In the second event, which is auditory, God addresses Jesus in the words of OT scripture and solemnly affirms that he (the Anointed One [Messiah] from the line of David) is his only, or unique, Son whom he has chosen for eschatological ministry (1:11). It is in thus highlighting the unique filial relationship which Jesus has to God that the title Son of God stands out as the central term in Mark's christology. With this solemn affirmation of 1:11, the reader has reached the culmination of the first main part of Mark's story (1:1–13) and a crucial point in the development of the motif of the secret of Jesus' identity. God himself has entered the world of Mark's story as "actor," and the reader has heard directly from him how he "thinks" about Jesus, that is, what his "evaluative point of view" concerning Jesus' identity is. Since Mark has already indicated in his epigraph that God's evaluative point of view is normative for his story (1:2), and since the reader can also observe that Mark's own narrational understanding of Jesus in 1:1 is in accord with that expressed by God in 1:11, the reader knows that he has, in the understanding of Jesus God has affirmed in 1:11, the standard against which he is to measure all other estimates of Jesus in Mark's story.

Whereas the baptismal pericope focuses on who Jesus is, the temptation focuses on what he is about (1:12–13). Led by the Spirit into the desert, the abode of Satan, Jesus, the royal Son of God, is put to the test for forty days. Sustained by angels, he withstands Satan's assault, which would have alienated him from God, and "binds" the "strong man" (3:27). In so doing, he breaks the rule of Satan and inaugurates the eschatological age of salvation.

Accordingly, Mark employs the climactic pericopes of the first main part of his story (1:9–13) to present Jesus to the reader as the royal Son of God who inaugurates the eschatological age of salvation. Nonetheless, while the reader and such transcendent beings as God (1:11) and Satan (1:12–13) know that Jesus is God's royal Son, the human characters in Mark's story, such as the Jewish people (1:5) and John as well, do not. Indeed, it belongs to the peculiar nature of Mark's story that the reader, assuming the posture of the silent observer, now looks on as Mark guides him through the events of the second and third main parts of his story in order to show him how it comes about that a human character will eventually acclaim Jesus in a manner which reveals that his "evaluative point of view" concerning Jesus' identity is in alignment with that of God and that he therefore "thinks" about Jesus as God "thinks" about him (1:11; 15:39; 8:33d).

Mark devotes the second main part of his story to the ministry of Jesus in and around Galilee (1:14—8:26). As the summary-passages indicate, Jesus embarks on an itinerant ministry throughout Galilee and beyond in which he preaches the gospel of God (1:14–15), calls disciples to follow him (1:16–20), teaches with incomparable authority (1:21–22), and heals the sick and exorcizes demons (1:32–34). Typically, the impact he has on those who hear him or witness his deeds is one of astonishment (1:22; 2:12; 6:2). The result is that his fame spreads far and wide (1:28; 3:8), people stream to him from all parts of Palestine and outlying regions (3:7–8), and the crowd gathers wherever he happens to be (1:45; 2:13; 6:53–56). Concomitantly, the spectacular nature of his activity also stirs people to ask themselves about his identity.

Mark treats the theme of Jesus' identity in 1:14—8:26 by fashioning a "contrapuntal pattern" according to which demonic shouts that Jesus is the Son of God alternate with questions human characters pose about who Jesus could conceivably be.[247] On the one hand, the demons, as transcendent beings, know the secret of Jesus' identity (1:34). Although their shouts are suppressed or uttered in private confrontation so that human ears remain untouched by them (1:25, 34; 3:12; 5:7), they nonetheless cry aloud that Jesus is the Son of God (1:24; 3:11; 5:7). Because their "evaluative point of view" concerning Jesus' identity is in accord with that of God (1:11, 34), the rhetorical effect of their intermittent shouts is constantly to remind the reader of who Jesus is.

On the other hand, alternating with these demonic shouts are the questions human characters pose as to who Jesus might be. In the synagogue at Capernaum, the people, astounded at the exorcism Jesus has just performed, inquire after his identity by querying one another about his powerful act: "What is this?" they exclaim, "A new teaching with authority?" (1:27). In the house in Capernaum, some of the scribes, provoked by the fact that Jesus should dare to forgive a paralytic his sins, reason in their hearts, "Why does this man speak thus? He blasphemes! Who can forgive sins but God alone?" (2:7). Caught in a storm on the sea, the disciples, having witnessed Jesus calm wind and wave, ask one another, "Who then is this, that even wind and

---

247. Cf. Mark 1:24, 27, 34; 2:7; 3:11; 4:41; 5:7; 6:3.

sea obey him?" (4:41, RSV). And in the synagogue at Nazareth, the villagers, amazed at the wisdom with which Jesus teaches and the reports they have heard about the wondrous deeds he has performed, ask among themselves, "Is not this the carpenter, the son of Mary?" (6:3).

Despite their diverse nature, the underlying sense of these various questions is the same. To begin with, they are posed by groups of characters who either constitute, or are representative of, the principal characters in Mark's story: the Jewish people (1:27), the Jewish authorities (2:7), the disciples (4:41), and the family, relatives, and acquaintances of Jesus (6:3). But however that may be, the spirit in which they are asked is, respectively, one of amazement born of incomprehension (1:27), of utter disapprobation (2:7), of fear springing from cowardice and lack of faith (4:40–41), and of repudiation rooted in unbelief (6:3, 6). In short, these questions are all symptomatic of "ignorance," of the inability to understand who Jesus is. On balance, therefore, the purpose of the contrapuntal pattern Mark has fashioned in 1:14—8:26 is to juxtapose demonic "knowledge" and human "ignorance": the reader, hearing the cries of the demons alternating with the questions of the human characters, is continually being reminded that Jesus is the Son of God even as he observes the Jewish people, the Jewish authorities, the disciples, and the family, relatives, and acquaintances of Jesus wonder uncomprehendingly who he is.

Reflective of the ignorance that beclouds the human characters in 1:14—8:26 are the "evaluative points of view" regarding Jesus' identity held by Herod and the Jewish public. Some, including Herod, take Jesus to be John the Baptizer raised from the dead; others take him to be Elijah; and still others take him to be a prophet (6:14–16). The reason the reader knows that these judgments are all false is that they are incongruous with the "normative" understanding of Jesus which governs Mark's story. As God himself has asseverated (1:11), as the "reliable narrator" Mark has stated (1:1), and as the demons, who "know Jesus," have repeatedly said (1:24, 34; 3:11; 5:7), Jesus is the royal Son of God. Then, too, because Mark makes "John the Baptizer" out to be a "prophet" (11:32) and, indeed, "Elijah" redivivus (1:6; 9:11–13), the ironic thing about these popular opinions is that they constitute gross confusion about both John and Jesus, the two agents whom God has sent to Israel (1:2).

In the third main part of his story (8:27—16:8), Mark tells of Jesus' journey to Jerusalem and of his suffering, death, and resurrection. Here it is the passion-predictions that describe the flow of events (8:31; 9:31; 10:33–34; cf. 11:18). As for the secret of Jesus' identity, Mark demonstrably alters the way in which he deals with this motif. Thus far, the human characters have not of themselves broached the question of Jesus' identity. Instead, it has been a powerful word or deed of Jesus or his fame that has prompted them to wonder who he is. Only the demons are privy to the mystery of his person. But in 8:27—16:8, a different pattern emerges. Demons no longer shout aloud Jesus' identity. Instead, human characters address this issue directly, and not all are without insight. Overall, in fact, Mark depicts, though only from the standpoint of the reader of his story, a progressive disclosure of Jesus' identity in three "stages." As the reader watches, Mark leads him through a series of scenes in which Peter confesses Jesus to be the Messiah (8:29), Bartimaeus appeals to him as the Son of David (10:47–48), and the Roman centurion declares him to be the Son of God (15:39). In addition, the disciples receive the promise that they will see Jesus in Galilee following his resurrection (14:28; 16:6–7). Still, because Mark firmly associates the secret of Jesus' identity with his divine sonship, it is neither with Peter's confession nor with Bartimaeus's appeal but solely with the centurion's declaration that the secret is at last penetrated.

The first stage, then, to which the reader is witness in the progressive disclosure of Jesus' identity is the "evaluative point of view" expressed by Peter on behalf of himself and the other disciples according to which Jesus is the Messiah (8:29). This confession Peter makes is "correct" and not "false," as is evident from several considerations. For one thing, it squares, as far as it goes, with Mark's own understanding of Jesus (cf. 8:29 to 1:1). For another thing, Jesus himself elicits it from the disciples (8:29). Third, Jesus suppresses it (8:30), a phenomenon that occurs, where it is a matter of his identity, only in relation to correct views of him (1:24–25, 34; 3:11–12; 8:29–30; 9:9). And fourth, the purpose this confession serves, situated as it is at the head of the third main part of Mark's story, is to draw the balance on the way in which Peter and the disciples, in contradistinction to the Jewish public, have come to view Jesus thus far in his ministry, that is, throughout 1:14—8:26: whereas the Jewish public wrongly imagines Jesus to be John the Baptist or Elijah or one of the prophets (cf. 8:27c–28 to 6:14–16), Peter and the disciples rightly understand him to be the Messiah (8:29), which is to say that they regard him as the one who, as God's Anointed, preaches, calls disciples, teaches, and heals and exorcizes demons.

But correct though it is, Peter's confession is also "insufficient." In what it connotes, it does full justice to neither the identity nor the destiny of Jesus. The insufficiency of Peter's confession relative to the destiny of Jesus is that it does not envisage his passion. In 8:31, Jesus teaches the disciples what for them is a "new word," telling them that he will be rejected by the Jewish leaders and be killed. Peter and the disciples repudiate this new word (8:32–33). Hence, while "Messiah" in 8:29 correctly describes Jesus in terms of his ministry in 1:14—8:26 as preacher, gatherer of disciples, teacher, and healer and exorcist, the notion of suffering lies beyond its purview.

The insufficiency of Peter's confession relative to the identity of Jesus is exemplified by the circumstance that it does not measure up to God's "evaluative point of view" concerning Jesus' identity. On the mountain of the transfiguration, God causes Jesus to be transfigured before Peter and James and John and also announces to them how he "thinks" about Jesus, namely, as his beloved Son (9:2–7). But Peter and the other two do not comprehend this revelation (9:5–6), and once the event of the transfiguration is over, Jesus enjoins them to silence about it (9:9). Nor would Mark have it otherwise in his scheme of things. For the disciples to be able to "think" about Jesus as God "thinks" about him they must, to be sure, see him as preacher, teacher, healer, and exorcist (1:14—8:26; 8:29) but, beyond this, they must also see him as the one who obediently submits to crucifixion and whom God raises to glory (9:9; 12:6–11; 14:27–28; 15:39; 16:6–7). Destiny and identity are inextricably bound together. Peter's confession at 8:29, therefore, does not constitute a "break" in the secret of Jesus' identity. On the contrary, it will only be at the projected meeting in Galilee with the risen Jesus, who remains the crucified one, that the disciples will be able to manage what escapes them prior to this time: to "think" about Jesus as the Son of God, as God "thinks" about him (1:11; 9:7, 9; 12:6–8; 14:27–28; 16:6–7; 8:33d).

With the pericope on the healing of Bartimaeus (10:46–52), the reader arrives at the second stage in Mark's progressive disclosure in 8:27—16:8 of the identity of Jesus. Bartimaeus, a blind beggar, cries out in great faith to Jesus as the Son of David to have mercy on him, that is, to grant him the gift of his sight, and Jesus accedes to his request and heals him. "Son of David" thus constitutes Bartimaeus's "evaluative point of view" regarding Jesus' identity, and in granting Bartimaeus his request of faith, Jesus in effect sanctions his evaluative point of view. This is Mark's narrative way of affirming that Jesus is in truth the Son of David.

Mark makes two points relative to the Davidic sonship of Jesus. In that it is "Jesus the Nazarene" whom Bartimaeus designates as the "Son of David" (10:47), Mark lays claim to Davidic lineage for Jesus, the man who is from Nazareth. And in that Jesus heals Bartimaeus, Mark shows that Jesus Son of David is not, say, a warrior king, but one who wields his royal authority in order to have mercy on an afflicted man such as Bartimaeus, to heal and in this manner to "save" (10:47–48, 51–52). It is in this "unexpected" fashion that Jesus fulfills the eschatological expectations associated with David.

The pericope on the triumphal entry (11:1–10) follows that on the healing of Bartimaeus. Publicly identified by Bartimaeus as the Son of David, Jesus approaches Jerusalem under the auspices of this title. Indeed, the entire narrative on the triumphal entry is replete with messianic allusions that Mark associates with Jesus as Davidic. Chief of these perhaps is the antiphonal acclamation of those who accompany Jesus. In this acclamation, Jesus is hailed with shouts to God that assume the form of a petition for salvation ("Hosanna") and is praised as the one who comes on the authority of God and is therefore the bearer of "the Kingdom of our father David" (11:9–10). Although Jesus is not explicitly named the Son of David in this pericope, he is undubitably being so presented.

But like "Messiah" in 8:29, "Son of David," though a "correct" title for Jesus, is also "insufficient." Mark makes this clear in the pericope on the question about David's son (12:35–37). No longer in debate with the Jewish leaders (12:34e), Jesus remains in the temple but begins teaching the crowd (12:35, 37c). He poses a problem of antinomy by setting forth two views about the Messiah which, while ostensibly contradictory, are in reality harmonious if related to each other in the proper way. The problem Jesus poses is this: How is it possible for the Messiah to be both the "son" of David and the "lord" of David? And the answer to this problem, which is anticipated but not explicitly stated, is this: the Messiah is the "son" of David because he is descended from David; by the same token, the Messiah is also the "lord" of David because he is the Son of God and, as such, is of higher station and authority than David. In Mark's logic, therefore, Jesus can "correctly" be called the Son of David (10:47–48; 12:35), and yet he is also "more" than this, for he is the Son of God (12:37). Proof of this is the fact that it is not, strictly speaking, as Son of David but as Son of God that Jesus dies and is raised, and it is not as Son of David but as Son of God that God "thinks" about Jesus (1:11; 9:7; 12:6). "Correct" as Bartimaeus's evaluative point of view concerning Jesus' identity is, it is "insufficient" when compared with God's evaluative point of view. And because Mark binds the secret of Jesus' identity to God's evaluative point of view, Bartimaeus's public appeal to Jesus as the Son of David does not "break" this secret.

It is not until the centurion declares at the foot of the cross that Jesus truly was the Son of God (15:39) that the reader finally reaches the third stage in the progressive disclosure of Jesus' identity in 8:27—16:8. Nevertheless, Mark skillfully develops his story prior to this declaration so as to set the stage for it. One pericope that stands in a direct line with this declaration is Jesus' parable of the wicked husbandmen (12:1–12). Addressing the chief priests and the scribes and the elders (12:1; 11:27), Jesus sketches in this parable God's dealings with Israel in the history of salvation. He portrays himself as the "beloved son" whom the owner of the vineyard calls "my son" and whom the wicked tenant-farmers kill (12:6–8). Quoting from scripture, Jesus furthermore predicts that this "stone-son" whom the "builders" reject God will place "at the head of the corner," that is, vindicate through the wondrous act of the resurrection (12:10–11). In reaction to Jesus' parable, the Jewish leaders want to arrest him (12:12). They understand that he has made himself out to be God's Son and themselves the murderous tenant-farmers (12:12c), and they repudiate these identifications. In so doing, they are likewise repudiating the truth-claim that Jesus' parable makes upon them. Because Jesus has characterized himself as the "beloved son" and has depicted the owner of the vineyard as designating him as "my son," he has imbued his parable with the evaluative point of view concerning himself which God had enunciated at both the baptism (1:11) and the transfiguration (9:7). Hence, in repudiating the truth-claim of Jesus' parable, the Jewish leaders are unwittingly repudiating God's evaluative point of view concerning Jesus' identity. Although they have grasped Jesus' parable intellectually, they have in no wise penetrated the secret of Jesus' identity, for they will not, and cannot, accept the notion that Jesus is the Son of God.

The parable of the wicked husbandmen points ahead to the pericope on the trial of Jesus before the Sanhedrin (14:53–65). At his trial, Jesus again faces the same three groups of Jewish leaders to whom he had delivered his parable (14:53, 55; 11:27; 12:1). As the spokesman for the Sanhedrin and these three groups, the high priest is privy to the claim to be the beloved Son of God which Jesus had advanced in allegorical form in his parable (12:6). When, therefore, the high priest asks Jesus, "Are you the Messiah, the Son of the Blessed [God]?" (14:61), he is at once reformulating Jesus' claim in non-allegorical terms and aiming to turn it against him in order to destroy him. Moreover, from his own standpoint the high priest succeeds, for Jesus' reply to his question is unequivocally affirmative ("I am!"; 14:62a). In consequence of Jesus' reply, the high priest and the Sanhedrin condemn him to death for blasphemy (14:63–64). And therein lies the irony of Jesus' trial, in regard to both Jesus and the Sanhedrin. In the case of Jesus, the irony is that although he is made to die for committing blasphemy against God, his "crime" has been to dare to "think" about himself as God had revealed, at his baptism and transfiguration, that he does in truth "think" about him (1:11; 9:7; 12:6; 8:33d). In the case of the high priest and the Sanhedrin, the irony is that in condemning Jesus to death for blaspheming God, they are alleging that they know the "thinking," of God; yet even while alleging knowledge of God's "thinking" they are effectively repudiating it. And in other respects, because the high priest and the Sanhedrin construe as "blasphemy" Jesus' affirmation that he is the Son of God, they reveal that they do not comprehend the secret of Jesus' identity but are "ignorant" of it. At Jesus' trial, therefore, there is, once again, no "break" in the secret of Jesus' identity.

If the Jewish Sanhedrin condemns Jesus to death for daring to claim to be the Son of God (14:61–64), the Roman centurion declares, upon seeing Jesus die, that he truly was the Son of God (15:39). Between these two passages that focus on the divine sonship of Jesus is a block of material in which Jesus is in the custody of Pilate and the Romans and is uniformly designated as the "King of the Jews [Israel]" (15:2, 9, 12, 18, 26, 32). As expressive of "evaluative point of view," this designation possesses two or even three meanings.

In 15:2–3, Mark fashions a scene in which (a) Pilate asks Jesus,

"Are you the King of the Jews?" and (b) Jesus replies, "(So) you say," and (c) the chief priests respond to Jesus' answer by accusing him of many things. What this scene reveals is that, although Jesus' reply to Pilate is one of reserve, all three parties nonetheless understand it to be affirmative.

As 15:26 suggests, in Pilate's eyes the term "King of the Jews" marks Jesus as an insurrectionist who aspires to political rule over the Jews. Still, the irony of Pilate's use of this term is that he shows in some five different ways that he gives no credence whatever to the notion that Jesus is in fact the King of the Jews, that is, an insurrectionist (cf. 15:2–15). At 15:32, the chief priests, together with the scribes, mock Jesus as "the Messiah, the King of Israel." From their vantage point, "King of Israel" seems to characterize Jesus as the one God has at last raised up and anointed to rule over his people Israel, a view they reject out of hand, as their scoffing indicates. In contradistinction to both Pilate and the chief priests, Jesus accepts as true the imputation to him of the title "King of the Jews [Israel]" (15:2). In what sense it is true Mark explains in 15:16–20b and 15:31–32: Jesus is indeed "King of the Jews (Israel)," but neither as one who foments rebellion against Rome nor as one who will restore to Israel its national splendor, but as one who, ironically, exercises his regal authority by submitting, in obedience to the will of God, to the mockery of his enemies and the death to which this leads (14:35–36; 15:25–26).

At the moment of Jesus' death upon the cross, Mark suddenly reverts to his use of the title "Son of God." His immediate purpose in doing so is to correlate the event of Jesus' death with that of his trial (cf. 14:61–62a). The centurion's acclamation, "Truly this man was the Son of God!" (15:39, RSV), ranks with God's announcements at the baptism (1:11) and the transfiguration (9:7) as one of the key christological statements of Mark's story.

The centurion's acclamation is embedded in the section 15:37–39. Uttering a second, wordless cry, Jesus expires. Upon his death, two events occur. In the one event, God reacts to Jesus' death by causing the curtain of the temple to be split in two (15:38). This presages the destruction of the temple (14:58; 15:29) and with it the cessation of the temple cult. In Marcan thought, this is God's will, for in his death Jesus has made final atonement for the sins of humankind (14:24; 10:45).

The second event is the acclamation of the centurion itself (15:39). What prompts it is the manner in which the centurion sees Jesus die (15:39a). More immediately, therefore, it is the final act of Jesus' dying that prompts his acclamation (15:37); more broadly, it is the several acts leading up to Jesus' death (15:29–32, 33–36). From the standpoint of the centurion alone, his words constitute the declaration of a "converted man." From the standpoint of the reader, they are replete with meaning beyond his own comprehension.

Thus, the exclamation that Jesus "truly" was the Son of God vindicates the claim Jesus made to this effect at his trial and refutes the contention of the Jewish Sanhedrin that this claim was blasphemous (14:61–64). Also, the centurion's use of the verb "was" underlines the circumstance that Jesus has, in his death on the cross, reached the end of his ministry. The end of Jesus' ministry, however, is at the same time its culmination, for in his death Jesus has at once atoned for sins and become the "builder" (14:58; 15:29) of the new community that is God's eschatological people (8:34; 10:29–30; 16:7).

But the peculiar importance of the centurion's words likewise resides in the fact that they close out the motif of the secret of Jesus' identity in Mark's story. For the first time, Mark allows a human character other than Jesus himself to adopt unreservedly God's "evaluative point of view" and to "think" about Jesus the way God "thinks" about him (1:11; 9:7; 12:6; 15:39; 8:33d). The result is that the centurion becomes the first human being to penetrate the secret of Jesus' identity and to comprehend aright that he is (was) the Son of God.

Mark devotes only one verse of his story to what may be termed the event of the resurrection (16:6). The terminology of this verse, however, is such as to impel the reader to infer that Mark would have him regard the Jesus God raises as also being the Son of God. Thus, the risen Jesus is "Jesus the Nazarene." Through the vehicle of this expression, Mark creates an "inclusion" that permits him to gather up his entire story and to indicate to the reader that the Jesus whom God has raised from the dead is no other Jesus than the one with whom he began his story, namely, the Jesus who is God's beloved Son (1:9, 11; 16:6). Again, the risen Jesus is "the one who has been crucified and remains the crucified one" *(ton estaurōmenon)*. By having Jesus so characterized, Mark deftly informs the reader that the crucified Jesus, who is said upon his death to have been the Son of

God (15:39), has been raised and so "is" the Son of God. And third, of the risen Jesus the young man announces that "he has been raised" (= "God has raised him"). By means of this announcement, Mark documents the fulfillment of OT prophecy and once more alludes to Jesus as being the Son of God: the resurrection is the act whereby God has vindicated the "rejected stone—his beloved Son" (12:10–11).

The young man in white next speaks of the disciples (16:7). The word they are to receive is that Jesus precedes them to Galilee, where they will see him. Because this word of the young man is based on a previous word of Jesus (14:28), and because Mark is careful in his story to show that Jesus' predictions come to pass, the attitude the reader is invited to take is that of assuming that this prediction, too, has its fulfillment. The question, then, becomes: What is the reader, given Mark's story, to project as taking place at this meeting of Jesus with his disciples in Galilee?

Apparently, three things. The first thing the reader can project is that the risen Jesus reconciles the disciples to himself and gathers the flock that, owing to his arrest and death, has been scattered. The second thing the reader can project is that the disciples penetrate the secret of Jesus' identity. In seeing the risen Jesus as being one with the crucified Jesus, the disciples are able at last to "think" about Jesus aright, that is, to "think" about him as God revealed to the three disciples atop the mountain of the transfiguration that he "thinks" about him, namely, as his royal Son (sent to die, to be raised and so vindicated, and to create for God a people living in the sphere of his eschatological Rule). And the third thing the reader can project is that the disciples also gain insight into themselves. In finally perceiving Jesus aright, the disciples likewise perceive themselves aright, which is to say that they grasp the meaning of true discipleship (8:34; 10:43–44). Endowed with this new self-understanding, the disciples will henceforth move from the events surrounding the resurrection into the "world" Jesus predicted for them in his discourse of chapter 13.

The lifting of the secret of Jesus' identity in the events surrounding his death and resurrection poses the question of the purpose of this motif, both narrationally and theologically. Narrationally, the purpose of this motif is so to guide the action of the story that the way God "thinks" about Jesus, that is, the "evaluative point of view" he enunciates to Jesus alone at the baptismal scene (1:11) and to the three uncomprehending disciples atop the mountain of the transfiguration (9:7), should, despite repudiation on the part of Israel's establishment leading to the death of Jesus (12:12; 14:61–64), nonetheless be espoused at the end by human characters: explicitly by the centurion (15:39), and anticipatively by the disciples at their projected meeting with the resurrected Jesus in Galilee (16:6–7). The motif of the secret is thus a device for showing, in the telling of the story of Jesus, how "human thinking" about Jesus is, under God's direction, brought into alignment with "divine thinking" (cf. 8:33d).

Theologically, the purpose of this motif is to invite readers to appropriate for themselves that "thinking" about Jesus which places them "in alignment" with God's "thinking" about Jesus. This takes place when the readers, through the "hearing" of Mark's story, are led to perceive that Jesus of Nazareth is of ultimate significance as far as their relationship to God is concerned. Jesus is so because he is God's Son through whom God proffers salvation and life in the sphere of his eschatological Rule. Should now the readers of Mark's story be brought to the perception of this ultimate significance of Jesus, they have presented them the possibility of entering upon, or being confirmed in, a life that is "in alignment" with the will of God because it is "in alignment" with the life of Jesus himself: "If anyone would come after me, let him deny himself and take up his cross, and let him follow me" (8:34).

In the prophetic-apocalyptic discourse of chapter 13, Mark has Jesus transport the four disciples (13:3) and the reader to a time in the history of salvation that lies beyond the resurrection and leads up to the Parousia. In telling of this future time, Jesus designates himself, as the one his followers fervently await, as the "Messiah" in one instance (13:21) and as "the Son" in another (13:32). Through such references, Mark encourages the reader to conceive of the Jesus who is awaited as the Messiah Son of God (cf. 1:1). At the same time, Mark also has Jesus refer to himself as the one to be awaited as "the Son of Man" (8:38; 13:26; 14:62). Accordingly, I can pursue the discussion of Mark's christology no further without addressing the issue of the use Mark makes of the title "the Son of Man." This is the subject matter of the final chapter.

4   THE CHRISTOLOGY OF MARK

The Son of Man

In Chapter 2, I noted that during the last quarter century the dominant method by means of which scholars have dealt with the christology of Mark, certainly in North America, has been in terms of the "corrective approach." Fundamental to this approach as generally applied is the belief that, for Mark, the title "Son of God" (and "Messiah" as well) is defective, erroneous, or ambiguous and therefore stands in need of correction. The problem with "Son of God," it is usually alleged, is that it casts Jesus in the mold of a divine man of glory who has no truck with suffering and death. To correct this title, Mark employs his theology of the cross and, what is of particular interest here, the title of "the Son of Man."[1] On this view, then, "the Son of Man" becomes the preeminent title for Jesus in Mark's Gospel, for it is the one title that requires no correction. Proof of its preeminence is the fact that Mark places it on the lips exclusively of Jesus, so that it constitutes his own self-understanding. In a word, therefore, "the Son of Man" is the title for Jesus in Mark's story which is "normative," for it "reinterprets" the other titles to depict Jesus as one whose divinely ordained fate is suffering and death (and vindication).

A major reason I contest the viability of the corrective approach is that it not only does not take into account, but indeed runs counter to, a factor that is pivotal to a proper grasp of the christology of Mark, namely, the "evaluative point of view" of God regarding the identity of Jesus. Mark, as implied author and reliable narrator, has imbued his story with his own "evaluative point of view." In addition, Mark

---

1. For a survey of the various ways in which the title "the Son of Man" is seen to "correct" the titles "Son of God" or "Messiah," cf., e.g., Keck, "Mark's Christology," pp. 354, 357; Weeden, *Mark*, pp. 64–69, 65 n. 20; Perrin, "Christology of Mark," pp. 110–21; Donahue, *Christ*, pp. 180–85; Achtemeier, *Mark*, pp. 41–47; Petersen, *Literary Criticism for New Testament Critics*, pp. 63, 67–68, 72, 75.

has also brought his own evaluative point of view into alignment with that of Jesus. But beyond this Mark has furthermore, and this is the crucial matter, brought his own evaluative point of view and that of Jesus into alignment with that of God. Accordingly, by authorial choice Mark establishes neither his own evaluative point of view nor even that of Jesus as "normative" for his story, but the evaluative point of view of God. In principle, therefore, the normative christological title for explaining who Jesus is in Mark's story will not, strictly speaking, be one that Mark grounds on his own authority as narrator and not even one that Jesus may apply to himself, but one that God attributes to Jesus. But if this is in fact the case, then two further conclusions follow. Should the normative title for Jesus in Mark's story be one that God gives him, it is this title that becomes determinative of Jesus' identity, and the circumstance that the title of "the Son of Man" occurs exclusively on the lips of Jesus ceases to be of telling force as far as assessing its importance is concerned. And second, should God affirm Jesus in Mark's story to be his Son, which of course he does, the exegete errs if he devalues or deflates the significance of this title by describing it as being defective, erroneous, or ambiguous in meaning. The reader can, to be sure, anticipate that Mark will utilize the flow of his story to elaborate the meaning of the title Son of God, but this is a different matter altogether from claiming that Mark intends with his story to "correct," "reinterpret," or "give [new] conceptual content to" the title Son of God.

In the baptismal account, Mark portrays God as entering the realm of his story as "actor" to affirm the identity of Jesus in private encounter with him. In uttering the words of Psalm 2, God implicitly describes Jesus as the Davidic Messiah-King, his beloved Son (cf. LXX Ps. 2:2, 6–7; also Mark 1:1). Explicitly, however, God declares Jesus to be "my beloved Son" (1:11). In narrating his story, Mark gradually reveals to the reader in what sense the fuller designation is true, but by the same token he binds the secret of Jesus' identity more narrowly to the insight that he is the Son of God. The upshot is that it is not until the centurion, at the foot of the cross, acclaims Jesus to be the "Son of God" (15:39) and the disciples "see" in the risen Son of God the crucified Son of God (16:6–7; 14:27–28; 9:7, 9) that Mark brings to its culmination and end the motif of the secret of Jesus' identity. Still, what Mark accomplishes by preserving this motif intact from the baptism of Jesus to his crucifixion and resurrection is that he guides the reader to the realization that human beings cannot "think" about Jesus of Nazareth the way God "thinks" about him, namely, as being God's royal Son (1:11; 9:7, 9; 15:39), until they perceive all of the following to be true of him: that God empowered him with the Spirit, named him Son, and chose him for messianic ministry (1:1–13); that he authoritatively preached, called disciples, taught, and healed and exorcized demons (1:14—8:26); and that he journeyed to Jerusalem, suffered, died and atoned for sins, was raised (8:27—16:8), and hence is the "creator" of God's eschatological people (10:29–30; 15:29; 16:7), the one with whom the reader is summoned to "align" himself (8:34). But if the title of the Son of God, lying as it does at the heart of the motif of the secret of Jesus' identity, conveys most adequately the understanding of Jesus that controls Mark's story because it constitutes God's understanding of Jesus mediated at last to human beings, what is one to make of the designation of "the Son of Man"?

"THE SON OF MAN" IN RELATION TO THE OTHER MAJOR TITLES

One of the most striking features of the title "the Son of Man" is that it stands apart, and thus is different in nature, from the other major titles ("Messiah," "Son of David," "King of the Jews [Israel]," and "Son of God"). Unlike the latter, "the Son of Man" does not function "confessionally" to specify "who Jesus is." Implausible as this statement may seem at first blush, the evidence to support it is undeniable.

Consider, for example, the way in which Mark works with the two personal names he ascribes to Jesus, "Jesus" and "Christ" ("Messiah"). Of interest is the fact that Mark closely associates these names at points in his narrative with christological titles, in this manner apprising the reader of the identity of Jesus. To take first the name "Jesus," Mark himself, as narrator, couples it with "Christ" in the caption-summary of his Gospel not only to form the name "Jesus Christ" but also to advise the reader that "Jesus [is] Christ (Messiah)" (1:1). Again, three times Mark places "Jesus" in the vocative case, so that for some human characters it becomes a means of address.

Once it is blind Bartimaeus who calls out the name "Jesus": "And when he heard that it was Jesus of Nazareth, he began to cry out and say, 'Son of David, Jesus, have mercy on me!' " (10:47). Rhetorically, the force of these words is to let the reader know that Jesus, the man from Nazareth, is the Son of David. On two occasions, it is men who are demoniacs who utter the name "Jesus": "What have you to do with us, Jesus of Nazareth?" shouts the one man, "I know who you are, the Holy One of God!" (1:24); and the second man exclaims, "What have you to do with me, Jesus, Son of the Most High God?" (5:7, RSV). Now demoniacs, the mouthpiece of demons, do indeed, as Mark insists in a "reliable" comment, "know" who Jesus is (1:34). Consequently, even if the function of these cries is to picture the demons as "naming" Jesus in order thereby to attempt to gain power over him and ward off destruction, they nonetheless serve, concomitantly, to inform the reader that Jesus, the man from Nazareth, is the Son of God. In other respects, the only major title with which the name "Jesus" is not conjoined is "King of the Jews (Israel)." Even here, however, the title "the King of the Jews" at 15:9 is the virtual substitute of the name "Jesus," and it is at least worthy of note that whereas in Mark the inscription on the cross reads "the King of the Jews" (15:26), in Matthew it reads "This is Jesus, the King of the Jews" (Matt. 27:37, RSV).

The point towards which we are steering is this: by fashioning a story in which the personal name "Jesus" is either conjoined or directly associated with "Christ" ("Messiah"), "Son of David," and "Son of God,"[2] Mark is subtly but unmistakably informing the reader of the identity of Jesus: Jesus, the man from Nazareth (1:24; 10:47), is the Davidic Messiah, the Son of God (1:1, 24; 5:7; 10:47; cf. 15:9). By contrast, conspicuous by its absence from Mark's story is the use of "the Son of Man" in conjunction with the personal name "Jesus." Thus, never does Mark write "Jesus Son of Man," and never does any character in his story call upon Jesus with the words, "Jesus Son of Man. . . ." If direct association with the personal name "Jesus" is any sign, the title "the Son of Man" stands apart, and hence is different in nature, from "Messiah," "Son of David," and "Son of

---

2. As 3:11 shows, at the level of Mark's story, "the Holy One of God" (1:24) and "Son of the Most High God" (5:7) are variant forms of the title "Son of God."

God"; it functions other than to instruct the reader as to the identity of this man from Nazareth.

When one turns to the term *christos,* which serves in Mark as a personal name ("Christ"; 1:1; 9:41) but especially as a title ("Anointed One," "Messiah"), one arrives at this same conclusion, based on a broader range of evidence which is even more compelling. Mark conjoins or closely associates *christos,* too, with other titles so as to communicate to the reader "who Jesus is." Three times, for instance, Mark employs the grammatical construction of apposition to explain, respectively, that Jesus Christ (Jesus [who is] Messiah) is the Son of God (1:1), or that the Messiah is the Son of the Blessed (God) (14:61), or that the Messiah is the King of Israel (15:32). In addition, Mark also has Jesus assert, while putting a question to the crowd and with reference to scribal opinion with which Jesus agrees, that the Messiah is the Son of David (12:35). By thus coloring his story with notations such as these, Mark is once again apprising the reader of the identity of Jesus: Jesus is the Davidic Messiah-King, the Son of God. And by the same token, conspicuously absent from the narrative of Mark are any such expressions that directly link *christos* with "the Son of Man." Never is it said, for example, that "the Messiah is the Son of Man," and never does Mark place "the Son of Man" in apposition to *christos* ("the Messiah, the Son of Man"). If Mark, through his use of the terms "Jesus" and especially *christos,* alerts the reader to the presence in his story of a family of "confessional titles" which comprises "Messiah," "Son of David," "King of the Jews (Israel)," and "Son of God" and which is meant to inform the reader of the identity of Jesus, it is blatantly apparent that "the Son of Man" stands outside the circle of this family and hence may be assumed to possess a different nature and to play a different role in Mark's story from these other titles.

A particularly telling datum that shows that Mark does not employ the title "the Son of Man" to set forth the identity of Jesus as such is the circumstance that the high priest designates Jesus at his trial before the Sanhedrin, not as "the Messiah, the Son of Man," but as "the Messiah, the Son of the Blessed [God]" (14:61). Earlier in his story, Mark had pictured Jesus as referring to himself in public as "the Son of Man." Thus, in one instance Jesus tacitly referred to himself before the "crowd with his disciples" as the Son of Man

(8:34, 38), but in two other instances, before the "crowd" and "some of the scribes" (2:2, 4, 6, 10) and before "the Pharisees" (2:24, 28), he pointedly referred to himself as the Son of Man. In the light of these public references, the reader cannot therefore presume that the fact that Jesus has called himself "the Son of Man" is something not known to the high priest and the Jewish Sanhedrin at the trial of Jesus. At this trial, in turn, the proceedings take a course that causes the whole process to hang on the one question of Jesus' identity (14:55–61). From the standpoint of the Sanhedrin, the high priest wants Jesus to own up to a statement regarding his identity which encapsulates the claim Jesus has himself advanced on his behalf through the activity of his ministry (cf. 12:1–12). Should Jesus own up to such a statement, the high priest aims to have him condemned to death, ironically, for daring to claim at his trial to be the one he really is (1:1, 11; 9:7; 12:6). Accordingly, in view of such a scenario, where, ironically, the interest of the high priest as a character in Mark's story converges with the interest of Mark as narrator and the point of this mutual interest is to crystallize the entire ministry of Jesus into one question concerning his identity, one can only account it as of paramount significance that this question should read not, "Are you the Messiah, the Son of Man?" but, "Are you the Messiah, the Son of the Blessed [God]?" (14:61). And it is of course to the latter that Jesus answers, "I am!" (14:62a). Let, then, the reader ask Mark, the implied author, who the Jesus of his story is and Mark's answer cannot be different from that found in 14:61–62a, because here, again, the issue of Jesus' identity becomes the climactic issue that sums up his entire ministry: Jesus is "the Messiah, the Son of God." Nor should this answer come as any surprise to the reader, for it tallies with God's "evaluative point of view" concerning Jesus' identity: at the baptism and the transfiguration God did not say that Jesus is the Son of Man but that he is the Son of God (1:11; 9:7). Mark does not employ "the Son of Man" to address the specific topic of the identity of Jesus.

With this discussion of the high priest's question and Jesus' answer (14:61–62a), we have already touched on one of an extended series of statements and questions within Mark's story which are of the nature of the "predication formula." This term, as I use it, refers to a statement, or to a question answered in the affirmative, which attributes to Jesus some name or title of majesty in the interest of divulging "who he is."[3] The numerous predication formulas Mark has sprinkled throughout his story suggest further that he does not draw on "the Son of Man" to inform the reader of how he is to construe the identity of Jesus.

Statements or questions answered in the affirmative which function in Mark as predication formulas are such as the following: (1) God affirms, "You are my beloved Son" (1:11); (2) the man with an unclean spirit cries out, "I know who you are, the Holy One of God" (1:24, RSV); (3) Mark comments, "And whenever the unclean spirits caught sight of him, they would fall down before him and cry out, 'You are the Son of God!' " (3:11); (4) Jesus speaks encouragingly to the disciples, "Take heart, it is I [Jesus];[4] have no fear!" (6:50, RSV); (5) Peter declares on behalf of the disciples, "You are the Messiah!" (8:29); (6) God announces atop the mountain of the transfiguration, "This is my beloved Son" (9:7, RSV); (7) Jesus states in a question he puts to the crowd, ". . . the Messiah is the Son of David" (12:35); (8) the high priest asks and Jesus responds affirmatively, " 'Are you the Messiah, the Son of the Blessed?' . . . 'I am!' " (14:61–62a); (9) Pilate asks and Jesus responds affirmatively, " 'Are you the King of the Jews?' . . . '(So) you say' " (15:2); (10) the centurion declares, "Truly this man was the Son of God!" (15:39, RSV); and (11) Jesus says in his apocalyptic discourse, "Many will come in my name, saying, 'I am he [the Messiah; 13:21]!' " (13:6, RSV).

As a group, the passages listed here as functioning as predication formulas are of primary importance for providing insight into the christology of Mark. Five things are worthy of note. The first thing is that, as shown in chapter 3 with respect to all of these passages except 13:6 (which there was no occasion to discuss), Mark would have the reader regard the titles they contain as "correctly," even if in 8:29 and 12:35 also "insufficiently," applying to Jesus. The second thing is that the spectrum of characters who utter these formulas is uncommonly broad: it includes God, a demoniac, demons, Peter,

---

3. I am thus adapting to the circumstances of the Marcan narrative a rhetorical phenomenon discussed by Norden, *Agnostos Theos*, pp. 177–201.

4. Cf. Howard, *Das Ego Jesu*, p. 84.

Jesus, and the centurion, all of whom make assertions, and the high priest and Pilate, who direct questions to Jesus to which he replies in the affirmative. The third thing is that the manner in which these formulas describe the identity of Jesus agrees with the results we have obtained above by pursuing other lines of investigation: Jesus is the Davidic Messiah-King, the Son of God. The fourth thing is that, because the very purpose of the predication formula is to divulge "who a person is," it is clear that Mark wants the reader to look upon the titles which appear in the passages in his story which function as predication formulas, namely, "Messiah," "Son of David," "King of the Jews (Israel)," and "Son of God," as being of the nature of "confessional" titles. And the fifth thing to note is that despite the broad range of characters who utter these formulas, no one, neither a transcendent being nor a human being, declares or asks with reference to Jesus, "You are (Are you? He is) the Son of Man." The absence of "the Son of Man" from the predication formulas of Mark's narrative is an exceedingly strong indication that, again, Mark does not use this term to specify "who Jesus is."

Additional evidence that Mark does not use "the Son of Man" to explain the identity of Jesus comes from yet other quarters. Take the disciples, for example. In the pericope on plucking grain on the sabbath (2:23–28), it is in the audience of the disciples that Jesus rebuffs the Pharisees with the remark that "the Son of Man is lord even of the sabbath" (2:23, 24, 28). But this notwithstanding, when the disciples, two chapters later, broach the question of Jesus' identity in the pericope on the stilling of the storm (4:35–41), they do not query whether he is "the Son of Man" but instead simply ask themselves, "Who then is this, that even wind and sea obey him?" (4:41).

Or take the Jewish public. Although, as we have observed, Jesus openly speaks of himself as "the Son of Man" in the full hearing of the "crowd" (2:2, 4, 10, 12), of "some of the scribes" (2:6, 10), and of "the Pharisees" (2:24, 28), neither in 6:14–16 nor in 8:28 does Mark write that one of the rumors circulating among the populace is that Jesus is "the Son of Man." On the contrary, we read only that various segments of the people hold Jesus to be John the Baptist raised from the dead or Elijah or a prophet. Accordingly, if the interpreter proceeds on the assumption that "the Son of Man" in Mark designates "who Jesus is," these episodes with the disciples and the Jewish public are positively baffling. But if "the Son of Man" does not serve to define the identity of Jesus, its absence from such passages as 4:41; 6:14–16; and 8:28 presents no problem.

Finally, consonant with the argument that "the Son of Man" is not meant to inform the reader of how to construe the identity of Jesus is the largely unobtrusive way in which Mark introduces this term into his narrative. "The Son of Man" appears for the first time in Mark's story in the pericope on the healing of the paralytic (2:1–12). Although the passage itself in which it occurs is rhetorically striking (2:10), neither this passage nor the pericope as a whole reaches its culmination in the "presentation" of Jesus as "the Son of Man" but in the assertion that this Jesus, who refers to himself as the Son of Man, possesses the divine authority to forgive sins (2:5, 6–7, 9, 10).[5] One can compare, by contrast, the pericope on the baptism (1:9–11), which is the place in his story where Mark first introduces the term "Son of God" ("my Son") (1:1 is a "narrative comment"). The pericope on the baptism is one of the most dramatic scenes Mark relates. He depicts God himself as participating in the action he describes, and the scene culminates in the divine asseveration of "who Jesus is." In other words, when it comes to introducing the confessional title of "Son of God" into his story, Mark arranges for none other than God to present Jesus as such. On balance, then, what we have is this: in the pericope in Mark's story in which "Son of God" ("my Son") first appears, it is itself the element on which the pericope turns; in the pericope in Mark's story in which "the Son of Man" first appears, it proves not to be the element on which the pericope turns. Accordingly, combined with the other evidence mustered above, the contrasting manner in which Mark introduces these two terms into his narrative is an additional sign that they do not serve the same purpose, and that if "Son of God" specifies "who Jesus is," "the Son of Man" does not.

In sum, the aim of the preceding discussion has been to make two points: First, the term "the Son of Man" stands apart, and therefore is different in nature, from the family of titles to which "Messiah," "Son of David," "King of the Jews (Israel)," and "Son of God"

---

5. On this point, cf. also the comments by Hooker, *Son of Man,* p. 92; Vermes, *Jesus the Jew,* p. 161; Dewey, *Public Debate,* p. 124.

belong. Second, whereas Mark clearly identifies Jesus, again, as the Davidic Messiah-King, the Son of God, there is no evidence that he employs "the Son of Man" to explain to the reader "who Jesus is."

"THE SON OF MAN": A TITLE?

I have argued that the christological term "the Son of Man" does not serve in Mark to address the specific topic of "who Jesus is." But if this is correct, can, then, "the Son of Man" even be considered to be a title of majesty? Does it not rather function non-titularly,[6] perhaps as the equivalent expression of "a man"[7] or as a circumlocution for the pronoun "I" (or "me")?[8] Such suggestions as these have obvious appeal, for if in perusing Mark's story one can legitimately substitute either the expression "a man"[9] or the pronouns "I" or "me" each time one encounters the designation "the Son of Man," the exegetical gain is immediately apparent: for one thing, it becomes plain why there is such a welter of evidence in Mark to suggest that the purpose of the term "the Son of Man" is not to apprise the reader of the identity of Jesus; and for another, there results a unified portrait of the Marcan Jesus revolving around the title Son of God.

---

6. For a non-titular understanding of "the Son of Man" which nevertheless differs in important respects from the views of the scholars mentioned in the following two footnotes, cf. Moule, *Christology*, pp. 14, 19.

7. On the force of this meaning of "the Son of Man," cf. Bowker, "Son of Man," pp. 44–48; Casey, *Son of Man*, pp. 226–39. Cf. also the related remarks of Hoffmann, "Mk 8,31," p. 199. For a view of "the Son of Man" which construes it as meaning "(this) man" and lays stress on the humanness of Jesus in contrast to his divinity, cf. Nickelsburg, "Passion Narrative," pp. 153–84, esp. 175–76. For a view of "the Son of Man" which contends that the element of "lowliness" is missing from Mark's use of the term, cf. Lührmann, "Biographie des Gerechten," pp. 33–35.

8. Cf., e.g., Martin, *Mark,* p. 191; Leivestad, "Son of Man," pp. 256, 263–64 (contra: Lindars, "Son of Man," pp. 52–72); Vermes, *Jesus the Jew*, pp. 177–86; idem, "The 'Son of Man' Debate," pp. 19–32 (contra: Fitzmyer, "The 'Son of Man' Debate," pp. 58–68; Hooker, "Son of Man problem," pp. 157–59, 165; cf. further Wilson, "Son of Man," pp. 28–52).

9. According to Casey (*Son of Man,* pp. 228–38), the only uses of "the Son of Man" in Mark in which this more general meaning does not shine through (i.e., what Jesus says to be true of himself as the Son of Man is true of other people as well) are the three apocalyptic sayings of 8:38; 13:26; and 14:62.

10. Jesus is the Davidic Messiah-King, the royal Son of God.

While I of course hold that the purpose of "the Son of Man" in Mark is not to apprise the reader of the identity of Jesus and that Mark does indeed present a portrait of Jesus which revolves around the title Son of God,[10] nonetheless I am also convinced that Mark would have the reader construe "the Son of Man" as a title of majesty. This is evident from such factors as the following: (a) through his use of "the Son of Man," Mark has wedded it to the peculiar contours of Jesus' ministry: Jesus designates himself as "the Son of Man" in association with his earthly activity (2:10, 28), with his suffering, death, and rising,[11] and with his anticipated Parousia (8:38; 13:26; 14:62); as a result, "the Son of Man" has become in Mark a unique term which applies to Jesus in a way in which it cannot be applied to any other human being; (b) in a literary-critical perspective "the Son of Man" is also unique because it constitutes the "phraseological point of view"[12] of Jesus: it occurs solely in his mouth, it is always definite in form (" 'the' Son of Man"),[13] and he utilizes it to refer to himself alone (but only in specific situations); (c) "the Son of Man," owing to its selective use, is not employed haphazardly in Mark but according to plan and design; hence, at risk of obscuring the pattern that governs its usage, the interpreter cannot readily reduce it in the various passages in which it occurs to the expression "a man" or the pronoun "I" (or "me"); and (d) in his role as "the Son of Man" in Mark's story, Jesus fulfills OT prophecy (9:12; 13:26; 14:21, 62), which is a not insignificant factor in Mark's use of major titles.[14]

With this assertion, that "the Son of Man" must be adjudged to be a title of majesty, we face now the crux of the problem in dealing with this term in Mark: How is it possible to honor both of the principal conclusions to which our discussion thus far has led us, namely, that "the Son of Man" is, on the one hand, a title of majesty, but that it does not, on the other, specify for the reader "who Jesus is"? The

---

11. Cf. Mark 8:31; 9:9, 12, 31; 10:33, 45; 14:21, 41.

12. For an explanation of the "phraseological plane of point of view," cf. Uspensky, *Poetics of Composition*, chap. 2.

13. Cf. Moule, "Neglected Features," pp. 419–21; idem, *Christology*, p. 11 n. 1.

14. Cf. Mark 1:11; 9:7; 12:35–37; also 11:1–10.

answer to this question lies in understanding how "the Son of Man" functions in Mark's story.

THE USE OF "THE SON OF MAN"

Above it was stated that such terms as "Messiah," "Son of David," "King of the Jews (Israel)," and "Son of God" are of the nature of "confessional titles" the main purpose of which is to inform the reader of the identity of Jesus. This is abundantly evident from, among other things, the passages in Mark which serve as predication formulas. By contrast, "the Son of Man" may be defined as the title of majesty by means of which Jesus refers to himself "in public" or in view of the "public" (or "world") in order to point to himself as "the man," or "the human being" (earthly, suffering, vindicated), and to assert his divine authority in the face of opposition. For purposes of translation, perhaps one way to capture the force of this term in Mark is to render it as "this man," or "this human being." In what follows, I shall examine in turn the four constituent elements of this definition of the Son of Man.

"The Son of Man" is a "public" title in Mark. It is in view of the "world," Jews and also Gentiles but especially his opponents, that Jesus so refers to himself. With respect to the earthly Son-of-Man sayings, it is in the audience of the "crowd" (2:2, 4), of "some of the scribes" (2:6), and of "the Pharisees" (2:24) that Jesus designates himself as the Son of Man (2:10, 28). As for the suffering Son-of-Man sayings, although Jesus' partners in discussion are the disciples, it is in view of Judas[15] and "sinners" (14:41), of the Jewish leaders,[16] of Gentile opponents (10:33–34), of hostile "men" (both Jewish leaders and Gentile opponents? 9:31), and of the rulers of the Gentiles (10:42, 45) that Jesus designates himself as the Son of Man. And as far as the apocalyptic Son-of-Man sayings are concerned, it is in view of all those who prove themselves to be "ashamed of me and of my words in this adulterous and sinful generation" (8:38), of all the peoples who will "see the Son of Man coming" at the latter day (13:26),

---

15. Cf. Mark 9:31; 10:33; 14:20–21, 41–42.

16. Cf. Mark 8:31; 9:9 and 9:12; 10:33; 14:62; also Tödt, *Menschensohn*, pp. 154, 182 (ET, *Son of Man*, pp. 166, 196–97).

and of the high priest and the Jewish Sanhedrin (14:55, 61–62) that Jesus designates himself as the Son of Man. Moreover, because the apocalyptic Son-of-Man sayings have to do with judgment they necessarily envisage, not just the "public," or "world," but also the followers of Jesus, for at his coming they, too, will be held accountable and will either be "gathered" and hence saved (13:27) or be rejected and hence condemned (cf. 8:38 to 8:34a; 9:43–48).[17]

Through his use of the self-designation of "the Son of Man," Jesus alludes to himself in Mark as "the man," or "the human being" (earthly, suffering, vindicated). In the earthly Son-of-Man sayings, Jesus stands before the Jewish public as the man who dares to exersize authority in a manner the Jewish leaders associate with God (2:7, 10, 12, 24, 28). In the suffering Son-of-Man sayings, Jesus speaks of himself as the man whom God has ordained that he should suffer and die at the hands of "men" but also rise;[18] indeed, he is the man who serves humankind by giving his life as a ransom for many (10:45). By contrast, in the apocalyptic Son-of-Man sayings, Jesus speaks of himself as the man vindicated by God whom God will have exalted to universal rule and who will, at the consummation, come in the sight of all for judgment.[19]

Prominent in the passages in which Jesus refers to himself as "the Son of Man" is also an assertion on his part of divine authority.[20] In the earthly Son-of-Man sayings, Jesus claims outright the authority to forgive sins (2:10) or to regulate the sabbath (2:28). In the suffering Son-of-Man sayings, Jesus displays his authority by obediently submitting to the divine necessity of going the way of the cross (8:31) and consequently of doing God's will as set forth in Scripture (9:12; 14:21). Indeed, as the one who employs his authority not to be served but to serve, even to the point of embracing death to atone for sins,

---

17. Cf. Tödt, *Menschensohn*, p. 38 (ET, *Son of Man*, p. 41).

18. Cf. Mark 8:31; 9:9, 12, 31; 10:33–34; 14:21, 41.

19. Cf. Mark 8:38—9:1; 13:26; 14:62; also Ps. 110:1; Dan. 7:13–27.

20. Cf. Tödt, *Menschensohn*, p. 200 (ET, *Son of Man*, p. 218); Hooker (*Son of Man*, pp. 109–14, 180), too, observes that Jesus' Son-of-Man sayings are imbued with a strong sense of divine "authority," but whereas this authority in the suffering Son-of-Man sayings is one that, on her view, the Jewish leaders and Satan "deny" Jesus, I should prefer to understand it in these sayings as coming to expression in the obedience to God (cf. 8:31) and the service to humankind (10:45) Jesus renders by willingly embracing suffering and death.

Jesus holds himself up as the example his disciples are to emulate in their life together (10:42–45). And in the apocalyptic Son-of-Man sayings, Jesus exercises his authority as one who effects judgment, whether to salvation (13:27) or to condemnation (8:38; 14:62).

Especially striking in the Son-of-Man sayings is the note of opposition.[21] In the earthly Son-of-Man sayings, "some of the scribes" charge Jesus with blasphemy (2:6–7), and "the Pharisees" attack him because the disciples have broken the sabbath law (2:24). In the suffering Son-of-Man sayings, Jesus tells his disciples what his opponents are going to do to him: Judas will betray him (9:31; 10:33; 14:21, 41), and the leaders of the Jews and Gentiles will cause him to suffer and put him to death (8:31; 9:12, 31; 10:33–34). Moreover, in variation on this theme of suffering Jesus also sets in opposition to each other his will to serve others through the giving of his life with the will of the rulers of the Gentiles to lord it over others (10:42–45). And in the apocalyptic Son-of-Man sayings, the very idea that Jesus will come as judge contains within it the note of opposition, although here, of course, the emphasis on opposition is counterbalanced by an emphasis on faithful discipleship: as judge of the world (13:26a), Jesus will oppose at the latter day all those who have been "ashamed" of him (8:38)[22] and the high priest and Jewish Sanhedrin who have repudiated him (14:55, 61–64), but he will likewise "gather the elect" who have persevered as faithful disciples (13:13, 26–27).

If, then, "the Son of Man" is a public title by means of which Jesus points to himself as the man, or the human being (earthly, suffering, vindicated), and asserts his divine authority in the face of opposition, what influence does Mark's use of this title have on the whole of his story? The answer is that it highlights the related elements of *conflict* and ultimate *vindication* which characterize Jesus' interaction with the "public," or "world," that is, the Jewish crowd and leaders, Gentiles, Judas, and, in fact, all people. In the earthly Son-of-Man sayings, Jesus defies the Jewish leaders by claiming for himself a right of authority which they regard as blasphemous or unlawful (2:7, 10, 24, 28). In the suffering Son-of-Man sayings, Jesus tells his

---

21. Hahn (*Hoheitstitel*, p. 48) follows Tödt (*Menschensohn*, pp. 43–44, 129–30, 199–201 [ET, *Son of Man*, pp. 47, 139–40, 217–18]) in calling attention to the element of opposition in the Son-of-Man sayings.

22. On the meaning of the term "ashamed," cf. Kee, *Community*, pp. 133–34.

disciples of the betrayal, rejection, abuse, and condemnation to death which God would have him endure at the hands of the "world," that is, especially the Jewish leaders—aided by Judas—and Gentiles.[23] By extension, Jesus likewise tells the disciples that even as the ways of the rulers of the Gentiles, or "world," are diametrically opposed to his ways, so they are to emulate him and not these others in their life together (10:42–45). And in the apocalyptic Son-of-Man sayings, Jesus solemnly predicts to the Jewish crowd and his disciples and to the Jewish leaders that he of whom "this adulterous and sinful generation" is ashamed (8:38) and whom the Sanhedrin condemns to death (14:55, 62–64) will, at the end of time, be vindicated, for he will return in royal power and glory to usher in the Kingdom of God and to exercise judgment, thus repudiating those who have repudiated him but also gathering to himself those who have remained his own (8:34a, 38; 9:1; 13:24–27; 14:62).

Because "the Son of Man" is a public title that focuses attention, overall, on Jesus' interaction with the "world," it cannot be stressed too strongly that it does not infringe upon the motif of the secret of Jesus' identity. When, therefore, Jesus designates himself as the Son of Man in the presence of the crowd (2:2, 4), of some of the scribes (2:6), and of the Pharisees (2:24), he is not thereby "breaking" the secret of his identity. Also, when Jesus designates himself as the Son of Man in the passion-predictions he delivers to his disciples, he is likewise not thereby "breaking" the secret of his identity.[24] And when Jesus tacitly speaks of himself as the Son of Man before the crowd and his disciples and predicts his return in glory for judgment and the inauguration of the Kingdom of God in splendor, he is, again, not thereby "breaking" the secret of his identity (8:34a, 38; 9:1). If the reader of Mark asks "who the Jesus is" who designates himself as the Son of Man, the answer is that he is the royal Son of God (or, more fully: the Davidic Messiah-King, the Son of God).[25]

Before I conclude, there is one passage that merits special consideration, namely, 8:38. Here Mark has Jesus say, "For whoever is

---

23 Cf. Mark 8:31; 9:12, 31; 10:33–34; 14:21, 41.

24. Cf. Mark 8:31; 9:9 and 9:12; 9:31; 10:33, 45; 14:21, 41.

25. Cf. Mark 1:1, 11, 24; 3:11; 5:7; 9:7; 10:47–48; 11:9–10; 12:6; 14:61–62a; 15:2, 39.

ashamed of me and of my words in this adulterous and sinful generation, of him will the Son of Man also be ashamed, when he comes
in the glory of his Father with the holy angels." Of interest are three
factors: (a) temporally, the point of reference is the Parousia, which
of course brings to an end the post-Easter age that begins with the
resurrection; (b) Jesus tacitly refers to himself as "the Son of Man";
and (c) Jesus speaks of the Son of Man as coming in the glory of
"his Father." Taken together, these factors show that also in the time
following the resurrection and ending with the Parousia, the Jesus who
designates himself as the Son of Man is the royal Son of God.

Thus, Jesus' self-designation in 8:38 is in fact that of "the Son of
Man." Nor should this occasion surprise. It is to the "crowd with his
disciples" that Jesus is speaking (8:34a), and in such circumstances
it is the "public title" of the Son of Man which he employs (2:4, 6,
10, 12, 24, 28). Then, too, it is also in view of all those "in this
adulterous and sinful generation" who will have repudiated him and
whom he, vindicated by God, will judge at the latter day that Jesus
is here referring to himself, and when he speaks non-parabolically of
the role he will play at his Parousia he likewise refers to himself as
the Son of Man (cf. 13:24–27; 14:62).

What is extraordinary about 8:38 is not Jesus' use of the self-designation of "the Son of Man" but the presence in this passage of the
expression "his Father." Within Mark's story, the reference to God
as "Father" does not call to mind Son-of-Man passages, but the
understanding of Jesus as the "Son of God." Never, as we have said,
does God enter the realm of Mark's story to affirm with respect to
Jesus, "You are (He is) the Son of Man," but twice he does this in
order to affirm that Jesus is "my beloved Son" (1:11; 9:7). Moreover,
Mark likewise depicts Jesus as also understanding himself to be God's
beloved Son, for in his parable of the wicked husbandmen Jesus first
repeats God's own words in speaking narratively of himself ("He had
yet one, a *beloved son*"; 12:6) and then, dialogically, assumes the
very position of God, identifying himself as God had identified him
("He [the owner of the vineyard = God] said, 'They will respect *my
son*'"; 12:6). But if God, according to Mark, "thinks" of Jesus as
being his Son, and Jesus, in turn, also "thinks" of himself as being
God's Son (cf. 14:61–62a), the obverse of this is that Jesus will
"think" of God as "Father," which is what we have in passages like

14:36 and 13:32. In other words, if we know from reading Mark's story that God "thinks" of Jesus as being "his Son" (1:11; 9:7) and Jesus "thinks" of God as being his "Father" (14:36; 13:32), then we have grounds for inferring, in relation to 8:38, that the Jesus who designates himself in public and in echo of Daniel 7:13 as "the Son of Man" and who designates God as "Father" is, in terms of his identity, the royal "Son of God" (12:6, 10–11; 13:32; 14:61–62a; cf. 1:1). Accordingly, the Jesus who at the Parousia fulfills the role of the royal Son of Man is the royal Son of God.[26]

CONCLUDING REMARKS

This study has shown that there are two major aspects to Mark's portrait of Jesus. The one major aspect Mark develops in conjunction with the motif of the secret of Jesus' identity. To this aspect belong such related titles as "Messiah," "Son of David," "King of the Jews (Israel)," and "Son of God." These titles are confessional in nature and have as their purpose to set forth the identity of Jesus, to specify "who Jesus is" (cf. predication formulas). In fullest measure, they describe Jesus as being the Davidic Messiah-King, the Son of God. Still, because Mark binds the secret of Jesus' identity more narrowly to the truth of his divine sonship, and because "Son of God" is the sole title that constitutes the "evaluative point of view" concerning Jesus' identity of supernatural beings and human characters alike, Mark may be said to describe Jesus more singularly as the royal Son of God. In the baptismal pericope at the beginning of his story, Mark depicts God as affirming Jesus to be his beloved Son. In the crucifixion pericope at the end of his story, Mark for the first time depicts a human being other than Jesus himself as recognizing that Jesus was

---

26. This conclusion also squares with the observation made earlier, namely, that Mark shows that, in the time following the resurrection and leading up to the Parousia, Jesus is "Messiah" and "Son of God." Thus, the "stone" which the builders reject but which God places at the head of the corner is the crucified "Son [of God]" whom God vindicates by raising him to life (12:6–8, 10–11; 16:6). Again, the expression "the Son" in 13:32 is, from a "phraseological point of view," a variant form of "Son of God." And when Jesus predicts that imposters will invade the community of his disciples in the time between the resurrection and Parousia and declare, "I am he!" (13:6), he reveals through his use of this predication formula, as 13:21 indicates, that also as the risen one he is the Messiah.

in truth God's Son. The point Mark makes is that for one to "think" about Jesus the way God "thinks" about him (8:33d), namely, to perceive him to be the royal Son of God, one must know him not only as authoritative preacher, gatherer of disciples, teacher, healer, and exorcist (1:14—8:26), but also as the one who has obediently gone the way of the cross (8:27—16:8). Then, too, raised by God and thus vindicated, Jesus remains the royal Son of God (Messiah Son of God) also in the time following the resurrection and leading up to the Parousia (12:10–11; 16:6; 13:6, 21; 13:32). Indeed, it is as the one who is the royal Son of God (cf. "Father"; 8:38) that Jesus will return at the end of time and perform the role of the Son of Man of OT prophecy (8:38—9:1; 13:24–27; 14:62). But be that as it may, what Mark stresses by developing the one major aspect of his portrait of Jesus in conjunction with the motif of the secret of Jesus' identity is that hearing aright the gospel-story of the divinely wrought destiny of Jesus, which has its center in the cross, is indispensable for understanding aright his identity.

The second major aspect of his portrait of Jesus Mark develops through his use of "the Son of Man." Peculiarly, "the Son of Man" is without content as far as the identity of Jesus as such is concerned, for it does not inform the reader of "who Jesus is." Despite this fact, it clearly constitutes a title of majesty in Mark, for it is applied exclusively to Jesus and in conformity with the unique contours of his life and ministry: earthly activity; suffering, death, and rising; and return for judgment and vindication. The distinctiveness of the title "the Son of Man" lies in the way in which it functions within Mark's story. It is of the nature of a "public title" in the sense that it draws attention to Jesus' interaction with the "public," or "world," Jews and Gentiles but especially his opponents. With this title, Jesus points to himself as the man, or the human being, and asserts his divine authority in the face of opposition. The overall impact of this title upon Mark's story is that it underlines the twin elements of conflict with the "world" and of vindication in the sight of the "world" at the Parousia.

These two aspects of Mark's portrait of Jesus, which feature, on the one hand, Jesus as being the royal Son of God and, on the other, the Son-of-Man sayings he utters, *complement*—not "correct"—each other within the plot of Mark's story. Thus, the Son-of-Man aspect has an "outward orientation," calling attention to Jesus' interaction with the "public," or "world." The Son-of-God aspect has an "inward orientation," focusing on the secret of Jesus' identity and on confessing him aright. In this connection, precisely because the function of the title of the Son of Man is not to explicate for the reader "who Jesus is," two important consequences for Mark's story follow: (a) the Son-of-Man sayings do not infringe upon, or undermine, the motif of the secret of Jesus' identity; and (b) the identity Jesus bears in Mark's story is unified: Jesus of Nazareth is the Davidic Messiah-King, the Son of God, or, more pointedly, the royal Son of God.

And secondly, the Son-of-God and Son-of-Man aspects of Mark's christology also complement each other by treating such fundamental topics as the public activity, death, and vindication of Jesus from different perspectives. In regard to the public activity of Jesus, the Son-of-God aspect concentrates on the identity of the Jesus who preaches, calls disciples, teaches, and heals and exorcizes demons by juxtaposing the shouts of demons that he is the Son of God with the uncomprehending questions human characters pose as to who he might be (1:24, 27, 34; 2:7; 3:11; 4:41; 5:7; 6:3, 14–16). The Son-of-Man aspect, in turn, highlights the element of conflict between Jesus and the leaders of the Jews, depicting Jesus as asserting his divine authority in the face of their opposition (2:6, 10, 24, 28). As for the death of Jesus, the Son-of-God aspect deals with it, again, from the standpoint of the identity of Jesus: the red thread that runs through such pericopes as the transfiguration, the parable of the wicked husbandmen, the trial of Jesus before the Jewish Sanhedrin, and the narrative of Jesus on the cross is the notion that Jesus is the Son of God (9:7; 12:6–8; 14:61–62a; 15:39). By contrast, the Son-of-Man aspect deals with the death of Jesus, characteristically, from the standpoint of conflict and, in one instance, from the standpoint of service: the Jewish and Gentile opponents of Jesus will "kill" him (9:31; 10:34), or he will be "killed" by them (8:31); and in coming not to be served, like Gentile rulers, but to serve, Jesus gives his life and so atones for the sins of humankind (10:42–45). And concerning the vindication of Jesus, the Son-of-God aspect stresses both that it is God who vindicates his Son Jesus and that it is in the resurrection that he does so (12:10–11; 16:6). In the Son-of-Man aspect, the stress is on vindication in the sight of the "world" when Jesus, who remains the Son of God (13:32), comes in the glory of his Father with the holy angels to carry out the role of the Son of Man of OT prophecy, that is, to exercise judgment and to usher in the consummated Kingdom of God (8:38—9:1; 13:24–27; 14:62).

Finally, I wish to take note of the contrasting ways in which the Son-of-God and the Son-of-Man aspects of Mark's portrait of Jesus engage the reader. The Son-of-God aspect invites the reader to join with the centurion (15:39) and the post-Easter disciples (14:28; 16:7) to "see," that is, to confess, Jesus of Nazareth to be the royal Son of God. So to confess Jesus is to realize that it is through him and his ministry, which culminates in the cross, that God proffers salvation, above all atonement for sins (14:24; 15:38; 10:45), and creates that eschatological community of disciples of Jesus which lives in the sphere of the Kingdom and under the aegis of the risen Son of God. To "see," or to confess, in hearing Mark's story, that Jesus of Nazareth is the royal Son of God is thus to "think" about Jesus as God "thinks" about him and hence to be "in alignment" with God's gracious will for all people (13:10).

For the reader who is led, in hearing Mark's story, to confess Jesus to be the royal Son of God, the Son-of-Man aspect of Mark's portrait of Jesus holds out the promise of being accounted at the Parousia as one of the "elect" and of "being gathered" into the consummated Kingdom of God (13:27; 9:1). Otherwise, this Son-of-Man aspect confronts the reader as a warning, or threat. Not to confess Jesus to be the royal Son of God after hearing Mark's story is to "align" oneself with those "in this sinful and adulterous generation" who are "ashamed" of Jesus and who will encounter him at the Parousia as the judge who will likewise "be ashamed" of them (8:38; 13:24–26; 14:62). In the final analysis, therefore, the story Mark tells proves to be "kerygmatic" in tenor: in becoming involved in the plot, the reader is urged to confess Jesus to be the royal Son of God, which, in turn, places him or her "in alignment" with God's gracious will for all people (13:10).

BEYOND MARK: MATTHEW AND LUKE

It was stated above that the crux of the problem in dealing with the title of "the Son of Man" in Mark lies in asserting the truth of two observations that, on the surface, seem to be in tension with each other, to wit: that "the Son of Man" must, on the one hand, be adjudged to be a title of majesty but that it does not, on the other, specify for the reader "who Jesus is." In bold strokes, I should like to show that this phenomenon is not restricted to Mark but occurs in Matthew and Luke as well.

Luke, for example, laces the entire Galilean section of his story (4:14—9:50) with questions or statements human characters voice which have to do with the identity of Jesus. The long series begins with the people of Nazareth and does not end until Peter, in reply to Jesus' own question to the disciples, climactically confesses who Jesus is. Thus, at 4:22 the worshipers in the synagogue at Nazareth, marveling at the words Jesus has just spoken, ask themselves, "Is not this the son of Joseph?" At 4:36, the people in the synagogue of Capernaum, having witnessed Jesus exorcize a demon, say to one another in astonishment, "What is this word? For with authority and power he commands the unclean spirits, and they come out!" (cf. Mark 1:27). At 5:21 (RSV), the scribes and Pharisees, taking offense at Jesus, begin to question one another, "Who is this that speaks blasphemies? Who can forgive sins but God only?" At 7:19 (RSV), John the Baptist asks of Jesus through two of his disciples, "Are you he who is to come, or shall we look for another?" At 7:49 (RSV), the guests at table with Jesus are provoked by him to wonder to one another, "Who is this, who even forgives sins?" At 8:25, the disciples in fear and astonishment query one another, "Who is this, that he commands even wind and water, and they obey him?" At 9:7–9 (RSV), a perplexed Herod, having heard rumors to the effect that Jesus is John raised from the dead, or Elijah redivivus, or one of the old prophets come back to life, wonders aloud, ". . . who is this about whom I hear such things?" Then, at 9:18 Jesus himself seizes the initiative and asks the disciples, "Who do the crowds say that I am?" When the disciples respond by repeating the same rumors Herod has heard (9:19), Jesus presses them with the question, "But who do you say that I am?" (9:20). To this Peter replies, "The Messiah (Christ) of God!" (9:20).

The noteworthy thing about this string of questions is that it is entwined with assertions of Jesus in which he openly refers to himself as "the Son of Man." For instance, in the audience of "the scribes and the Pharisees" (5:21, 24), of "some of the Pharisees" (6:1, 5), of "his disciples" and the "people" (6:20, 22; 7:1), and of the "crowds" (7:24, 34), Jesus unabashedly designates himself as "the Son of Man." If, then, "the Son of Man" were understood by Luke as addressing the topic of Jesus' identity, it is incomprehensible (a) why he would extend this string of questions in which people puzzle over the identity of Jesus long after Jesus has publicly referred to himself as "the Son of Man," and (b) why Luke would describe "Herod" and the Jewish "crowds" as "guessing" that Jesus is, not "the Son of Man" as he has openly designated himself, but John the Baptist raised from the dead, or Elijah, or one of the ancient prophets who has arisen (9:7–9, 18–19). Clearly, for Luke as for Mark, "the Son of Man" does not give answer to the question of "who Jesus is."

The same is true of Matthew. It is as "the Son of Man" that the Matthean Jesus designates himself in the plain hearing of "a scribe" (8:19–20), of "some of the scribes" (9:3, 6), of "the Pharisees" (12:2, 8), of the "crowds" and "the Pharisees" (12:23–24, 32), and of "some of the scribes and Pharisees" (12:38, 40). But this notwithstanding, when Jesus asks the disciples at Caesarea Philippi who "men" say that he, who has openly called himself the Son of Man, is, the disciples do not reply that "men" think of him as being "the Son of Man" but as being John the Baptist or Elijah or Jeremiah or one of the prophets (16:13–14). Once again, "the Son of Man" proves not to give answer to the question of "who Jesus is" despite the fact that Jesus has designated himself as such in public.

But although "the Son of Man" informs the reader of the identity of Jesus as little in Matthew and Luke as it does in Mark, it cannot in Matthew and Luke, as it also cannot in Mark, simply be reduced in meaning to "a man" or to a circumlocution for the pronoun "I" (or "me"). The reasons for this are the same in the case of Matthew and of Luke as in the case of Mark: in Matthew and Luke, too, (a) Jesus refers to himself as "the Son of Man" in connection with the various aspects of his unique vocation (earthly activity, passion and resurrection, and future Parousia) with the result that "the Son of Man" applies to him in a way in which it can be applied to no other human being; (b) "the Son of Man" constitutes, literarily, the "phraseological point of view" of exclusively Jesus, occurring in his mouth alone and referring solely to him; (c) "the Son of Man" is used with plan and design, so that the very pattern controlling its usage resists a facile reduction in meaning to "a man" or to a circumlocution for the personal pronoun "I"; and (d) Jesus fulfills OT prophecy in his role as "the Son of Man," which is a further indication that the term is seen to be a title of majesty.

Accordingly, despite obvious differences there is an underlying commonality in the way in which "the Son of Man" is used in the Synoptic Gospels: although it does not provide the reader with an explanation of "who Jesus is," it is nonetheless a title of majesty (a "public title") employed by Jesus with reference to himself in order to allude to himself as the man, or the human being, and to call attention to some aspect of his interaction with the "world," Jews and Gentiles but especially his opponents.[27] As far as the identity of Jesus in Matthew and Luke is concerned, in Matthew Jesus is the Davidic Messiah-King, the royal Son of God,[28] and in Luke he is the Davidic Messiah-King, the Son and Servant of God (Lord and Savior).[29]

---

27. Cf. Kingsbury, *Jesus Christ*, pp. 38–40, 70–73, 106–110.

28. Cf. Kingsbury, *Matthew: Structure, Christology, Kingdom*, chaps. 2–3; idem, *Matthew*, chap. 2.

29. Cf. Danker, *New Age*, passim; idem, *Luke*, chaps. 2–4; idem, *Benefactor*, esp. pp. 317–493 and the comments in each section devoted to Luke; Fitzmyer, *Luke I–IX*, pp. 192–219.

SELECTED BIBLIOGRAPHY

(This list contains those works cited in the footnotes.)

Achtemeier, Paul J. "'And He Followed Him': Miracles and Discipleship in Mark 10:46–52." *Semeia* 11 (1978): 115–45.

———. "Gospel Miracle Tradition and the Divine Man." *Int.* 26 (1972): 174–97.

———. *Mark*. Proclamation Commentaries. Philadelphia: Fortress Press, 1975.

———. "The Origin and Function of the Pre-Marcan Miracle Catenae." *JBL* 91 (1972): 198–221.

———. "Toward the Isolation of Pre-Markan Miracle Catenae." *JBL* 89 (1970): 265–91.

Aune, David E. "The Problem of the Messianic Secret." *NovT* 11 (1969): 1–31.

Baltensweiler, Heinrich. *Die Verklärung Jesu*. ATANT 33. Zurich: Zwingli Verlag, 1959.

Barrett, C. K. *The Holy Spirit and the Gospel Tradition*. London: SPCK, 1947.

Behm, Johannes. "*Kainos*." *TDNT* 3 (1965): 447–50.

———. "*Metanoeō*." *TDNT* 4 (1967): 999–1006.

Berger, Klaus. "Zum Problem der Messianität Jesu." *ZTK* 71 (1974): 1–30.

Best, Ernest. *Following Jesus: Discipleship in the Gospel of Mark*. JSNTSup 4. Sheffield, Eng.: JSOT Press, 1981.

———. "Mark's Preservation of the Tradition." In *L'Évangile selon Marc*, edited by M. Sabbe, pp. 21–34. BETL 34. Louvain: Louvain University Press, 1974.

———. "The Role of the Disciples in Mark." *NTS* 23 (1977): 377–401.

———. *The Temptation and the Passion*. SNTSMS 2. New York and Cambridge: Cambridge University Press, 1965.

Betz, Hans Dieter. "Gottmensch II." *RAC* 12 (1982): 234–312.

————. "Jesus as Divine Man." In *Jesus and the Historian: In Honor of Ernest Cadman Colwell,* edited by F. T. Trotter, pp. 114–33. Philadelphia: Westminster Press, 1968.

Betz, Otto. "Die Frage nach dem messianischen Bewusstsein Jesu." *NovT* 6 (1963): 20–48.

————. "The Concept of the So-Called 'Divine Man' in Mark's Christology." In *Studies in New Testament and Early Christian Literature: Essays in honor of Allen Wikgren,* edited by D. Aune, pp. 229–40. Leiden: E. J. Brill, 1972.

Bieler, Ludwig. *Theios Anēr.* 2 vols. Vienna: Oskar Höfels, 1935–36.

Bieneck, Joachim. *Sohn Gottes als Christusbezeichnung der Synoptiker.* ATANT 21. Zurich: Zwingli Verlag, 1951.

Black, Matthew. "The Christological Use of the Old Testament in the New Testament." *NTS* 18 (1971/72): 1–14.

Blank, Josef. "Die Sendung des Sohnes. Zur christologischen Bedeutung des Gleichnisses von den bösen Winzern Mk 12, 1–12." In *Neues Testament und Kirche: Festschrift für Rudolf Schnackenburg,* edited by J. Gnilka, pp. 11–41. Freiburg: Herder, 1974.

Blinzler, Josef. "Zur Syntax von Markus 6, 14–16." *Philologus* 96 (1943/44): 119–31.

Boobyer, G. H. "The Secrecy Motif in St Mark's Gospel." *NTS* 6 (1959/60): 225–35.

Booth, W. C. *The Rhetoric of Fiction.* Chicago: University of Chicago Press, 1961.

Bornkamm, Günther. *Jesus von Nazareth.* Stuttgart: Kohlhammer, 1956; (*Jesus of Nazareth.* Eng. trans. Irene and Fraser McLuskey. New York: Harper & Row, 1960).

Boucher, Madeleine. *The Mysterious Parable.* CBQMS 6. Washington, D.C.: The Catholic Biblical Association of America, 1977.

Bowker, John. "The Son of Man," *JTS* 28 (1977): 19–48.

Bretscher, Paul G. "Exodus 4:22–23 and the Voice from Heaven." *JBL* 87 (1968): 301–11.

Brown, Schuyler. "'The Secret of the Kingdom of God' (Mark 4:11)."*JBL* 92 (1973): 60–74.

Bultmann, Rudolf. *Die Geschichte der synoptischen Tradition.* FRLANT 29. 4th ed. Göttingen: Vandenhoeck & Ruprecht, 1958; (*The History of the Synoptic Tradition.* Eng. trans. John Marsh. New York: Harper & Row; Oxford: Basil Blackwell, 1963).

————. *Theologie des Neuen Testaments.* 3d ed. Tübingen: J. C. B. Mohr (Paul Siebeck), 1958; (*Theology of the New Testament.* Eng. trans. K. Grobel. 2 vols. New York: Charles Scribner's Sons, 1951–55).

Burger, Christoph, *Jesus als Davidssohn*. FRLANT 98. Göttingen: Vandenhoeck & Ruprecht, 1970.

Burkill, T. A. *Mysterious Revelation*. Ithaca, N.Y.: Cornell University Press, 1963.

Carlston, Charles E. *The Parables of the Triple Tradition*. Philadelphia: Fortress Press, 1975.

————. "Transfiguration and Resurrection." *JBL* 80 (1961): 233–40.

Casey, Maurice. *Son of Man*. London: SPCK, 1979.

Catchpole, D. R. "The Answer of Jesus to Caiaphas (Matt. xxvi. 64)." *NTS* 17 (1970/71): 213–26.

Chatman, Seymour. *Story and Discourse: Narrative Structure in Fiction and Film*. Ithaca, N.Y.: Cornell University Press, 1978.

Chronis, Harry L. "The Torn Veil: Cultus and Christology in Mark 15:37–39." *JBL* 101 (1982): 97–114.

Colpe, Carsten. *"Ho Hyios tou Anthrōpou."* *TDNT* 8 (1972): 400–477.

Colwell, Ernest C. "A Definite Rule for the Use of the Article in the Greek New Testament." *JBL* 52 (1933): 12–21.

Conzelmann, Hans. "Gegenwart und Zukunft in der synoptischen Tradition." *ZTK* 54 (1957): 277–96.

————. "Historie und Theologie in den synoptischen Passionsberichten." In *Zur Bedeutung des Todes Jesu*, pp. 35–53. Gütersloh: Gerd Mohn, 1967.

Cranfield, C. E. B. *The Gospel according to Saint Mark*. CGTC. New York and Cambridge: Cambridge University Press, 1963.

Crossan, John Dominic. "Redaction and Citation in Mark 11:9–10 and 11:17." *Papers of the Chicago Society of Biblical Research* 17 (1972): 33–50.

Dana, H. E., and Julius R. Mantey. *A Manual Grammar of the Greek New Testament*. New York: Macmillan Co., 1927.

Danker, Frederick W. *Benefactor: Epigraphic Study of a Graeco-Roman and New Testament Semantic Field*. St. Louis: Clayton Publishing House, 1982.

————. *Jesus and the New Age*. St. Louis: Clayton Publishing House, 1972.

————. *Luke*. Proclamation Commentaries. Philadelphia: Fortress Press, 1976.

————. "The Demonic Secret in Mark: A Reexamination of the Cry of Dereliction (15:34)." *ZNW* 61 (1970): 48–69.

Daube, David. *The New Testament and Rabbinic Judaism*. London: University of London, Athlone Press, 1956.

Dautzenberg, Gerhard. "Die Zeit des Evangeliums." *BZ* 21 (1977): 219–34; 22 (1978): 78–91.

Derrett, J. Duncan. "Law in the New Testament: The Palm Sunday Colt." *NovT* 13 (1971): 241–58.

Dewey, Joanna. *Markan Public Debate.* SBLDS 48. Chico, Calif.: Scholars Press, 1980.

Dibelius, Martin. *Die Formgeschichte des Evangeliums.* 3d ed. Tübingen: J. C. B. Mohr (Paul Siebeck), 1959; (*From Tradition to Gospel.* Eng. trans. B. L. Woolf. New York: Charles Scribner's Sons, 1935).

Donahue, John R. *Are You the Christ?* SBLDS 10. Missoula, Mont.: Scholars Press, 1973.

————. "Temple, Trial, and Royal Christology (Mark 14:53–65)." In *The Passion in Mark,* edited by W. H. Kelber, pp. 61–79. Philadelphia: Fortress Press, 1976.

Dormeyer, Detlev. *Die Passion Jesu als Verhaltensmodell.* NTAbh 11. Münster: Aschendorff, 1974.

Drury, John. "The Sower, the Vineyard, and the Place of Allegory in the Interpretation of Mark's Parables." *JTS* 24 (1973): 367–79.

Dunn, J. D. G. "The Messianic Secret in Mark." *TynBul* 21 (1970): 92–117.

Ebeling, Hans Jürgen. *Das Messiasgeheimnis und die Botschaft des Marcus-Evangelisten.* BZNW 19. Berlin: Töpelmann, 1939.

Egger, Wilhelm. *Frohbotschaft und Lehre.* Frankfurter Theologische Studien 19. Frankfurt am Main: Knecht, 1976.

Ernst, Josef. "Petrusbekenntnis—Leidensankündigung—Satanswort (MK 8,27–33): Tradition und Redaktion." *Catholica* 32 (1978): 46–73.

Feneberg, Wolfgang. *Der Markusprolog.* SANT 36. Munich: Kösel, 1974.

Feuillet, A. "Le Baptême de Jesus d'après l'Évangile selon Saint Marc (1, 9–11)." *CBQ* 21 (1959): 468–90.

Fitzmyer, Joseph A. *A Wandering Aramean.* SBLMS 25. Missoula, Mont.: Scholars Press, 1979.

————. "Another View of the 'Son of Man' Debate." *JSNT* 4 (1979): 58–68.

————. *The Gospel according to Luke I–IX.* AB 28. Garden City, N.Y.: Doubleday & Co., 1981.

Fowler, Robert M. *Loaves and Fishes.* SBLDS 54. Chico, Calif.: Scholars Press, 1981.

Fuller, Reginald H. *The Formation of the Resurrection Narratives.* Philadelphia: Fortress Press, 1980.

————. *The Foundations of New Testament Christology.* New York: Charles Scribner's Sons; London: Lutterworth Press, 1965.

Funk, Robert, W. "The Wilderness." *JBL* 78 (1959): 205–14.

Georgi, Dieter. *Die Gegner des Paulus im 2. Korintherbrief.* WMANT 11. Neukirchen-Vluyn: Neukirchener, 1964.

Gnilka, Joachim. "'Bräutigam'—spätjüdisches Messiasprädikat?" *TTZ* 69 (1960): 298–301.

———. *Das Evangelium nach Markus.* EKKNT 2. 2 Parts. Zurich: Benziger, 1978–79.

———. *Jesus Christus nach frühen Zeugnissen des Glaubens.* Biblische Handbibliothek 8. Munich: Kösel, 1970.

Greeven, Heinrich. "*Peristera.*" *TDNT* 6 (1968): 63–72.

Grundmann, Walter. "*Chriō,*" *TDNT* 9 (1974): 530–31.

———. *Das Evangelium nach Markus.* THKNT 2. Berlin: Evangelische Verlagsanstalt, 1962.

———. "*Ischyō,*" *TDNT* 3 (1965): 397–402.

Haenchen, Ernst. *Der Weg Jesu.* Berlin: Töpelmann, 1966.

Hahn, Ferdinand. *Christologische Hoheitstitel.* FRLANT 83. Göttingen: Vandenhoeck & Ruprecht, 1963; (*The Titles of Jesus in Christology.* Eng. trans. New York: World Pub. Co.; London: Lutterworth Press, 1969).

Hartman, Lars. "Taufe, Geist und Sohnschaft." *Jesus in der Verkündigung der Kirche,* edited by A. Fuchs, pp. 89–109. Studien zum Neuen Testament und seiner Umwelt 1. Linz: Fuchs, 1976.

Hay, Lewis S. "The Son of Man in Mark 2:10 and 2:28." *JBL* 89 (1970): 69–75.

Hengel, Martin. *Der Sohn Gottes.* Tübingen: J. C. B. Mohr (Paul Siebeck), 1975; (*The Son of God.* Eng. trans. J. Bowden. Philadelphia: Fortress Press, 1976).

———. *Nachfolge und Charisma.* BZNW 34. Berlin: Walter de Gruyter & Co., 1968; (*The Charismatic Leader and His Followers.* Eng. trans. J. Greig. New York: Crossroad; Edinburgh: T. & T. Clark, 1981).

Hesse, F., A. S. van der Woude, and M. de Jonge. "*Chriō,*" *TDNT* 9 (1974): 496–521.

Hoehner, Harold W. *Herod Antipas.* SNTSMS 17. New York and Cambridge: Cambridge University Press, 1972.

Hoffmann, Paul. "Mk 8,31. Zur Herkunft und markinischen Rezeption einer alten Ueberlieferung." In *Orientierung an Jesus: Festschrift für Josef Schmid,* edited by P. Hoffmann, pp. 170–204. Freiburg: Herder, 1973.

Holladay, Carl H. *Theios Aner in Hellenistic Judaism: A Critique of the Use of This Category in New Testament Christology.* SBLDS 40. Missoula, Mont.: Scholars Press, 1977.

Hooker, Morna D. "Is the Son of Man problem really insoluble?" In *Text and Interpretation: Studies in the New Testament Presented to Matthew Black,* edited by E. Best and R. McL. Wilson, pp. 155–68. New York and Cambridge: Cambridge University Press, 1979.

———. *The Son of Man in Mark.* Montreal: McGill University Press, 1967.

Horstmann, Maria. *Studien zur Markinischen Christologie.* NTAbh 6. Münster: Aschendorff, 1969.

Howard, Virgil. *Das Ego Jesu in den synoptischen Evangelien.* Marburger Theologische Studien 14. Marburg: Elwert, 1975.

Hubaut, Michel. *La parabole des vignerons homicides.* CRB 16. Paris: J. Gabalda et Cie, 1976.

Jeremias, Joachim. *Die Gleichnisse Jesu.* 6th ed. Göttingen: Vandenhoeck & Ruprecht, 1962; (*Parables of Jesus.* Eng. trans. S. H. Hooke. Rev. ed. New York: Charles Scribner's Sons; London: SCM Press, 1963.

―――. *Die Verkündigung Jesu.* Vol. 1 of *Neutestamentliche Theologie.* Gütersloh: Gerd Mohn, 1971; (*New Testament Theology: The Proclamation of Jesus.* Eng. trans. J. Bowden. New York: Charles Scribner's Sons, 1971).

―――"*Nymphē.*" *TDNT* 4 (1967): 1099–1106.

―――. "*Pais Theou.*" *TDNT* 5 (1967): 677–717.

―――. "*Poimēn.*" *TDNT* 6 (1968): 487–93.

Johnson, Earl S. "Mark 10:46–52: Blind Bartimaeus." *CBQ* 40 (1978): 191–204.

Juel, Donald. *Messiah and Temple.* SBLDS 31. Missoula, Mont.: Scholars Press, 1977.

Käsemann, Ernst. "Das Problem des historischen Jesus." In *Exegetische Versuche und Besinnungen.* Vol. 1. Göttingen: Vandenhoeck & Ruprecht, 1960. Pp. 187–214; ("The Problem of the Historical Jesus." *Essays on New Testament Themes.* Eng. trans. W. J. Montague. Philadelphia: Fortress Press, 1982; London: SCM Press, 1964. Pp. 15–47).

Kazmierski, Carl R. *Jesus, the Son of God.* FB 33. Würzburg: Echter, 1979.

Keck, Leander E. "Mark 3:7–12 and Mark's Christology." *JBL* 84 (1965): 341–58.

―――. "The Introduction to Mark's Gospel." *NTS* 12 (1965/66): 352–70.

―――. "The Spirit and the Dove." *NTS* 17 (1970/71): 41–67.

Kee, Howard C. "Aretalogy and Gospel," *JBL* 92 (1973): 402–22.

―――. *Community of the New Age.* Philadelphia: Westminster Press, 1977.

―――. *Jesus in History.* 2d ed. New York: Harcourt Brace Jovanovich, 1977.

Kelber, Werner H. "Mark and Oral Tradition." *Semeia* 16 (1979): 7–55.

―――. *The Kingdom in Mark.* Philadelphia: Fortress Press, 1974.

Kertelge, Karl. "Die soteriologischen Aussagen in der urchristlichen Abendmahlüberlieferung und ihre Beziehung zum geschichtlichen Jesus." *TTZ* 81 (1972): 193–202.

―――. *Die Wunder Jesu im Markusevangelium.* SANT 23. Munich: Kösel, 1970.

Kingsbury, Jack Dean. *Jesus Christ in Matthew, Mark, and Luke.* Proclamation Commentaries. Philadelphia: Fortress Press, 1981.

————. *Matthew.* Proclamation Commentaries. Philadelphia: Fortress Press; London: SPCK, 1978.

————. *Matthew: Structure, Christology, Kingdom.* Philadelphia: Fortress Press; London: SPCK, 1976.

————. "The 'Divine Man' as the Key to Mark's Christology—The End of an Era?" *Int* 35 (1981): 243–57.

————. "The Gospel of Mark in Current Research." *RelSRev* 5 (1979): 101–7.

Klauck, Hans-Josef. *Allegorie und Allegorese in synoptischen Gleichnistexten.* NTAbh 13. Münster: Aschendorff, 1978.

————. "Das Gleichnis vom Mord im Weinberg." *Bib Leb* 11 (1970): 118–45.

Klausner, Joseph. *Jesus of Nazareth.* Eng. trans. Herbert Danby. London: George Allen, 1925.

Koch, Dietrich-Alex. *Die Bedeutung der Wundererzählungen für die Christologie des Markusevangeliums.* BZNW 42. Berlin: Walter de Gruyter, 1975.

Koester, Helmut. *Einführung in das Neue Testament.* Berlin: Walter de Gruyter, 1980; (*Introduction to the New Testament.* 2 vols. Eng. trans. H. Koester. Philadelphia: Fortress Press, 1982).

Kraus, Hans-Joachim. *Psalmen.* BKAT 15. 2 Vols. Neukirchen-Vluyn: Neukirchener, 1960.

Kuhn, Heinz-Wolfgang. *Aeltere Sammlungen im Markusevangelium.* SUNT 8. Göttingen: Vandenhoeck & Ruprecht, 1971.

————. "Das Reittier Jesu in der Einzugsgeschichte des Markusevangeliums." *ZNW* 50 (1959): 82–91.

Kümmel, Werner Georg. "Das Gleichnis von den bösen Weingärtnern (Mk 12, 1–9)." *Heilsgeschehen und Geschichte.* MTS 3. Pp. 207–17. Marburg: Elwert, 1965.

————. *Die Theologie des Neuen Testaments nach seinen Hauptzeugen: Jesus, Paulus, Johannes.* GNT 3. Göttingen: Vandenhoeck & Ruprecht, 1969; (*The Theology of the New Testament According to Its Major Witnesses: Jesus—Paul—John.* Eng. trans. J. E. Steely. Nashville: Abingdon Press, 1973).

Lagrange, M.-J. *Évangile selon Saint Marc.* Rev. ed. Paris: J. Gabalda et Cie, 1947.

Lane, William L. *Commentary on the Gospel of Mark.* NICNT. Grand Rapids: Wm. B. Eerdmans, 1974.

Leder, Hans-Günter. "Sündenfallerzählung und Versuchungsgeschichte."

ZNW 54 (1963): 188–216.

Leivestad, Ragnar. "Exit the Apocalyptic Son of Man." *NTS* 18 (1972): 243–67.

Lentzen-Deis, Fritzleo. *Die Taufe Jesu nach den Synoptikern.* Frankfurter Theologische Studien 4. Frankfurt am Main: Knecht, 1970.

Lightfoot, Robert Henry, *History and Interpretation in the Gospels.* London: Hodder and Stoughton, 1935.

Lindars, Barnabas. *New Testament Apologetic.* London: SCM Press, 1961.

———. "Re-Enter the Apocalyptic Son of Man." *NTS* 22 (1975): 52–72.

Linnemann, Eta. *Studien zur Passionsgeschichte.* FRLANT 102. Göttingen: Vandenhoeck & Ruprecht, 1970.

Ljungvik, H. "Zum Markusevangelium 6:14." *ZNW* 33 (1934): 90–92.

Loader, W. R. G. "Christ at the Right Hand—Ps. CX 1 in the New Testament." *NTS* 24 (1978): 199–217.

Lohmeyer, Ernst. *Das Evangelium des Markus.* MeyerK 2. Göttingen: Vandenhoeck & Ruprecht, 1957.

———. *Gottesknecht und Davidsohn.* FRLANT 43. Göttingen: Vandenhoeck & Ruprecht, 1953.

Lohse, Eduard. "Hosianna." *NovT* 6 (1963): 113–19.

———. "*Hyios Dayid.*" *TDNT* 8 (1972): 478–88.

———. "*Rabbi.*" *TDNT* 6 (1968): 961–65.

Longenecker, Richard N. "The Messianic Secret in the Light of Recent Discoveries." *EvQ* 41 (1969): 207–15.

Lotman, J. M. "Point of View in a Text." *New Literary History* 6 (1975): 339–52.

Lührmann, Dieter. "Biographie des Gerechten als Evangelium." *Wort und Dienst* 14 (1977): 25–50.

———. "Markus 14. 55–64: Christologie und Zerstörung des Tempels im Markusevangelium." *NTS* 27 (1981): 457–74.

Luz, Ulrich. "Das Geheimnismotiv und die markinische Christologie." *ZNW* 56 (1965): 9–30.

Manson, T. W. "The Life of Jesus: Some Tendencies in Present-Day Research." In *The Background of the New Testament and Its Eschatology: In honour of C. H. Dodd,* edited by W. D. Davies and D. Daube, pp. 211–21. New York and Cambridge: Cambridge University Press, 1956.

———. *The Teaching of Jesus.* New York and Cambridge: Cambridge University Press, 1931.

Manson, William. *Jesus the Messiah.* London: Hodder and Stoughton, 1943.

Marshall, I. Howard. "Son of God or Servant of Yahweh?—A Reconsideration of Mark I. 11." *NTS* 15 (1968/69): 326–36.

Martin, Ralph. *Mark: Evangelist and Theologian.* Grand Rapids: Zondervan, 1973.

Marxsen, Willi. *Der Evangelist Markus*. FRLANT 67. Göttingen: Vanden-hoeck & Ruprecht, 1956; (*Mark the Evangelist*. Eng. trans. R. Harrisville. Nashville: Abingdon Press, 1969).

————. *Einleitung in das Neue Testament*. Gütersloh: Gütersloher Verlags-haus Gerd Mohn, 1963; (*Introduction to the New Testament*. Eng. trans. G. Buswell. Philadelphia: Fortress Press, 1968).

Matera, Frank J. *The Kingship of Jesus*. SBLDS 66. Chico, Calif.: Scholars Press, 1982.

Meagher, John C. *Clumsy Construction in Mark's Gospel*. Toronto Studies in Theology 3. New York: Edwin Mellen Press, 1979.

————. "Die Form- und Redaktionsgeschichtliche Methoden: The Principle of Clumsiness and the Gospel of Mark." *JAAR* 43 (1975): 459–72.

Meye, Robert P. *Jesus and the Twelve*. Grand Rapids: Wm. B. Eerdmans, 1968.

Minette de Tillesse, G. *Le secret messianique dans L'Évangile de Marc*. LD 47. Paris: Cerf, 1968.

Moule, C. F. D. *An Idiom Book of New Testament Greek*. New York and Cambridge: Cambridge University Press, 1953.

————. "Neglected Features in the Problem of 'the Son of Man.'" *Neues Testament und Kirche: Festschrift für Rudolf Schnackenburg*, edited by J. Gnilka, pp. 413–28. Freiburg: Herder, 1974.

————. "On Defining the Messianic Secret in Mark." *Jesus und Paulus: Festschrift für Werner George Kümmel*, edited by E. E. Ellis and E. Grässer, pp. 239–52. Göttingen: Vandenhoeck & Ruprecht, 1975.

————. *The Origin of Christology*. New York and Cambridge: Cambridge University Press, 1977.

Müller, Ulrich B. "Die christologische Absicht des Markusevangeliums und die Verklärungsgeschichte." *ZNW* 64 (1973): 159–93.

Neill, Stephen. *The Interpretation of the New Testament 1861–1961*. New York and London: Oxford University Press, 1964.

Neugebauer, Fritz. "Die Davidssohnfrage (Mark xii. 35–37 Parr.) und der Menschensohn." *NTS* 21 (1974): 81–108.

Nickelsburg, George W. E. "The Genre and Function of the Markan Passion Narrative." *HTR* 73 (1980): 153–84.

Nineham, D. E. *The Gospel of St Mark*. The Pelican Gospel Commentaries. Harmondsworth, Middlesex: Penguin Books, 1963.

Norden, Eduard. *Agnostos Theos*. Leipzig: Teubner, 1913.

Nützel, Johannes M. *Die Verklärungserzählung im Markusevangelium*. FB 6. Würzburg: Echter, 1973.

Peake, Arthur S. "The Messiah and the Son of Man." *BJRL* 8 (1924): 52–81.

Percy, Ernst. *Die Botschaft Jesu*. LUA 49/5. Lund: C. W. K. Gleerup, 1953.

Perrin, Norman. "The Christology of Mark: A Study in Methodology." In *A Modern Pilgrimage in New Testament Christology*, pp. 104–21. Philadelphia: Fortress Press, 1974.

————. "The Creative Use of the Son of Man Traditions by Mark." In *A Modern Pilgrimage in New Testament Christology*, pp. 84–93. Philadelphia: Fortress Press, 1974.

————. "The High Priest's Question and Jesus' Answer (Mark 14:61–62)." In *The Passion in Mark*, edited by W. H. Kelber, pp. 80–95. Philadelphia: Fortress Press, 1976.

————. "The Wredestrasse becomes the Hauptstrasse: Reflections on the Reprinting of the Dodd Festschrift." *JR* 46 (1966): 296–300.

Pesch, Rudolf. "Anfang des Evangeliums Jesu Christi." *Die Zeit Jesu: Festschrift für Heinrich Schlier*, edited by G. Bornkamm and K. Rahner, pp. 108–44. Freiburg: Herder, 1970.

————. *Das Markusevangelium.* HTKNT 2. 2 Parts. Freiburg: Herder, 1976–77.

————. "Das Messiasbekenntnis des Petrus (Mk 8,27–30)." *BZ* 17 (1973): 178–95; 18 (1974): 20–31.

Petersen, Norman R. *Literary Criticism for New Testament Critics.* Guides to Biblical Scholarship. Philadelphia: Fortress Press, 1978.

————. "Literary Criticism in Biblical Studies." In *Orientation by Disorientation: Studies in Literary Criticism and Biblical Literary Criticism—Presented in honor of William A. Beardslee*, edited by R. A. Spencer, pp. 25–50. Pittsburgh: Pickwick Press, 1980.

————. " 'Point of View' in Mark's Narrative." *Semeia* 12 (1978): 97–121.

————. "The Composition of Mark 4:1—8:26." *HTR* 73 (1980): 185–217.

————. "When is the End Not the End?" *Int* 34 (1980): 151–66.

Petzke, G. *Die Traditionen über Apollonius von Tyana und das Neue Testament.* SCHNT 1. Leiden: E. J. Brill, 1970.

Powley, B. G. "The Purpose of the Messianic Secret: A Brief Survey." *Exp Tim* 80 (1969): 308–10.

Rad, Gerhard von. "Das judäische Königsritual." In *Gesammelte Studien zum Alten Testament*, I: 205–13. TBü 8. Munich: Chr. Kaiser, 1958.

Räisänen, Heikki. *Das "Messiasgeheimnis" im Markusevangelium.* Schriften der Finnischen Exegetischen Gesellschaft 28. Helsinki: Länsi-Suomi, 1976.

Rawlinson, A. E. J. *St Mark.* Westminster Commentaries. London: Methuen & Co., 1925.

Reploh, Karl-Georg. *Markus—Lehrer der Gemeinde.* SBM 9. Stuttgart: Katholisches Bibelwerk, 1969.

Rhoads, David. "Narrative Criticism and the Gospel of Mark." Unpublished

Paper: SBL Seminar on the Gospel of Mark (1980), pp. 1–24; (Revised version in *JAAR* 50 (1982): 411–34).

Richter, Georg. "Zu den Tauferzählungen Mk 1:9–11 und John 1:32–34." *ZNW* 65 (1974): 43–56.

Robbins, Vernon K. "The Healing of Blind Bartimaeus (10:46–52) in the Marcan Theology." *JBL* 92 (1973): 224–43.

————. "Summons and Outline in Mark: The Three-Step Progression." *NovT* 23 (1981): 97–114.

Robertson, A. T. *A Grammar of the Greek New Testament in the Light of Historical Research*. Nashville: Broadman Press, 1934.

Robinson, James M. *The Problem of History in Mark*. SBT 21. London: SCM Press, 1957; (Reprinted in *The Problem of History in Mark and Other Marcan Studies*. Philadelphia: Fortress Press, 1982).

Robinson, John A. T. "The Parable of the Wicked Husbandmen: A Test of Synoptic Relationships." *NTS* 21 (1975): 443–61.

Robinson, William C., Jr. "The Quest for Wrede's Secret Messiah." *Int.* 27 (1973): 10–30.

Roloff, Jürgen. "Kuhn: Aeltere Sammlungen im Markusevangelium." *TLZ* 98 (1973): 517–19.

Sanday, William. *The Life of Christ in Recent Research*. London: Oxford University Press, 1907.

Schenk, Wolfgang. *Der Passionsbericht nach Markus*. Gütersloh: Gerd Mohn, 1974.

Schenke, Ludger. *Der gekreuzigte Christus*. SBS 69. Stuttgart: Katholisches Bibelwerk, 1974.

————. *Die Wundererzählungen des Markusevangeliums*. SBB. Stuttgart: Katholisches Bibelwerk, 1974.

Schmidt, Karl Ludwig. *Der Rahmen der Geschichte Jesu*. Berlin: Trowitzsch, 1919.

Schneider, Gerhard. "Die Davidssohnfrage (Mk 12, 35–37)." *Bib* 53 (1970): 65–90.

————. *Die Passion Jesu nach den drei älteren Evangelien*. Biblische Handbibliothek 11. Munich: Kösel, 1973.

Schniewind, Julius. *Das Evangelium nach Markus*. NTD 1. Göttingen: Vandenhoeck & Ruprecht, 1936.

Schreiber, Johannes. "Die Christologie des Markusevangeliums." *ZTK* 58 (1961): 154–83.

————. *Theologie des Vertrauens*. Hamburg: Furche, 1967.

Schulz, Siegfried. *Die Stunde der Botschaft*. Hamburg: Furche, 1967.

Schweitzer, Albert. *Von Reimarus zu Wrede*. Tübingen: J. C. B. Mohr (Paul Siebeck), 1906; (*The Quest of the Historical Jesus*. Eng. trans. W. Montgomery. New York: Macmillan Co., 1961; London: A. and C. Black, 1910).

Schweizer, Eduard. *Das Evangelium nach Markus*. NTD 1. Göttingen: Vandenhoeck & Ruprecht, 1975; (*The Good News According to Mark*. Eng. trans. D. H. Madvig. Atlanta: John Knox Press, 1970).

————. *"Hyios."* *TDNT* 8 (1972): 363–92.

————. "Neuere Markus-Forschung in USA." *EvT* 33 (1973): 533–37.

Simonsen, Hejne. "Zur Frage der grundlegenden Problematik in form- und redaktionsgeschichtlicher Evangelienforschung." *ST* 27 (1972): 1–23.

Sjöberg, Erik. *Der verborgene Menschensohn in den Evangelien*. Lund: C. W. K. Gleerup, 1955.

Smith, Morton. "Prolegomena to a Discussion of Aretalogies, Divine Men, The Gospels and Jesus." *JBL* 90 (1971): 174–99.

Steichele, Hans-Jörg. *Der leidende Sohn Gottes*. Biblische Untersuchungen 14. Regensburg: Pustet, 1980.

Stein, Robert H. "Is the Transfiguration (Mark 9:2–8) a Misplaced Resurrection-Account?" *JBL* 95 (1976): 79–96.

Strecker, Georg. "Zur Messiasgeheimnistheorie im Markusevangelium (1964)." In *Das Markus-Evangelium*, edited by R. Pesch, pp. 190–210. Wege der Forschung 411. Darmstadt: Wissenschaftliche Buchgesellschaft, 1979.

Suhl, Alfred. *Die Funktion der alttestamentlichen Zitate und Anspielungen im Markusevangelium*. Gütersloh: Gerd Mohn, 1965.

Swete, Henry Barclay. *The Gospel according to St Mark*. 2d ed. London: Macmillan, 1908.

Tannehill, Robert C. "The Disciples in Mark: The Function of a Narrative Role." *JR* 57 (1977): 386–405.

————. "The Gospel of Mark as Narrative Christology." *Semeia* 16 (1979): 57–95.

Taylor, Vincent. *The Gospel According to St. Mark*. London: Macmillan, 1959.

————. "The Messianic Secret in Mark." *Exp Tim* 59 (1947/48): 146–51.

————. "The Messianic Secret in Mark: A Rejoinder to The Rev. Dr. T. A. Burkill." *HibJ* 55 (1956/57): 241–48.

————. "W. Wrede's The Messianic Secret in the Gospels." *Exp Tim* 65 (1953/54): 246–50.

Theissen, Gerd. *Urchristliche Wundergeschichten*. SNT 8. Gütersloh: Gerd Mohn, 1974; (*The Miracle Stories of the Early Christian Tradition*. Eng. trans. F. McDonagh. Philadelphia: Fortress Press; Edinburgh: T. & T. Clark, 1983).

Tiede, David L. *The Charismatic Figure as Miracle Worker.* SBLDS 1. Missoula, Mont.: Scholars Press, 1972.

Tödt, Heinz Eduard. *Der Menschensohn in der synoptischen Ueberlieferung.* Gütersloh: Gerd Mohn, 1959; (*The Son of Man in the Synoptic Tradition.* Eng. trans. D. M. Barton. Philadelphia: Westminster Press; London: SCM Press, 1965).

Trocmé, Etienne. *The Formation of the Gospel according to Mark.* Eng. trans. P. Gaughan. Philadelphia: Westminster Press, 1975.

Turner, C. H. "*Ho hyios mou ho agapētos.*" *JTS* 27 (1926): 113–29.

―――. *The Gospel according to St. Mark.* London: SPCK, n.d.

Turner, Nigel. *Syntax.* Vol. III of *A Grammar of New Testament Greek.* By James Hope Moulton. Edinburgh: T. & T. Clark, 1963.

Tyson, Joseph B. "The Blindness of the Disciples in Mark." *JBL* 80 (1961): 261–68.

Uspensky, Boris. *A Poetics of Composition.* Eng. trans. V. Zavarin and S. Wittig. Berkeley and Los Angeles: University of California Press, 1973.

van Iersel, B. M. G. "*Der Sohn*" *in den synoptischen Jesusworten.* NovTSup 3. Leiden: E. J. Brill, 1964.

van Unnik, W. C. "Die 'geöffneten Himmel' in der Offenbarungsvision des Apokryphons des Johannes." *Apophoreta: Festschrift für Ernst Haenchen,* edited by W. Eltester, pp. 269–80. Berlin: Töpelmann, 1964.

Vermes, Geza. *Jesus the Jew.* New York: Macmillan Co., 1974.

―――. "The 'Son of Man' Debate." *JSNT* 1 (1978): 19–32.

Vielhauer, Philipp. "Erwägungen zur Christologie des Markusevangeliums." In *Aufsätze zum Neuen Testament,* pp. 199–214. TBü 31. Munich: Chr. Kaiser, 1965.

―――. "Tracht und Speise Johannes des Täufers." In *Aufsätze zum Neuen Testament,* pp. 47–54. TBü 31. Munich: Chr. Kaiser, 1965.

Vögtle, Anton. "Die sogenannte Taufperikope Mk 1,9–11. Zur Problematik der Herkunft und des ursprünglichen Sinnes." In *Evangelisch-Katholischer Kommentar zum Neuen Testament. Vorarbeiten Heft 4,* pp. 105–39. Neukirchen/Zurich: Neukirchener/Benziger, 1972.

von Martitz, Wülfing. "*Hyios.*" *TDNT* 8 (1972): 334–40.

Weder, Hans. *Die Gleichnisse Jesu als Metaphern.* FRLANT 120. Göttingen: Vandenhoeck & Ruprecht, 1978.

Weeden, Theodore J. *Mark: Traditions in Conflict.* Philadelphia: Fortress Press, 1971.

―――. "The Heresy That Necessitated Mark's Gospel." *ZNW* 59 (1968): 145–58.

Wetter, Gillis P. *"Der Sohn Gottes."* FRLANT 26. Göttingen: Vandenhoeck
& Ruprecht, 1916.

Wilson, Frederick M. "The Son of Man in Jewish Apocalyptic Literature."
SBTheol 8 (1978): 28–52.

Windisch, Hans. *Paulus und Christus.* UNT 24. Leipzig: J. C. Hinrichs'sche
Buchhandlung, 1934.

Wink, Walter. *John the Baptist in the Gospel Tradition.* SNTSMS 7. New
York and Cambridge: Cambridge University Press, 1968.

Wrede, William. *Das Messiasgeheimnis in den Evangelien.* 3d ed. Göttingen:
Vandenhoeck & Ruprecht, 1963; (*The Messianic Secret.* Eng. trans. J. C.
G. Greig. Library of Theological Translations. London: James Clarke,
1971).

———. *Vorträge und Studien.* Tübingen: J. C. B. Mohr (Paul Siebeck),
1907.

Zerwick, Maximilian. *Biblical Greek.* Scripta Pontificii Instituti Biblici 114.
Rome: Pontifical Institute, 1963.

INDEXES

NAMES

Achtemeier, P. J., 27, 30, 32, 37, 103–5, 109, 122, 157, 181
Aland, K., 14, 55, 82
Arndt, W. F., xv, 17, 63, 76, 98, 104, 109–10, 133
Aune, D. E., 7, 10, 181, 182

Baltensweiler, H., 99, 181
Barrett, C. K., 68, 69, 110, 181
Barton, D. M., 193
Bauer, W., xv, 17, 63, 76, 98, 104, 109–10, 133
Beardslee, W. A., 190
Behm, J., 73, 76, 181
Berger, K., 34, 181
Best, E., 7, 10, 68, 74, 103, 105, 181, 185
Betz, H. D., 27, 30, 99, 181
Betz, O., 6, 34, 36, 182
Bieler, L., 26, 27, 182
Bieneck, J., 33, 182
Billerbeck, P., xvi, 130
Black, M., 36, 115, 182
Blank, J., 115, 182
Blinzler, J., 85, 182
Boobyer, G. H., 18, 83, 103–5, 182
Booth, W. C., 1, 47, 57, 182
Bornkamm, G., 6, 182, 190
Boucher, M., 17, 117, 182
Bowden, J., 185, 186
Bowker, J., 166, 182
Bretscher, P. G., 65, 182
Brown, S., 11, 182

Bultmann, R., 7, 8, 26–28, 37, 40, 43, 61–62, 67, 83, 105, 111, 129, 182
Burger, C., 104–5, 107, 112, 183
Burkill, T. A., 5, 7, 13, 19, 95, 99, 103, 183, 192
Buswell, G., 189

Carlston, C. E, 17, 99, 115–16, 183
Casey, M., 124, 166, 183
Catchpole, D. R., 125, 183
Chatman, S., 1, 47, 183
Chronis, H. L., 129, 183
Colpe, C., 84, 183
Colwell, E. C., 109, 129, 182, 183
Conzelmann, H., 8, 121, 183
Cranfield, C. E. B., 83, 92, 95, 183
Crossan, J. C., 107, 183

Dalman, G., 62
Dana, H. E., 131, 183
Danby, H., 187
Danker, F. W., xv, 34, 130, 179, 183
Daube, D., 109, 183, 188
Dautzenberg, G., 183
Davies, W. D., 188
de Jonge, M., 185
Derrett, J. D., 107, 184
Dewey, J., 15, 165, 184
Dibelius, M., 7, 8, 67, 184
Dodd, C. H., 188, 190
Donahue, J. R., 32, 36, 121–22, 132, 157, 184

195

SYNOPTIC PASSAGES